D0256679

28

W

Thi
Libr
v

# SINNER
# AND
# SAINT

# SINNER
## AND
# SAINT

*The Inspirational Story of Martin Murray*

**PAUL ZANON**

First published by Pitch Publishing, 2018

Pitch Publishing
A2 Yeoman Gate
Yeoman Way
Worthing
Sussex
BN13 3QZ
www.pitchpublishing.co.uk
info@pitchpublishing.co.uk

© 2018, Martin Murray and Paul Zanon

Every effort has been made to trace the copyright.
Any oversight will be rectified in future editions at the
earliest opportunity by the publisher.

All rights reserved. No part of this book may be reproduced,
sold or utilised in any form or transmitted in any form or by
any means, electronic or mechanical, including photocopying,
recording or by any information storage and retrieval system,
without prior permission in writing from the Publisher.

A CIP catalogue record is available for this book
from the British Library.

ISBN 978-1-78531-385-1

Typesetting and origination by Pitch Publishing
Printed in India by Replika Press

# CONTENTS

# DEDICATED TO

My amazing children Archie, Amelia and Aisla. You make me so proud and everything I do, I do it for you. Thanks for being my inspiration. You're my absolute world and I love you more than you'll ever know. xxx

Mum and Dad. Thanks for the great memories growing up and standing by me in the lowest points in my life. I'll never be able to repay you but I just hope you understand how much I appreciate what you've done for me and how much I love you. xxx

To my beautiful wife and best friend Gemma. Thanks for giving me the life I could only have dreamt of and for always being by my side. But most of all, thanks for being you. I love you so much.

As long as we've got each other, we've got it all.

xxx

# TOO MANY TO MENTION

A BIG thanks to everyone who took the time to share some stories about my mad life. Special thanks to my Father Buller Greenhalgh, my incredible parents Dek and Carol, my sister Katie, and my brothers Danny and Ricky.

Thanks to Ian Robinson (Robbo), Bernard Platt, Frank Martin, Mark Robinson, Sergio 'Maravilla' Martinez, Gennady Gennadyevich Golovkin, Liz Dickenson, Pete Dickenson, Stu McCulloch, Ian 'Zapper' Roberts, Jonny Fear, Alex Matvienko, Jimmy Williams, Ricky Murray, my beautiful wife Gemma Murray, Nathan Brough, Mike Glynn (Glynny), Alan Burke (Burky), Luca Rosi for great editing, David Price (Pricey), John Hassall, Mark Bitcon (Bittaz), Andy Pinkerton (Pinky), Martin Blondel (Steve Prescott Foundation), Tony Bellew, Tony Dodson, Peter Eden (Mill Green School), Ian Moore (Mozez), John Wilson (Willo), Craig Lyon (The General), Ian Davies, Craig Lyon (The boxer), Dean Hillman, Mick Farrell, Stuart Bamford (Digger), Lee Prior, Oliver Harrison, Paul Brown (Brownie), David Garvey, Mark Picton (Picko), Mick Farrell, Rodney Berman, Jamie Moore, Andy Mikhail, Carl Davis (Davo), Ant O'Neill, Steve 'No Brakes' Howell, Derry Mathews, Sean Green, Daniel Sharkey, John Lyon, Kevin Bacon, Johnney Roye, Jimmy Christian, Dave Sands (Sandsy), Steve Larrisey (Stav), Darren Chisnall, Paul McCracken, Nav Mansouri, Rocky Fielding, Phil Roberts (Butty), Dennis 'Victor Meldrew' Foster, Alex Hagen, Carol Thompson.

Thanks to my management team MTK, especially Daniel, Anto and Matt.

I'd also like to give a special mention to my physios, Pinky, Rob Harris, Doug Jones, Darren Roberts and Nathan Mills (Millsy) for taking care of me and a big thanks to Mike Hayton for always looking after my hands. Thanks also to Dr Chris Brooks (Brooksi) for always giving me excellent advice.

A big thanks to all my sponsors who've helped me along the way for having the faith to invest in me.

The Barmy Army. There's literally not enough space to thank you all, but I need to say this. You're a cracking bunch of people who've always made a good impression. Some of you I've never even met, but that doesn't mean to say I'm not appreciative of you. Together, you are my support in that ring and no matter what the result or where I go, you've always got my back. When I stop boxing, hopefully we can all stay in touch. By that time, I hope there will be some new up-and-coming fighters from St Helens who we can all go and support and then I can become a member of the Barmy Army myself.

A few words about my ghostwriter, Paul Zanon. Even when going through episodes of my life I would have rather forgotten, you've made writing this book so enjoyable and put a positive spin on it. Thanks for not judging me and for being someone I now call a friend. x

There's a long list of people who are not mentioned above who I want to say thank you to. You've supported me when I was down, in trouble and in my success. You know who you are and I'll never forget you.

Last but certainly not least, I need to mention a man who has been through blood, sweat and tears with me in the boxing ring. I'll never forget the buzz of Oliver's gym. The likes of Jamie Moore, Amir Khan and Alex Matvienko training in there and Oliver Harrison's brother Humphrey making sure we didn't cut any corners. But there was one man in there who made it something special: Oliver himself. I have so much love and respect for this man.

At the time of writing this book, he was seriously ill and we nearly lost him at one point. He showed me what being in a 'real fight' is all about. He represents everything a fighter is. I just want to say thank you for all your time and commitment over the past ten years. There's been some highs and lows, we've travelled the world together and shared some incredible experiences. What a journey it's been.

#MemoriesForLife

# INTRODUCTION

*7 May 2016 – Manchester Arena*

*Martin Murray v Cedric Spera*

'**D**OUBLE jab, right hand, left hook to the body. One, two, three, four.'

Bam, bam, bam, crack.

'And again.'

With 30 minutes to go before the first bell, these were the sounds of Oliver Harrison and Martin Murray warming up.

After a lively pad session, Martin took his gloves off and passed them to long-term friend Andy Mikhail to stretch them out one last time. Oliver turned to Martin and said in his calm voice, 'Shadow box Martin. Nice and easy.' As Martin started to occupy most of the floor space in the changing room going through various drills behind the jab, he looked down at Andy's son's friend, who was about seven and staring at Martin in awe. Martin stopped throwing punches, knelt down in front of the lad and said, 'Your laces are undone. Let's do them up, otherwise you could trip over.' Andy took a photo, then turned to me and said, 'That will be one for that lad's scrapbook when he gets older.'

After a two-round demolition of Spera, Martin conducted an interview with IFL TV. After a few questions about the fight, Martin was asked by interviewer James Helder, 'Are you going to hang around and watch Crolla?' 'No. I wish him all the luck, he's a top lad, but I'm going to shoot off home with the family,' Martin replied.

That kind of sums up Martin Murray. Family comes first and his passion for boxing is a close second. But there was a time when neither played a part in his life and living beyond his 20s was something he believed would never happen. *Sinner and Saint* has allowed me to shine a torch into some of the darker parts of his life, but also details the immense effort he has put into turning his chaos into a life lesson for all. The book goes from 0-60 fast. Really fast. Hold on, it's a bumpy ride.

Paul Zanon
January 2018

NB: Martin's book doesn't always tick the editing style guide. For example, one minute he might say 'Our Archie', then next line simply 'Arch'. That's how Martin speaks and he wanted the dialogue to sound as close to his real voice as possible. I hope you have as much pleasure walking in Martin's shoes for the next 46 chapters as I did. He's an upstanding man who has certainly been an inspiration to me.

# FOREWORD

*'The Epitome Of A Man'*

T HE LAST time I sparred as a professional was in preparation for my fight against Sergey Khomitsky in 2010. Leading up to it, my training had gone well and although I had a few pounds to shed I was in good condition. The only problem was that I hadn't sparred hard for 12 months because my brain scans had come back with reported movement. Although I was deemed fit to fight and had been cleared by the doctors and the British Boxing Board of Control, I didn't want to overdo it unnecessarily, just to keep the mileage on the clock down.

Khomitsky was a notoriously tough nut and as fight day approached my trainer Oliver Harrison said, 'We're going to have to get at least one hard spar before this fight. Instead of doing sprints on Friday, you and Martin can spar and I'll close the doors so no one else is here.'

Martin had boxed Khomitsky, so had a valuable insight. That Friday, Oliver reminded us of what he wanted. Over the previous 12 months or so, nearly all the sparring we had done together had been more technical and I'd underestimated how much Martin had come on during that time.

We did six rounds, and I mean six proper rounds. We tore lumps out of each other. In many of the previous sessions, because of my style, Martin would be competitive and fire back for the first two or three rounds, but then he'd start to tire. This time he was virtually unbreakable. His defence was so tight that every time I seemed to get a punch through, he'd counter me with a body shot or an uppercut each time.

After the third round, when my pressure usually took its toll, he grew stronger. Then he started to catch and counter with shots, before starting his own attack, pushing me on to my back foot. He'd made huge strides during that year, so much so that I wasn't able to use my experience to pull him around. He was not only able to weather the storm and come through the other side but pushed me into deep waters, a complete role reversal.

That day, I definitely came off second best. I ended up with a shiner and the spar was one of those defining moments. Up to that point, I was recognised as the top fighter in the gym. It was like the changing of the guard. I knew that Martin was now the main man in Oliver's gym.

Before the spar, I'd said to Oliver, 'I still want to get my sprints in, so why don't we do them afterwards?' 'OK,' Ol replied. Fucking hell, did I regret saying that. After that sparring, the only thing we both needed was to go home and take a bath. We still went and done them and as we were waiting to do the first one, Martin turns to me and says, 'Was this your fucking idea?' We both erupted in laughter.

I've never been the sort of person to be envious of the success of other boxers, far from it. I wish anyone success in this tough sport. I never got to fight for a world title, whereas Martin has on more than one occasion, and was unlucky not to have been a world champion. Being able to follow him along the way, helping when I can and commentating on his fights, has given me a lot of personal satisfaction. And to then be a part of his last few fights with Oliver was very special. It was like a mini reunion of the old Salford days.

I'd love to be a part of his journey right the way through to him winning a world title, but if he decides to retire tomorrow, I'd be so proud just to have known him. Not just as a great fighter, but as a great human being. Having success in your career and being able to buy expensive things and brag about it is not what he's about. If you see the way he expresses his love for his missus and kids, that's the mark of a true man for me. Martin does that. He epitomises how a man should behave.

Martin has been involved with everyone you could think of in boxing terms, at the very highest level. People who have added so much value to the sport. For him to ask me to do this foreword is the ultimate compliment, and I feel privileged not only to be able to do it, but also to be able to call him my friend. If this book is half as successful as he is, that will be a massive accomplishment.

MOORESY (Jamie Moore)
Former Commonwealth, Irish, British and
European Light-Middleweight Champion

# PROLOGUE

*Banged Up Abroad*

*Martin Murray, Aged 18 – May 2001*

I WAS on remand in Ayia Napa police station waiting to find out where I'd be moved on to next. There was only one cell, which was really rough, and I got treated like shit. Every time the guards saw me, they'd give me bits and bobs of hidings and slap me around.

I got one meal a day, usually some kind of tinned food like corned beef. They didn't give me any cutlery, so I had to eat it with my hands. When you're that starving, you just get your fingers in there and eat. The shower in the cell was something else. It was a little hole in the wall without a shower head. The water trickled down and you had to press your body up against the wall and spin underneath it to get some water on you.

The beds were hanging. I got bitten that much by insects that I was full, and I mean *full*, of bites all over my body. When I got to the main jail a couple of weeks later, between only eating one meal a day and because the bite marks had turned to blisters and scabs, people thought I was a smackhead.

I now needed to get court representation and didn't know where to start. When I got nicked, this horrible-looking skinny man with dead-long, greasy straight hair had heard about my case and offered to be my lawyer. He looked like a total creep. I had a meeting with him and he asked if I had any money. I had about 500 quid in Cypriot pounds and he took that. I didn't know, but this guy had been banned from every other police station for being a conman. I never saw him again.

In the middle of the night they took me to this other remand centre, in a place called Paralimni, which was about 45 minutes away. My mate had got nicked a few days before me and was already there. The guards drove round the back and there was this little wing of four cells, with a toilet at the end of the landing. This is where I spent the next week.

After a couple of nights, they told me I was going to join my mate. What had happened was, two girls from Birmingham had arrived at the remand centre I was at and they needed to put them in the same cell, and I needed to be moved out as we couldn't share a room with girls. I was buzzing to see my mate.

I hadn't seen him in ages by this stage and it was about three in the morning. When I got in, I shouted dead excited, 'Alright pal!' He was stretching and walking on the way to the toilet for a piss and said, half asleep like, he couldn't be arsed, 'Y'alright cock.' So much for the big Hollywood-style reunion.

Most of us hadn't had a proper wash in ages, so you can imagine what the smell was like. There was also this Scottish lad in our cell called Bruce, who was in his 30s and had been nicked for smoking a bit of weed. Lovely lad. He'd never been in trouble in his life and couldn't believe he was behind bars.

The catering wasn't any better. Still one meal a day. They used to give us a couple of tins of ham, a cucumber and a bit of bread to share between us. We used to have our meal and then try and save a bit for later, even though it would be stale.

The exercise area was this cage above the cells, outside of the prison, but was still part of the complex. We'd have one hour a day out there, as people would drive past and look at you like animals.

We ended up getting this other lawyer from the British Embassy, who my mum sorted and paid for. He said, 'You're under 21 and British.' Apparently, as British citizens, they would go more leniently on us. They wanted us to get a folder together to help prove that back home we were good people. My mate said, 'I'm not getting anything sent over. Let's just do our bird, innit.'

When it came to the court, the lawyer, reading from my folder, said, 'Martin Murray. He's done a bit of boxing, won the schoolboys title, went a little bit off the rails,' all that kind of stuff. Then, when it came to my mate's defence, the brief pulled out this massive folder that his mum had sent over, which included his record of achievement from school and everything he'd done since he'd left. I couldn't believe it. It was that detailed, it had everything from when he'd won a Blue Peter badge.

We were up for importation, supplying and possession of drugs. We were advised to plead guilty for possession only. When the judge announced that we'd have to serve an eight-week sentence, I was buzzing. From what the locals had said, I thought I was going to be behind bars for at least ten, maybe 15 years. After being sentenced, we were escorted to this car by armed security, which would then transport us to the main prison in Nicosia a couple of hours away.

At the time, I was smoking and there was this big meathead of a guard sitting at the front of the car and one sitting in between us. As we headed off, I opened the window and the burning end of my cig flew off and landed on the shoulder of this meathead in front. The guard in between us hadn't spotted what happened.

I didn't want to touch the guard in front because he might have thought we were attacking him, so we just watched it burn away there on his shoulder until it got through his top and on to his skin. The second it burned through, he jumped up and went ballistic, turned around and gave us a slap.

The prison in Nicosia was mental. It was exactly like one of them prisons you see on telly when someone's been arrested abroad. There were people on towers with guns and helicopters circling the jail a couple of times a day. When we arrived, they did the full search on us. We then went in, got put in our wing and were given bits and bobs like clothes, a towel and a toothbrush.

There was one roll call in the morning before breakfast and then one before dinner. In between you'd be out in the sun, having the craic with the other prisoners to pass time and playing a bit of football.

The jail was dirty. Seriously dirty. There were 16 men with a mixture of races and religions crammed into our cell, with eight bunk beds and four toilets per wing, which were basically holes in the ground. The showers were hanging. People used to take a crap in there and not think anything of it. The only luxury we had was a telly room at the end of the wing, which had one film on at night with English subtitles.

The routine for the next few weeks was identical. We'd get up in the morning and have a bit of breakfast, which was the best meal of the day. They're mad for their coffee out there and they'd have these big jugs of it for you. We were allowed to use the freezer in the screws' office at the end of the landing and we'd put some coffee into two-litre plastic bottles and pop them in, so we could have cold coffee throughout the day.

People from all round the world were in that jail. We had this Ukrainian who spoke nine languages, which came in very handy as we had about eight nationalities in our cell alone and he ended up translating everything for us. There were also two lads from England on our wing called 'Big Gus' from Middlesbrough and a proper old-school Cockney called John. They both lived in Cyprus and were sound fellas. However, out of all the prisoners, the two I'll never forget were Algerian refugees. We named one Dracula, because he was obsessed with Christopher Lee in that film. His front teeth were missing and you could only see his canine teeth, like fangs. The other Algerian we called Maradona, because he was really good at football and had that curly hair like him.

Dracula was proper funny. A natural comedian. When he was in bed, he'd pull the white sheet over himself and then Maradona would do the chime like it was 12 o'clock, and he'd slowly rise up. We'd be in stitches and would be up until 1am most mornings having the craic. So much so that the screws would often be telling us to keep quiet as we were keeping the other prisoners awake with our laughter.

It turned out Dracula was a policeman in Algeria but due to the civil war he went over to Cyprus illegally for a better life. He got caught and had been in jail for ages while the prison system decided what to do with him. If he'd have been British, he'd have probably never even gone to jail.

When we went into that cell on the first day, straight away, Dracula and Maradona gave us some food, cigs and something to drink. These guys had hardly anything, but what they did have they shared out.

Not everyone was nice, though. There was this big firm of Russians and there was this one lad in particular who thought he was the big bully, but he was just a muppet. He came up to us once while we were having a fag and said,

'Where are you from?'

'England.'

My mate had a tattoo on his arm and this lad said, 'Where we're from in Russia, we cut tattoos out of you.' Basically trying to intimidate us.

'But we're not in Russia now, are we, ye prick,' I said.

Fast forward a few weeks and I'd been told I was leaving the prison in the morning. I knew I wouldn't be able to sleep, so I got a Diazepam from the medical room to help me and then went to chill out and watch the telly.

For some reason, the tablet was giving me a bit of a bad turn and every time I looked over at that same Russian guy, it seemed he was laughing at me. I started to get paranoid and thought, 'What's he looking at?'

I went out of the telly room and waited for him. As he came out, I threw it on him. I didn't hit him, I just fronted him. As bullies do, he shit it and swallowed what I told him. In the meantime, Cockney John was keeping the peace with the other Russians, explaining that it was just a misunderstanding. Thankfully, that's as far as that episode went.

Over in Cyprus there was only one jail and if you got in trouble for violence inside the jail, they'd move you to Block Four, which is where all the lifers were. The lifers' block had a real bad reputation and rumour had it that people got raped, seriously hurt, or both. That's why everyone tried to keep their head down, do their bird and stay out of trouble as much as possible.

On the day of my release, I tried transferring all the money I had left over in my account into Dracula's, but the guards wouldn't let me. As I left, Dracula was there by the gates. It was like something off a film. For every day of the six weeks I'd been there, he was great to me. He was a lovely man who I'd grown close to. We had a little moment, almost knowing we'd never see each other again. I put my hand on the railings of this steel gate and he did the same from his side and we had a talk. It upsets me now even to think about it. Dracula was in his 50s at the time and I'll never know what happened to him, and will never be able to find out. I just hope, if he's still alive, wherever he is, he's OK.

Me and my mate then got handcuffed by two coppers, thrown into a van and driven straight to the airport. When we arrived, we were marched through, still in cuffs. All the holidaymakers were looking over at us. Looking back, it was proper embarrassing.

The guards then told us which flight we'd be on and also let us know we were banned from Cyprus for three years. Just before they left us, they said, 'Go home. Don't think about coming back. If you do, we'll find you and you'll get jailed for a long time.'

The flight back to the UK was a five-hour journey with free ale, so we ended up getting bladdered. I learned nothing from being behind bars and that became very obvious, very quickly, when I got back home.

# CHAPTER 1

# CHILDHOOD ROBBERY

*'Remember what to do, Martin. Get under the table,*
*make out you're playing around a bit, then put that*
*20 quid into your dad's sock'*

Carol Murray – Martin's mother, 1988

THAT was always my mission when visiting my dad at HM Prison Kirkham. My mum always used to say that I was the only one who could get away with it. Our Danny and Katie were too shy, whereas I was a cheeky little six-year-old and could make it look like I was messing about. The sock thing was like a game to me.

I'll always remember that journey to get to Kirkham. We used to pass a load of greenhouses in the middle of some massive fields on the motorway. Mum used to say, 'That's where your dad works.' She never once said he was in prison. Not that I really understood what prison or jail was at that age anyway. All I knew was that he was inside somewhere and we all wanted him home with us.

The fact is, my dad didn't get a great start in life. When he was a kid, his mum got divorced early and she met a man called Mike, who wasn't very nice to my dad. They were never at home. They spent most of their time going to the club up the road getting pissed, instead of saving enough money to pay for the leccy [electricity], which was always disconnected.

First chance my dad's mum had, she put him into a home in Gloucestershire. A great big institution, like you see in them old

Victorian movies. I can't imagine how rejected he must have felt. He started thieving and spent a lot of his teenage years bouncing between borstals, or approved schools, as they preferred to call them. When he did start to go back home, Mike soon picked up on my dad's thieving and realised he'd always have a few quid. He used to go into my dad's bedroom and steal everything. In the end, my dad moved out and stayed at a YMCA.

By now, he'd got into a routine of thieving and when you drive down a one-way street, you tend to just keep on driving forward, as it's difficult to turn. When my dad came out of prison for the last time, his brother, my uncle Dave, said to him, 'You've got this chance, Dek. Don't fuck it up.' He was referring to a new start with a new job. He got the job, stuck at it and never looked back. He's always been a grafter and like myself, all his life, if he did something, he did it proper, whether it was positive or negative. Considering he's had no education, I'm very proud of where he is today in his life. All I can say is that the love of a good woman straightened him up. Something I'd appreciate myself a few years down the line.

Back to Kirkham. When my dad came home from prison a year later, he kept himself 'busy'. He had a good mate who he'd go grafting with. Mainly stuff from warehouses and factories. The strict rule was never to steal from anyone on our estate in Fingerpost, St Helens. Nobody would rob off their own, nobody would grass on each other and everyone looked after each other. I've never heard of a story of anyone getting mugged on our estate. If an old lady was beaten up, God help them. The whole estate would be tracking them down.

Due to my dad's activities, our house was always full of boxes. All kinds of stuff. It was like Del Boy's flat from *Only Fools and Horses*. Funny that, as my dad's name is Derek. Despite the police raiding the house from time to time, I never questioned what my dad was up to. All I knew was that he never forgot about me after a good night's work.

There used to be this place near us which used to distribute magazines, papers and pretty much everything you'd see on the shelves in the likes of WHSmith. My dad had decided to visit in the middle of the night with his partner in crime, Ste Lynch.

At the time, I was massively into collecting the Teenage Mutant Ninja Turtle cards and Panini football stickers, as the 1990 FIFA World Cup was on. On this particular day, my dad woke me up and gave me some stickers. Not just a few packets but boxes of them. I was absolutely buzzing. I stayed up the whole night ripping open every packet. Let's just say both the Turtles and Panini albums were complete by breakfast time and I made a few quid selling any doubles at school.

I can't complain about my childhood or where I grew up. There was always stuff to get up to with your friends on the estate, but as a little kid I was too young to really understand the difference between right and wrong. It was all a bit of fun. However, there was one man who did his very best to show kids that there were different choices that could give them a better start in life.

## CHAPTER 2

# CHIZZY

*'There were a lot of people and distractions around him. Sport helped keep him on the straight and narrow. Or perhaps straighter and narrower, as it was always going to be a struggle growing up in Fingerpost'*

Ian Davies – Martin's former PE teacher

FOR as long as I can remember, there had always been a pair of boxing gloves in our house. As little kids, me and our Danny would always be battering each other. We also used to have one of those punch balls on a stand, which you had to step on to keep it from falling over, but it wasn't until a couple of years later that it became more than just a game in the house.

My very first boxing trainer was a man called John Chisnall. I didn't know it at this point but Chizzy would become a lifelong influence, inside and out of the ring. He was one of four brothers who were heavily involved in sport and were well known in the area. However, he was the only one who boxed – the others were all into rugby.

Chizzy turned professional when he was 26 and fought by the name of Johnny James. He had an eight-fight career as a light-heavyweight, cut short just over a year after his debut due to a burst blood vessel in his nose. Soon after, he decided to set up a boxing gym and train kids in the local area. I'm so glad he did.

All he cared about was getting kids off the street and into a boxing ring. In Fingerpost, there was no community centre or anything like that. He could see a lot of lads were growing up thieving, drinking and smoking, many before they'd even become teenagers. Even if the mums and dads had no money for their kids' subs, he used to let them train anyway, just so they'd be away from bad influences.

However, the way he got the kids to his gym, you wouldn't get away with now. He had this mad boogie bus/van and he used to drive around our estate shouting to the kids, 'Go and tell your mum I'm taking you boxing, then jump in th'van.' Can you imagine that happening these days? John and his van were a well-known double act in the area, so when I ran into the house and said to my mum, 'Can I go boxing? It's with John Chisnall,' I knew the answer would be 'Yes'.

The gym was St Helens Town Amateur Boxing Club (ABC). The first voice you'd hear at the door was my grandfather on my mum's side, Buller. I've always called him 'Father'. Becomes confusing when I'm talking about my dad (my dad) and my father (my grandfather). My 'Mother' is my grandmother and my mum is my mum.

My father used to collect the money at the boxing club. 'Where's your subs? Pay your subs. You don't get free passes for being my grandchildren. Turn that music down.' He was a proper grumpy old man. Still is now. But I love him to bits. My father grew up on the same avenue as Chizzy and were always fighting as kids. Nothing serious, the usual stuff. As adults, the two of them never strayed too far from each other. They both used to work at the market, with my father selling lino flooring and Chizzy selling fruit. They'd go for a pint in the evening and rumour has it they'd been known to get into a scrap or two.

I was only seven when I went to that first boxing session. You should have seen the trainers my mum found for me. They were massive. It looked like nobody owned me. They were easily my dad's. There's a video knocking about somewhere of the session and when I watched it a few years later with my mum, I said laughing, 'What the fuck were they on me feet?'

From the get go, I loved it, but you could also see Chizzy was buzzing. 'Go on, cocker. Hit it like this,' as he'd show me a move on the bag, or, 'Keep your hands up, lad. Hands up!' as he was teaching me my guard.

The first thing that struck you about Chizzy was that he was a hard man with a tough exterior, but a big heart. He probably scared more kids away than the ones who joined the gym. He'd start winding you up saying, 'I'm gonna get you a big lad for your first fight. It's gonna be tough.' Although he was half joking, it gave you discipline. Reminded you that there's always someone bigger, stronger and more experienced.

For the next three years, my father took me to Chizzy's to train. Mainly in the winter, though, because I preferred playing with my mates on the estate during the summer. It wasn't until I was ten that I started taking the boxing seriously. So seriously that I managed to knock myself out. The gym had now moved to Bobbies Lane and there was this big heavy bag which we used to swing and then catch. First time I swung it, it came flying back and hit me bang on the chin. All I remember was waking up on my back.

I started to look at boxing in a different way now. As kids, me and my brothers, Danny and Ricky, had bunk beds. Mine was the top one. I had a piece of paper pinned to the ceiling which said, *If you want to be a champion, you've got to train like a champion.* It would give me that little surge of motivation to get up and go for a run before school when I couldn't be arsed.

The fighters around me in St Helens were also a massive inspiration. My good friend at the time, Ste Birch, was boxing and I used to tag along. Ste was a real talent and a year older than me, so I really looked up to him. It wasn't just Ste, though. Bearing in mind how small the population of the local area was, we had some cracking fighters. The likes of John Lyon, Darren and Wayne Chisnall (Chizzy's sons), Mike Thompson, Lee Connor and Carl Pennington. I used to look at how good they were and realised that if I wanted to be like them, I needed to dedicate myself. But it was Chizzy who was the driving force behind all of us.

'Get gloves on. You're in next.' That was the first time I sparred. I remember just having it with this lad, with both of us windmilling, really going for it. Getting hit and wanting to give my own back in a competition setting was a massive buzz, although my discipline might not have been the best.

About a year or so later, our Danny started boxing and we used to spar pretty regular. We'd always be messing about with our boxing gloves at home, even though we only had one pair between us. It was one glove each. I'd always have the left one and Danny would have the right. At the weekend, we used to stay in to watch all the big fights, the likes of Nigel Benn, Chris Eubank, Steve Collins and Prince Naseem Hamed. We'd be hitting each other before, during and after watching the fights, while saying, 'If we take our licks now, this will make us able to take a shot when we're older.'

Back to the sparring session. Our Danny was a sneaky little kid, but in a silly way. If he wasn't locking you out the house, he'd be pouring water on you when you were walking in. This time at Bobbies Lane, the bell went for the end of the round and he blatantly walloped me after it. I hit him back, then he kicked me and it turned into a street fight. My father jumped in and gave us a massive bollocking. 'If it was down to me I'd kick you both out,' he said. My mate Picko (Mark Picton) was standing at the side watching, absolutely pissing himself. My father then gave me a clip round the ear and I had to walk three and a half miles home. That was the last time me and Danny sparred.

Chizzy also used to do this thing where he'd have four people in the ring at the same time. We'd all start off in different corners, then when the bell went we'd start sparring with the person in the opposite corner. The second he said, 'Switch,' you'd turn around to the nearest person and try and wallop them. It taught you to keep your guard up at all times, that's for sure. I loved it.

I had my first amateur fight when I was 11. The date was our Danny's birthday, 5 November, 'Bombie' Night [St Helens slang for Bonfire Night] 1993. A lot seemed to happen on that very day in my life for some unknown reason, most of it best forgotten. My father took me to that first fight, which was in Northwich. I fought at 4st 9lbs, against a lad called Michael Blackmore. In fact, I ended up fighting Michael four times over the next couple of years.

I don't recall any instructions Chizzy gave me that night in the changing room. All I remember was getting kitted up and pacing up and down the room, dead nervous. My father told me to sit down, but instead I was moving around even more and ended up having an argument with him. The fight itself went alright. I won on points and everyone was cheering me as I stepped out of the ring. I couldn't wait for the next one.

Someone I'd like to give a mention to is Brian Tonks. At the time, I was always the little runt of the boxers at Bobbies Lane. I hadn't developed physically as quick as the other boxers and I was surrounded by some genuine talent, lads who had all the skills to become world champions.

I only found this out recently. Chizzy asked Brian, 'Who do you reckon will make it out of them?' referring to me and a few of the lads in the gym. Brian pointed at me and said, 'He'll go far, him.' Chizzy was almost a bit shocked as there was the likes of Ste Birch, Craig Lyon and Gary Davies, who were smashing it at the time. Brian died in December 2016 and I'll be forever grateful of the faith he had in me and the encouragement he used to give me as a kid. RIP mate.

* * * * * * *

Chizzy was a master at bringing people together. The club was more than boxing. He knew that most of the kids coming into his gym would only learn the basics and maybe only compete in a few amateur fights, if at all. It wasn't just about creating champions. Chizzy wanted to get kids off the street, flush out bullies, build confidence and teach everyone discipline. Most importantly, he wanted to build a community under that roof.

No matter how busy he was, whatever the finances of the club were like, or how many boxers had fights coming up, he'd always do something for the end-of-season presentations. All the families and friends of the kids were also invited and we used to look forward to it. The parties were hosted at the social club next to the gym and during the evening there were presentations. Every kid got given a trophy. Chizzy never left anyone out and realised there were different levels of ability and that every person was as important as the next. Good memories.

Problem was, with the best will in the world, there was only so much he could do. When you grow up in an area where everyone is doing things they shouldn't, you start to become curious. And that curiosity can soon get you into a whole lot of trouble.

# CHAPTER 3

# FISH AND CHIPS

*'You know I'm always in trouble'*

Tony Yayo

FIRST time I got arrested, I was ten. There was a girl around our area who only had one arm. On this day, I sneaked into town with her and another girl, who were both a couple of years older than me. We went to the shop Stationery Box, split up and nicked a few bits like a compass box, a few pens and some highlighters.

Somehow, our group broke up and I got lost in the shop. I asked the lady who worked at Stationery Box, 'Scuse me. Have you seen a girl with one arm?' 'Yeah, yeah. Follow me.' She took me to this room around back, opened the door and threw me in. There they were. The police appeared in no time, nicked us, then took us home. My dad went mad. The policeman said, 'He's been caught thieving in town.' All I remember is my dad rattling me and sending me to bed. From there on, it was a slippery slope.

Have you seen that programme on the telly, *Shameless*? Well, they had fuck all on us growing up. Work was almost non-existent in Fingerpost, as was money. However, the place always seemed to be rich in scrap. For as long as I can remember, me and my dad would always be on the lookout for any chances to take something to the scrapyard and make a few quid. The best job we ever picked up turned out to be on our doorstep.

Across the road from my mum and my dad's place used to be a load of derelict three-storey houses, which were literally falling apart. One day, they started demolishing them and we were in and out of there non-stop. We'd rip up floorboards and pull out all the leccy cables, then we'd burn off the plastic to get to the copper inside. There would also be a shitload of copper piping under the floorboards, which is where you could make some good cash. Once we'd pulled the piping out, we'd smash it one end so it was flat and then fill the open end with sand to make it heavier for when we took it to the scrapyard. Worked every time.

We absolutely rinsed those houses and they ended up putting a security guard on patrol. The guy turned out to be a nice fellow, which worked to our advantage. One day he had to nip home but looked a bit worried, so we said, 'Don't worry, mate. You go home and we'll make sure nobody touches the site.'

The second he left, I sprinted back home and told my dad. This was our chance to go for the copper boilers. Within no time, none of these houses had boilers or aluminium windows. The security guard came back a couple of hours later and was none the wiser. In fact, he even thanked us for our help. 'Any time, mate!' I said.

When we were done with the houses, we took whatever other work was available. There was a man called Teddy Noonan, who was a right character and would usually have some kind of 'job' for us, although he didn't pay the best wages. Not long after we'd finished with them houses, Teddy came over to me and Glynny (Mike Glynn). 'Do you lads want to get some scrap and earn yourselves some money?' We were like, 'Yeah, yeah,' all excited.

We all pedalled up on our bikes and drove down this little pathway until we reached this building site. When we got there, he pointed at this small gap which he couldn't get through and said, 'I need you to go through there and get that scaffolding.' Me and Glynny squeezed in, then passed Teddy all this scaffolding as he strapped it up to his bike. We worked pretty hard that day and were expecting a good few quid, at least a fiver each. Guess what we got? Twenty-five pence each and a chip butty. Good old Teddy.

Scrap aside, there always seemed to be stuff to do as a kid. If we weren't playing football on the Bowly (bowling green), we'd be down the swimming baths on our estate, annoying the staff. I originally got banned from the baths for a few months for smashing the fire alarm, but I soon got barred for life. Dive bombing next to the 'Don't dive' sign, winding up the lifeguards and getting caught sneaking in without paying repeatedly probably didn't help.

With the pool now out of bounds, we'd head to the big canal near us, which we called 'stinky brook'. It was proper minging. Years ago, we thought nothing of it. We'd get our scruffy clothes on and wade through it. My mum wasn't impressed when me and our Danny would walk through the front door dripping and stinking of shit. We also used to play 'man hunt', which was the St Helens version of 'hide and seek'. We'd hide all over the estate and in people's gardens, but we had areas we couldn't go past. I remember once having a top hiding place and decided not to move from it for hours. When I did come out, everyone had gone home.

Getting banned from the baths didn't stop us from having a laugh. I've always liked my cars and bikes from a young age. Difference is, as opposed to most ten-year-olds, I wasn't playing with the miniature toy versions. Honda 90s (Plackies) gave us hours of fun – although we never actually bought one. The moment we saw one around the area, word would spread like wildfire and it would be nicked and stripped.

My most memorable ride on a Plackie was also my most painful. Glynny turns up on his bike with another mate of mine, Ste Moore, and there was this other guy we used to call Hunky Funky Avo, who turned up on his Plackie. Avo was about my dad's age and was well into his bikes. Why he was called Hunky Funky I have no idea.

Glynny starts bombing it down this dirt track on his Plackie, with me and Avo chasing them down. Ahead of us was this dirt hump, followed by a dip, then another hump. Glynny hits the accelerator, revs the shit out of the bike and clears both humps. As we approached, Avo started accelerating, but didn't have the balls to go through with it and slowed down. We cleared the first hump, but the front wheel hit the second hump and we went flying. We weren't wearing helmets, but somehow walked away with just a few scratches. Not so funky after all.

\* \* \* \* \*

Although I started boxing at seven, I'd been scrapping on the streets for a lot longer. Lads from Fingerpost used to lay down their markers against neighbouring areas like Parr and fights would often take place. Believe it or not, I was never a big fighter back then. Yes, I was boxing, but I was just a jack the lad, a confident kid up for some fun.

I had my first straightener (a fight you'd have with someone to put an end to an argument) with a lad from Parr when I was barely 11, over a football. We had a fight and I ended up keeping the ball.

Not all my fights finished with a good ending, though. One time, there was a small group of us in town and a similar number from Parr. We saw them in the shop Index and approached them for a straightener at the bus depot. I ended up having a fight with a lad who'd turn out to be a mate years later, but as we were fighting, a couple of his mates jumped in. It was that time when rollerblades were in and one of their lads smashed me in the face with one. I've still got a chipped tooth from that and a lump on the inside of my lip that never went down.

I've always been a bit of a trendsetter, in my mind anyway, and that chipped tooth and fat lip didn't do anything for my image back then. Thankfully, I was still miles ahead on the haircut front. A lot of people had the mushroom cut. It was big back in the day. Literally. My hair was always dead thick, so my mushroom was massive. Then I had an undercut, to be that bit cooler. There was some decent mushrooms knocking about in my area, but without a doubt mine was the best, although my mate Mozez (Ian Moore) did try to take it to another level to be that bit cooler.

He'd always been into the whole American hip hop gangsta vibe and one day when we were at school, he took the day off to get the full mushroom braided. He said, 'I'll come over at dinner time and show it to ya.' When he appeared, with the whole swagger walk going on, we couldn't stop laughing, although, not as much as we did when it caught fire once when we were all smoking weed under a bridge. Seeing him putting out his beloved mushroom was priceless. Good old Mozez.

Our Danny soon followed and then my mum made our Katie have the mushroom as well. Why my mum would do that to a little girl I don't know. Some people would consider that child cruelty.

By the time I turned 14, I started to get into more and more trouble on all fronts. Not major stuff, but enough to get me a bad reputation and a constant clip round the ear. I'd moved on from Honda Plackies and was looking for bigger thrills. One of the older lads known in our area had got a cat killer (three-wheeled car). So, there we were in the car with his best mate going down Cowley Hill Lane. It quickly became obvious that this guy didn't know how to drive. He was smashing all the wing mirrors off all the other cars because he was driving that close. We got near our house and said, 'Gis a go.' He said, 'OK. I'll wait outside pub for yous.'

He soon realised we weren't coming back in a hurry. We took it over to a nearby field and decided to have a competition, each taking turns to see who could roll it. I couldn't wait for my go. I strapped myself in, drove about 500 yards, then turned it really quick and rolled it. Everyone was dead quiet as they thought I might have been seriously injured. After about 20 seconds, I got out and started jumping up and down with my arms up like Rocky Balboa. Everyone started cheering like mad. I was proper made up with myself. What we didn't realise was that the lad who owned the car had sneaked up a tree with a video camera to show the police what we'd done to his car. We wasn't arsed as we were just a bunch of kids having fun.

After rolling it a few times, we ripped all the doors off and sawed the roof clean off. All that was left was the shell. We ended up going everywhere in it and I mean everywhere. If the police had seen us, we'd have been nicked in a heartbeat. We went past Maccy's drive-thru down Linc Way, six of us inside and four hanging off the shell. People were looking at us just shaking their heads. At one point, we spotted Chizzy and everyone was trying to cover me up as we passed him.

We got as far as Thrifty's store in Fingerpost and the cat killer kind of conked out. We ended up wheeling it down to the park, then rolled it down into stinky brook, where it crashed into a load of shopping trollies and burnt-out Plackies. Somehow, I never got nicked for anything to do with the Plackies or the cat killer. I would, however, become over the coming months and years a regular at the police station because of my street fighting. Back then, if you'd been arrested that week, you'd be in the name and shame section of the *St Helens Reporter*. I was featured in pretty much every edition. My father soon started to call me 'fish and chips' because I was always in the paper. Unfortunately, that side of my life was only going to get worse for the next few years.

# CHAPTER 4

# WHEELER DEALER

*'Every day I'm hustlin''*

Rick Ross

BOXING wasn't the only sport in my life as a kid. I tried Jiu Jitsu when I was six for a couple of months, but it wasn't for me. I wasn't that good at football either, but I was good at winding people up.

One summer's day, we were all playing down the Bowly and at half-time we all sat down. I said to everyone, 'I'll fill the water bottles,' and snuck over to the allotment where the tap was. I came back and Picko starts swigging his. After the third sip, you could see him thinking, 'This don't taste right.' He took the lid off and saw that I'd chucked in a lump of mud. He put his hand inside and pulled out about ten worms. We were all pissing ourselves as Picko chased me all over the Bowly shouting, 'Come here you little shit!'

It was only when I went to St Augustine's (Guzzies) School that I realised that rugby was something I wanted to really get stuck into. They had some good players, but it wasn't really a rugby school. I'd get on the field, have a bit of fun and always made the first team. I even played for the year above a couple of times. In terms of my position on the field, I'd play anywhere. I say anywhere but I was really small, so tended to be part of the backs, on the wing. Basically away from the really big guys.

In fact, when I was a young lad, there was a standing joke about me because I was short and bow-legged. My auntie Pam whispered to my mum one day, 'He's only little, isn't he?' 'He must take after his dad,' my mum said. Auntie Pam replied, 'I don't think it's that. I think he might be a dwarf,' as my mum and auntie Pam slowly looked over at me. In the end, my mum took me to the doctor's and had me checked out. He measured me against one of them height charts and said, 'He's a bit under his height, but he's OK.'

When I was at Guzzies, they chose the best rugby players from all the schools in the area, who would then get to play for the St Helens town squad. My PE teacher Ian Davies and Eric Chisnall (Chizzy's brother) used to run some of the town teams together. Eric used to play for the St Helens rugby league team and also represented Great Britain. He knew me through the boxing club and thought it would be a good idea to get me involved in the rugby town club set-up.

Even though I didn't get as much game time as the other kids, I managed to play for the town and was really proud of that. I used to go there and train hard all the time, but looking at the other lads I could tell I was no good. I was nearly always sub. My claim to fame is that I managed to play on the old Saints ground in Knowsley Road.

I stayed at Guzzies until the age of 14 and then got expelled. Bar one or two, I had no respect for my teachers. I was actually a bright kid, but I was always pissing about. I used to spend my break time outside my head of year Mr Twist's office, and then every dinner time I used to have to go into the canteen and eat my dinner with him in front of all the school. This went on for a few weeks while I was on report.

When I got kicked out, it was the inevitable waiting to happen. The teachers did their best to try and keep me through to 16, but after suspending me a number of times for misbehaving they had no option really but to expel me.

Soon after, I went with my mum to Cowley School and had a meeting with the headmaster. They were wary to take me on, but I explained that I genuinely wanted a clean break. Thankfully, they took me in. The only person who wasn't happy that I got into Cowley was our Katie. Me and our Danny have always been very protective and when we were at school, nobody could say anything bad to her or we'd be on them. She hated that. She's got a strong character and certainly didn't need her older brothers sticking up for her. She was made up when she went to Cowley without us, but when me and our Danny got expelled and ended up following her, she was fuming. No escaping us.

I became quite a popular kid at Cowley pretty quickly, but that wasn't purely down to my charm. I was always doing a bit of wheeling and dealing, making a few quid whenever I saw the chance. Chizzy's missus, Carol Thompson, always used to call me 'The Little Hustler'. At some of the boxing dinner shows, they'd sell raffle tickets. Sometimes you couldn't get people to part with their money, so Chizzy used to get me to do it. Carol used to say, 'You could charm the birds out of a tree.'

When I was at Guzzies, I used to pinch stuff from shops, like pens and lip balms, then I'd sell them to the other kids. But when I got to Cowley, that's where my tuck shop took off. My mum once gave me a pack of Hobnobs from Thrifty's and I took them to school. Someone said, 'They look sound. I'll give ya 50p for them.' They only cost 10p, so of course I agreed. I went back to Thrifty's that same evening and bought loads of them, then took them into school the morning after. They went in a heartbeat. I thought, 'I've got a business here.' Next weekend, I went back and spent a fiver in there. By the time I'd sold it all at school, I'd made 25 quid profit and that became a daily occurrence. In my mind, the stuff I was selling in Guzzies was illegal, whereas I was buying the stuff now, so that made it legal ...ish.

Closest I ever came to getting caught was when me and our Danny went to Wales for a boxing show. We found a few rolls of tickets, which looked similar to the dinner tickets we had at school. When we got back to Cowley on the Monday, we sold them for 50p each and made a killing. There was even an assembly about it, with the headmaster shouting, 'Who's selling these tickets?' Thankfully, we never got caught.

In terms of rugby at Cowley, they were shit hot. It's now called Cowley International College and their training facility is that good, it's currently being used by St Helens rugby team. From having always made the first team at Guzzies, I struggled to even make the B team at Cowley. What I would say, and still maintain to this day, is I was shit at everything else, but I had a world-class side-step. My mates still go on about that side-step to this very day. Or maybe I do. Either way, it was class.

\* \* \* \* \*

Although I was boxing at the time and was always confident at school, as a 14-year-old I knew when I was out of my depth, especially against three 18-year-old lads. Here's what happened. A big group of us from school used to get Zonies (all zones travel passes). They used to cost about a pound and it was one of them that you had to scratch off which day and month you were using it on. We'd then jump on a bus and go round St Helens and Liverpool, just having a laugh together.

On this occasion, we were walking through Lime Street Station after getting off the train and these three older lads spotted us and saw us as easy prey. They came straight over to the biggest in our group, took his Zonie off him and whatever money he had. I'm not really into football, but I was wearing a Manchester United top at the time and thought if these lads saw it, because we were in Liverpool, they'd do me in, so I started slowly zipping my jacket up. The leader of the older lads had his hand up his jumper as if he was about to pull something out, proper intimidated us. He started saying, 'Give us your fucking money.' He must have done some type of kickboxing, as he started throwing big high kicks to the side of my mate's head.

Thankfully, a passer-by spotted what was going on and shouted, 'Oi. Leave them alone.' These lads made a run for it and seconds later, the police turned up and started running through Lime Street trying to catch them. Problem now was that these lads had nicked our Zonies and we had no money to get home. When the police realised what had happened, they wrote us out a note each, basically saying we could travel for nothing.

Thing is, the copper never dated it, so I took that note everywhere with me and used it for about a year. Happy days.

# CHAPTER 5

# GO SHORTY

*'It's not the size of the dog in the fight, it's the
size of the fight in the dog'*

Mark Twain

ALTHOUGH my rugby career came to a standstill, I was always there or thereabouts when it came to boxing competitions. In my first 22 amateur fights, I only lost one. If I have to be honest, though, I never reached my full potential back then, simply because I started messing about. Smoking weed and having a few drinks didn't help.

We used to go to this girl's house about a mile from our house, whose walls were covered in tin foil. Very strange. We used to buy a fiver's worth of weed, put two cigs in it and that made the 'two cigga mix'. That would go in the homemade bong, then we'd pass it around. There'd be about ten of us puffing away and we could barely see each other because of all the smoke.

Back to the boxing.

From the age of 14 to 15, I'd got to the semis and the finals, but never won the National Amateur Boxing Championships (NABCs). However, when I turned 16 I knuckled down in training and reached the finals at the Barnsley Metrodome. My opponent was John Corcoran, from Stowe ABC, and all I remember about the fight was going back to the corner at the end of the second round and Chizzy shouting, 'You've got this!' I went out for the third round buzzing and won on points.

This was my first major win and title. I was made up. I'd trained hard and it showed me the results I could get when I really dedicated myself. I had a real feeling of achievement, especially as I'd fought around 60 times as an amateur by now and had something to show for it. More than anything, I was over the moon for Chizzy after all the time and effort he'd put in with me.

Here's an interesting fact. When I was 16, I won the schoolboys competing at 45kg (seven stone) and was only a shade over five feet tall. How I grew into a middleweight frame is beyond me. On the subject of weight, it wasn't until I started to compete that I started to realise just how tough a sport boxing was. Not just the fighting bit, but everything that comes with it.

The hardest part for me in boxing at this stage was making weight. I'd eat the wrong food, then make myself sick in the toilet, just to make sure I didn't put any weight on. Stupid really. One day, I picked some books up at school and immediately fainted because I had no energy in me. Next thing I remember was opening my eyes and seeing the ceiling.

As to how we used to make weight, there was no science back then. We never tried working out how much a pint of fluid weighed and which foods retained water. Back then, I'd leave the gym in the evening having checked my weight and was buzzing when it was bang on. Then I'd go home and eat a little bit extra and panic like mad when I had to jump on the scales the day after. I used to put on a massive pair of boots which went up to my knees and get all my kit on, including my wraps. I was basically trying to say, 'I'm OK. I don't need my weight checked.' But the second Chizzy saw you, he'd say, 'Take it all off and get on them scales. You can't kid the kid that's kidded thousands.' Great.

If I was a little bit heavy, he'd kick up the biggest stink you could ever imagine. He'd then get me on the heavy bags with a sweat suit on, walk over to my father and anyone else standing at reception, and you could hear him saying, 'He's a glutton. Doesn't give a shit.' I was throwing a punch then looking over at reception to see him pointing at me in a rage, shaming me up in front of everyone. It got worse. You'd be at home watching the telly when you'd hear a hard knock on the door. There was Chizzy with the scales in his hand. 'Surprise! Check weight.' There was no escaping him. It seemed like borderline bullying, but I now look back with a smile on them days.

Sounds strange, but a big memory of me making weight is the smell of bin bags. The gym at Bobbies Lane was massive, with no central heating. We used to have one of those Calor gas fires and we'd be skipping in front of it on Saturdays and Sundays, wearing bin bags trying to get weight off. They don't do that much now, but back in the day that's how we made weight. We'd never take our bin bags home with us at the end of a session because you'd only use them in the gym, then chuck them away. When I used to forget to take new ones the morning after, I had to wear the same ones I'd left the night before. As I said, the gym was ice cold and where there was sweat and condensation built up inside them, it was now rock-solid ice. Even to this day, when I smell a bin bag, it takes me back to those days at the gym.

Making weight turned out to be the reason our Danny quit boxing. Shame really as he had loads of talent. He'd fought some good lads in the amateurs like Derry Mathews. In fact, he was responsible for me losing one of my teeth, although that wasn't strictly boxing.

Remember the programme *Gladiators*? When it first came out, we all used to sit round the telly as a family and buzz off it on a Saturday night. As soon as it would finish, me and our Danny would have our own version. We'd jump on to our mum's bed and wrestle each other off. The one who wrestled the other off three times was the winner.

On this occasion, I jumped up to get him, but the problem was he'd gone just before me. Our heads clashed and when I pulled away, my front tooth was stuck in his head. Realising what had happened, Danny went quiet for a few seconds with his mouth wide open as he stared at the gap in my teeth. I went downstairs and said to my mum, 'I've lost me tooth. It's stuck in our Danny's head.' She looked at me a bit concerned, took a look at me to make sure I was OK, then I went back and said to Danny, 'It's still only 2-1. Let's crack on!'

Back to Danny's weight. Around this time, we were due to weigh in for the schoolboys' boxing competition. We'd just finished training on that Saturday and knew we had to diet to make weight for Sunday. That night, we were watching telly when something looked a bit suspicious. Our Ricky was only a little kid at the time and always used to sit on the floor in front of the telly with a cup of tea and some biscuits on a tray.

Our Danny was laid down next to Ricky and every now and then I kept seeing Danny very subtly leaning to one side, dropping his head down slightly and then lifting it up again. I decided to ask him, 'You're quiet tonight. You alright?' He nodded his head. I asked again, 'You OK?' He nodded again. I then said, 'Why aren't you talking or looking at us?'

Next time he dropped his head down, I leant over and saw he was eating a biscuit each time and dipping it into his brew. I said, 'What you doing? We're weighing in tomorrow.' As he turned around, his cheeks were full, and a big pack of biscuits appeared from under his t-shirt that he'd been hiding. Our Danny then said in a right huff, 'I can't diet any more. I've got Chizzy at the gym giving me shit and you're like the Chizzy of this house. I'm not boxing any more. I've had enough.'

That was the last episode in his boxing career.

\* \* \* \* \*

If there's one thing boxing did open my eyes to, it's travelling. I got to visit countries I could have never dreamed about or afforded as a lad. One of my most memorable trips was to Uzbekistan, not long after I won the schoolboys [championship]. It probably wasn't Chizzy's favourite, though. There was a selection of us from the North West who went over. From our gym there was me, Birchy, Craig Lyon and Gary Davies, and from other gyms the likes of Paul Smith Jr (Smigga), Ste Ungi, Lee Jennings and Joe Vaughn.

It was proper rough in Uzbekistan back then, but we got treated unbelievably well. We had this round-the-clock bodyguard who didn't look like your typical big meathead. He was just a normal young lad. I don't know exactly who he was, but wherever we went he had massive respect. You'd be walking down the street and people would be slamming on the brakes just to get out and shake his hand. Not sure if he was some kind of gangster, or well connected, but he was certainly a well-known face in the area.

Growing up in Fingerpost, money was scarce, but it wasn't until we came here that we realised how wealthy we were. They were badly poverty stricken. When you changed up ten US dollars, you'd get a massive load of notes back. It was about 3,000 Uzbekistani Som to a dollar and notes started from one Som upwards.

These kids were begging you for something like a 25 Som note, which was not even a penny in English currency. This one kid asked for 25 Som and I gave him 200. His face lit up. He was buzzing. He ran round the corner and you could hear him shouting something. Next thing a whole tribe came running out and it was total chaos. I ended up having to get them to queue in single file, while Lee Jennings was pissing himself saying, 'Look at you dishing out notes like you're the president.'

Back to the boxing competition and I did alright. My first fight was against the Uzbekistani champion, who I beat. I couldn't make my 45kg weight for the next fight, which was strange because my check weight was usually spot on. That night, I went and trained, ran back to the hotel, ran up the stairs, had a boiling hot shower, got changed and went to check my weight and was a pound over.

I woke up the morning after and the scales were now saying I was heavier than the night before. That made no sense. I went for another run and did another weight check, but nothing came off, so I ended up fighting in the 48kg category for my next bout. Even though I won my fight against a lad from Korea, I didn't get any prizes because my last fight wasn't officially part of the competition.

The worst done by was Lee Jennings. Lee weighed bang on 60kg but when he jumped in the ring, there was this monster in front of him who was at least 20kg heavier. Lee was looking at him across the ring, while we were all looking at each other thinking, 'Surely this is the wrong guy. They'll bring in the right one in a minute.' Next thing the bell went and you could see the expression on Lee's face thinking, 'Oh shit.'

Fair play to Lee. He could have walked out, but he went in there and gave it his best. Every time he landed a punch, the other guy never moved an inch. The fight was stopped in the second round, which was certainly a good thing for Lee. Our team asked for the opponent to be put on the scales as he walked out of the ring, but they got him out of the venue immediately. They agreed to send him to the hotel the day after to be weighed, but a totally different lad turned up, who was half his size and still heavier than Lee. Funnily enough, there's not a trace of that fight in any of the records. I still joke with Lee now when I see an Uzbekistani heavyweight on the telly. I'll pop him a text and say, 'Isn't that the bloke you fought in 1999?'

Craig Lyon, on the other hand, had no problems and ended up winning the tournament. The people who won were given massive rugs and loads of other mad stuff. The rest of us were all given one of them big cloaks like you see Gennady Golovkin wear for his ring entrance. I wore it all round my estate for weeks when I got back and when anybody knocked on our door, there I was wearing it.

The trip was a great experience, but unfortunately it didn't have a great ending. Chizzy was very ill. All I remember was waking up this one morning and someone saying, 'John's been taken ill. He's gone to hospital.' The late, great boxing coach from Rotunda ABC, Jimmy 'Albo' Albertini, was there with him. Those old-school trainers, even though they were in different gyms, they all had a lot of respect for each other. Albo was very worried about him, but Chizzy being Chizzy tried to brush it under the carpet and came home with us a few days later, most likely against the doctors' orders. It wasn't until we got home that we found out Chizzy had had a heart attack.

I hated seeing Chizzy ill, but at least I was around to see him and help him if he needed it. It was something I wouldn't be able to do at a later date, which would become one of my biggest regrets in life.

# CHAPTER 6

# BARMY ARMY

*'Your country needs you'*

Lord Kitchener

ALL the way through school, I wanted to join the army. When I was 16, I left Cowley and about a year later I applied at the army careers office in town. I went to Warrington to do the standard English and maths tests, and all that carry-on, and passed with no bother. In fact, I came second in the class and was told I'd be on track to get into the army and the police if I wanted. I then had another couple of meetings with the army officers and it was agreed for me to go to Sutton Coldfield to do my basic training.

First day was the medical and the second was the physical tests, which I was looking forward to. Problem is, I never got the chance to do them. I failed the medical because I'd put on the form that I had eczema on my legs. Turns out when I went to the doctor's a few weeks later, it was just dry skin.

A couple of weeks before, I was fighting in the NABC quarter-finals and one of the refs was an army physical trainer. On the day I failed the medical, he recognised me and came over and had a chat. I told him I was getting discharged and next thing I know, I'm in the sergeant major's office having a meeting. 'Please come back. We love boxing in the army and we'd love you to come back. We've heard you've got real talent and we'd love for you to fight for the army team. You'll have a great life and get looked after.'

By now I was a bit disheartened having been discharged. I'd trained for all their tests, passed everything, then I was on a train home because of the dry skin. I was genuinely pissed off, so I turned them down. The thing is, I had no idea what I was going to do with my life now.

If I'd not told them it was eczema, I could have been in the army and none of the madness which was about to unfold in my life would have happened.

CHAPTER 7

# OLD FART

*'It's quite nice to have a place to leave things.*
*You can be a permanent gypsy, but it's nice to go home'*

Daphne Guinness

WITHOUT the army to fill my time, I started taking any work available. Problem was, there was rarely anything permanent going locally. Also, if I wanted to get a job with a company as a brickie or something like that, nobody would take me on full time because I was too young and didn't have experience. How was I supposed to come to a job with experience if nobody gave me experience in the first place? It was the classic 'Catch 22' situation.

The number of jobs I had as a lad was ridiculous. One of my first was a milk round, which worked out at a pound an hour. I used to get up at 4.45am and work until 8am, come home, change and go straight to school. All for three quid a day.

I went on to work in a chicken factory, order picked at a warehouse and soon after leaving school ended up in a place called Salford Meat Packing. The factory, which wasn't in Salford and doesn't exist any more, looked like something out of the Rocky movies. Either way, it was my first proper job and I loved it. I'd do the morning shift from 6am until 2pm and then, if it was available, I'd do another shift from 2pm until 10pm to get overtime. Legally, I wasn't allowed to do a double shift at that time because I wasn't 18.

They had a building in the factory where they diced the meat and another building where they minced it. All frozen. You name it, chicken, turkey, rabbit, any type of mince. We'd then bag it up, put it through the sealer and box it. That was then shipped off to the big supermarket chains.

When you walked into the cubing place, you had to put your overalls on, take your shoes off and put your boots on. There was this fella called Phil and he had a bad temper on him. Proper psycho. He worked all the doors around town and was known to be a hard man. For some reason, me and Zapper (Ian Roberts) used to torment Phil, winding him up. I ended up with a black eye from him on more than one occasion.

Here's one of the things that we'd do to wind him up. I'd pop some frozen diced meat in my pocket and then tell the supervisor I needed to go to the toilet. I used to then get Phil's shoes and fill them with the frozen cubes. Two or three hours later, we'd all go and put our shoes on to come out for our break. By now, all the cubes had melted and Phil had loads of soggy meat in his shoes. When he found out it was me, he flipped.

'Fucking you again,' he said. He was throwing me around this room and trying to make me eat this soggy meat out of his shoe. At one point, I was on the floor laughing as he was trying to make me eat this meat and he ended up kicking me. Because the floor was all wet and slippery, the second he booted me, I slid from one length of the room to the other, still laughing.

\* \* \* \* \*

Not long after the army episode, I was in and out of jobs. A group of gypsies who I knew would always have a bit of work for me and our Danny. Stuff like guttering and roofing. They'd knock on our door, pick us up and then give us 30 quid at the end of the day, 50 if we were lucky.

One day, they came for our Danny, but he wasn't there, so they said to me, 'Do you wanna go? The job's in Gateshead.' I'd just woken up and was still pissed from the night before. 'OK,' I said. I got a bag together quickly, threw loads of stuff in it and jumped in the back of the

Tranny (Transit) van and fell asleep. Next thing, I woke up almost 200 miles away from home, sober, but really rough. As we pulled into this field, I suddenly thought, 'Fuuuucking shit. What am I gonna do now?'

I ended up spending the next five weeks up there doing jobs like roofing and at night I'd be sleeping in the back of the Tranny van, which was proper rough. We weren't allowed to use the toilet in the caravans, so every time we had to go, we'd head to the bushes. In terms of a shower – forget it. There was a Maccy's in Gateshead and we used to walk into the disabled toilet to have a full body wash.

Our Danny ended up coming after a couple of weeks and we had a laugh, but it was not a great quality of life. I'd go to work, then go to the pubs in Gateshead, walk home pissed, get in the back of the Tranny van and get my head down. A few hours later, I'd wake up and do the same the day after.

After a few weeks, life on the gypsy campsite was starting to get me down and one night I decided to leave and head back home. I didn't have any money and was pissed, so I walked all the way to Newcastle, right over the Gateshead Millennium Bridge and got to the train station. It was about a five-mile walk.

Without any money, I thought I could pay on the other side. That in itself made no sense, because I still wouldn't have had any money when I did reach the other side. Anyway, the station was shut, so I decided to go to sleep until it opened. I got my head down and within no time the police appeared.

'What you doing?'

'I'm going to sleep. Train station's shut. I'm waiting for me train.'

'Alright,' then they walked off.

Twenty minutes later, the train pulled up and I jumped on. Get in! Then the conductor came over and said, 'Where's your ticket?'

'I don't have a ticket.'

'Got any money?'

'No. Got no money.'

'No ticket or money, you're not coming on.'

So that was that. Hardly the masterplan, was it? Just as quickly as I was on, I was off and walking the five-mile trek back to the gypsy camp.

By the time I arrived, it was starting to get light. As I was walking through, all these dogs on their chains on site were barking like mad at me. I went back to the Tranny van and put my head down for a couple of hours, feeling really deflated.

In the end, as daft as it sounds, it was a fart that made me leave the gypsies. I was in the Tranny van, when someone let one rip. It wasn't me, though, honest to God. The guy who owned the van, John, turned around in his thick Irish accent and said at a hundred miles an hour, 'Who the fuck farted? Who? Who? Who?'

I was sitting behind him and burst out laughing.

'It's you Martin, it's you, innit?' he said.

'John. It's not me,' I replied while giggling.

'One more fart in this van and you've all had it.'

Next minute, someone farted. You couldn't hear it, just smell it. It really stunk. I was thinking, 'It's gonna kick off now.' I was the first to smell it and started laughing nervously, then a couple of seconds later John smelt it. He hit the roof and thought it was me. 'No! It's not me!' He started trying to hit me while driving. At first it was a bit of a laugh as I was dodging the blows, but then he hit me with an elbow in the head. That was it. I felt like getting stuck into him, but I wouldn't have made it very far from the caravan site if I had. Instead I said, 'Fucking take me home, now.'

One day and one fart later, they drove me back and that was the end of my gypsy adventure.

# CHAPTER 8

# DEAD LUCKY

*'Before you leave, the fortune teller reminds you that
the future is never set in stone'*

Erin Morgenstern

FIRST time I got really drunk was when I was 14. I left the house and said to my mum, 'I'm going out. I won't be late.'

I wasn't meant to be drinking because I obviously wasn't old enough, but our good family friends Ste and Kim Lynch had just took over the local pub and were having an opening party, and me and my mates decided to go behind the bar and pour our own pints.

At 3am my mum and dad received a knock on the door. A policeman was standing there with an ambulance behind him. 'Your son has been picked up on the side of the road, drunk. Really out of it. We would like for you to come to the hospital with us.'

My mum spent the whole night there. They didn't pump my stomach, but the doctors were genuinely concerned because I was completely unresponsive. In other words, I was sloshed. Thankfully I came to a few hours later, in a bad way.

From that episode, up to the time of the army, I'd not really been into getting drunk or out of my head on drugs, even though they were always available on my estate. Yeah, the odd joint and beer, but not getting proper out of it. That was about to change pretty quickly.

A couple of months after being discharged from the army, I went down Wigan Pier clubbing with a few of my mates, including Johnno and Butty (aka Phil Roberts, Zapper's brother). Butty got his nickname because he's always been dark skinned and would tan really quickly. We used to say he looked like a burnt sausage. Then it went to sausage, then sausage butty, now it's just 'Butty'.

At the time, the rave scene was big at Wigan Pier and one night I was that deflated after the whole army thing that I turned to one of my mates and said, 'Give us something.'

'I don't think you should, mate,' he replied.

He kept refusing as he knew I'd never taken it before, but in the end I convinced him to give me half an Ecstasy tablet. After I took it, the first thing he said was, 'Don't let this fuck up your boxing.'

Problem was, it did. I started going to Wigan Pier every Friday and Saturday from then on and between the new experience of drugs, the clubbing and alcohol, it became a euphoric feeling every time I went out. There was a big gang of us and we became known as 'Pier-Heads'.

A couple of months before I'd decided to join the army, my mum went to see this fortune teller who was well known in the area for predicting the future with accuracy. When my mum came home, I asked, 'How did it go?'

My mum replied, 'She was brilliant. I was sat there and she asked, "Have you got boys?" "Yes." "Does one of them do drugs?" "One of them smokes pot," and she replied, "No. The other son. The one who's good at sports. He's taking cocaine. He's going to get into drugs big time and go off the rails soon. He'll get in a lot of trouble. But don't worry, it will only last about 18 months and he'll be back to his usual self."'

I couldn't believe how far-fetched it all sounded. Bearing in mind I'd recently won the schoolboys, was training like mad and was trying to get on the England squad, I replied, 'Well, she's got that all wrong.' Truth is, she was spot on. A few months later, I started resenting being at home and wanted my own place. Mum said, 'Go and get your own place then. You'll soon see how hard it is.' I thought I was king of the world and said, 'I'll be alright. Just you see.'

When I stopped boxing, I kind of went the other way and decided that I was going to catch up on everything I'd missed out on and rebel. I don't know why, as I'd had a good upbringing and always been close to my mum and dad. I ended up applying for my own council flat and getting it in a matter of weeks. It was in Peasley Cross and the bonus was that Zapper also had a pad in the same block. Within no time, I had Garvey (David Garvey), Adam Moore and Digger (Stuart Bamford), who was on the run at the time, all living with me. Four of us in a one-bedroom flat. Every day was like a weekend.

We used to go out, then sometimes come back with up to 50 people, including a good few friends from Salford, and have an all-night session. We hardly ever slept and it was sometimes hard to tell what time of the day it was. The music was on full blast right through to late morning and we soon started getting into trouble with the neighbours and police. We didn't give a shit, though, because everything was either funny or a joke.

Everyone who came into the flat had to sign their name on the wall and within a few weeks, it was almost full. The place started to stink and I remember our Katie once saying, 'It looks like a doss house in here.' She wasn't far wrong.

I had some laughs at the flat, but there is one episode I'd love to be able to reverse. There was this small immersion heater cupboard in the flat, which was pitch black and had one chair in it. If anyone was missing from the party, you could almost guarantee they'd be in that cupboard bladdered. I used it like a little boardroom. You'd often hear me say, 'Meet me in the cupboard in a minute for a team talk,' or a TT as it soon became known. On this particular night, I called Digger in for a TT about boxing. I started off by saying, 'I hate boxing.' I didn't really, but I'd just had an argument with Chizzy and hadn't cooled off yet. Digger replies, 'I only ever started boxing for me dad. I'm bored of it.'

I walked out of the cupboard, picked up a baseball bat and smashed the shit out of all my trophies I had on these shelves. Digger ran over trying to stop me as he said, 'Fucking 'ell, mate. I was only joking. Don't. You'll regret this one day.' And how right he was.

I put all the broken bits and pieces in black bin bags, threw them off the third-floor landing we were on and got back on the ale. A few hours later, I went down with Digger and dumped them by the railway track. Seven years of boxing achievements gone just like that. What a dickhead.

Looking back, it breaks my heart thinking what I put everyone through. The likes of Chizzy, my mum and dad, and close friends could all see I was getting out of control, but I thought it was them who were wrong. Who did they think they were telling me what to do? 'Don't hang around with this person. Stop with the ale and drugs. Get back into your boxing.' I didn't want to hear any of it.

Despite all my carryings on, while I was down Wigan Pier all the time my mum and our Katie would go round and clean my flat. Not once, but all the time. The place stunk and was always in a state, but they never made any fuss of it. One morning they came in after an all-night session and Butty was laid face down in the kitchen, in his own sick. Although it wasn't funny for our Katie to see, when it happened it was hilarious.

Butty knew he was going to be sick and ran to the kitchen, but didn't make it to the sink. He fell on the carpet, puked up, then lay there with his head on its side, with his cheek fully in his own sick. He was smashed but still aware of the music and was nodding his head to the beat, with all this sick sloshing around him.

Even with all that, and about 20 people sprawled all over the place, our Katie and my mum somehow still managed to give the flat the once-over. Nobody even remembered them coming in. They would have made great burglars.

\* \* \* \* \*

I was known for being a good boxer from the local area who had a good future ahead. So when I started to bump into people in town who didn't know I was on drugs, family or people who were proud of me, I'd be really ashamed as I was standing there out of it.

After a while, that feeling just evaporated. I started thinking, 'Yeah, I'm doing drugs. You got a problem with it? It's my fucking life.' I wasn't addicted to drugs. I was never itching to take them. It was the scene I loved. The music, the atmosphere, partying with my mates. The lifestyle. The thing was, with the style of life I was living, aged only 18, I was already thinking, 'I won't make it to 30. Why change what I'm doing?'

I only found this story out recently, and again, it gets me really upset to think what I put my mum through in those early days. I was standing in town with a group of mates, with a can of lager in my hand looking like shit. Really bad. I always took tip-top pride in my appearance and there I was, off my head, looking like I'd been wearing the same clothes for a couple of days. Mum started crying and thought to herself, 'What is he doing?' She then walked off home in a total state and I never knew she'd been watching. That's how bad I was. A complete wreck-head.

The parties were fun, but the comedowns were awful. Think of it when you've been on the ale, now multiply that by 100 when you're off your head on drugs and have been up for days. You'd go from that feeling of buzzing to feeling lost. I also started having night terrors. I was afraid to go to sleep because every time I did, it was as if I felt like I was getting strangled. If I did fall asleep, it wouldn't be for long and when I woke up, I'd be panicking as if I was being killed. Then I didn't want to go back to sleep because I was having massive anxiety attacks. That's what drugs can do to you.

* * * * *

Usually, it was my mum who would dish out a bollocking at home. My dad would only say something if he felt it was really necessary, usually when I'd done something very wrong. Now he was trying to give me advice all the time, because he could see I was off the rails.

Take, for example, the time I bought this shitty little ghetto Mk1 orange Ford Fiesta with Zapper. I put a PlayStation down as the deposit as I didn't have all the money at once. We thought we wouldn't get pulled by the police. What were we thinking? Two young kids in a proper shit car. I used to get the keys and take it for a spin, even though I hadn't passed my test. Even worse, I'd usually be drunk and on drugs. My dad would say, 'What are you doing? You can't drive that car.'

'I can do what I want. I'm fucking 18,' I would say. I was apparently a big man now. A proper grown-up. A few weeks later, that arrogance almost cost me my life. Five of us squeezed into the shitty Fiesta, which included Zapper and our Danny. The intention was to finish off at Wigan Pier.

We went for a few drinks locally and just before getting into the car took some Ecstasy. The drive to Wigan Pier was about 20 minutes, so we used to time it just right in terms of taking them, so by the time we arrived we were 'coming up' and feeling the high.

As we were driving down the motorway, all I remember was our Danny shouting, 'It's coming into us,' but none of us could understand what he was going on about because the tablets had kicked in. What we didn't realise was that a big artic lorry was coming our way.

BANG. It crashed flush into us.

It all happened dead quick. The second it hit us, we've started spinning around and around on the motorway. Then it got worse. All of a sudden it felt like the car was crushing in on us, like it was about to cave in. The windows started cracking and you could hear the metal crunching in on us.

What we didn't realise, while we were spinning, was the lorry was braking and had caught up with us. We were now wedged firmly underneath its front cabin, being crushed and dragged along the motorway. Every one of us was screaming and I mean screaming.

The lorry ended up coming to a standstill, with loads of cars behind us, which had also come to a halt. We jumped out of the car and went on the hard shoulder of the M6, checked each other out to make sure nobody was hurt, then all hugged, buzzing, that we were still alive. It was a miracle how none of us had a scratch. The car looked like a mangled matchbox in the middle of the motorway.

I looked at the lorry, then realised our Danny had run over to try and drag the driver out. As he's trying to get to the driver, this car pulls up next to us and this guy gets out to check we're OK.

We were all buzzing from drugs, had more tablets in our pockets, none of us had a licence, the car wasn't registered to us and it had no insurance. Without answering to this guy who'd just pulled up, I turned to everyone and said, 'Come on, let's go.'

We bombed it down the motorway on foot, up this little grass verge, crossed this road and next minute we'd gatecrashed some 21st birthday party at a community hall in the middle of nowhere. There were loads of people there drinking, so when we walked in, nobody batted an eyelid. We immediately called a taxi and headed straight down to Wigan Pier. As we pulled up, there was a massive queue outside and loads of police were hovering around. The guy from the car who'd pulled over to check on us must have grassed us up to the police, telling them what we looked like and the direction we headed off in.

Our Danny and my other two mates took a look at the police and said, 'Fuuuuck that. I'm not going in there. No way. There's bizzies all over it.' Me and Zapper took the gamble and went inside Wigan Pier. When we were queuing up, the police were still walking up and down checking everyone out. They were probably looking for people covered in scratches and bruises, so we never got looked at once. Very lucky.

The episode with the car crash didn't stop me driving and it wasn't long before I started getting nicked and stopped regularly by the police. The first time I got done for a car offence, it wasn't even my fault or car. My mate was banned and was driving, so he gave my details in. That's how I got my first ban. It certainly wasn't my last, though.

A few weeks later, five of us, including our Danny, were driving on the way to Warrington, proper bladdered. We got pulled over by the police and they asked us who was who. I was on warrant, so I said I was our Danny. That used to be our thing. We used to give each other's details when the other was on the run or had been in plenty of trouble. Funnily enough, we were never on warrant or on the run at the same time.

Anyway, the policeman got to my brother and asked, 'What's your name?' 'Danny Murray,' he replied. The policeman shouted at him, 'Stop lying. That's him (pointing at me). He's Danny Murray.' They ended up nicking him, even though he was the real one.

It got to the stage around then when they'd start to nick us both. We didn't have any tattoos at the time and loads of people used to say that we looked dead similar, so the police didn't take any chances.

I had my routine down to a tee.

'Have you passed your test?' the copper would ask.

'Of course I have. I just don't have me licence on me.'

'You've got seven days to produce it at the police station.'

'No worries. I'll sort it.'

I never did, though. I lost count of how many times I pulled this routine. I thought I was being clever, but these things always catch up with you one way or another.

CHAPTER 9

# BAD TRIP

*'Morality is not only taught, it is caught'*

Neil Kurshan

I'M mad into *The Antiques Roadshow,* me. Love programmes like that, although I certainly paid above the asking price one night.

On 30 October 2000, me, Zapper and Butty decided to go to KFC, which was about a mile from the flat. Halfway to KFC, there was this little dip under a bridge and because of the floods at the time some cars had tried to drive through it, broken down and were just left there stranded.

We went over to the cars and decide to have a rummage. First car, nothing. Then we managed to get into the boot of a Nissan Micra and inside was this mad church painting type thing. I looked and thought, *'Antiques Roadshow!'* I turned to Zapper and said, 'It's gotta be worth a fortune, that. Gotta be.'

I got it out of the boot and put it by the side of the road and carried on walking, with the intention of picking it up on the way back. What we didn't realise was that the police had seen everything on CCTV. There we were in KFC when this police van pulls up outside. I said straight away, 'They're here for us.' I had some drugs down my pants, so I dropped them on the floor and kicked them away. In they came and bang, we were nicked.

Two days later, I was in St Helens Magistrates' Court. I'd been arrested loads of times before but this was the first time I had ended up in court. I came away with a conditional discharge for six months and a 40 quid fine. It turned out the car belonged to a priest. Made sense. The painting was apparently worth £1.99. So much for *The Antiques Roadshow*.

Drugs by this stage had become a massive thing in my life. I'd tried most available recreational drugs out there at the time, so tripping was a regular thing. That said, there are some strange and weird trips which stick in my mind.

One night, we came out of Wigan Pier and I jumped in a car with a few lads from Leyland who I used to knock around with. We ended up at this massive house party, with a load of people I didn't know. They were all taking these tablets called 'Fish', which were basically ketamine, the type of drug they use to knock out horses with. I took one.

I was sat there on the couch and this lad was talking to me and I don't remember what he was saying, but his head just kept morphing into different faces. Like when you walk around town sometimes and you stop and stare at someone and think, 'Where do I know that person from?' It was like that. I was staring at this guy as his face started morphing into someone I thought I knew, then a few seconds later it changed into another familiar face.

That was my first bad trip, but it certainly wasn't my last. The next big one came with a lot more drama. A hell of a lot more.

# CHAPTER 10

# HOLIDAY WRECK

*'Little bit of fun, little bit of joke,*
*Little bit of drink, little bit of smoke'*

DJ Pied Piper – 'Do You Really Like It'?

STE Birch lived above my flat in Peasley Cross. He and Craig Lyon were flying all over the world fighting for the England squad, making a real name for themselves. I should have been with them. It wasn't that long before that I was in Uzbekistan with Craig and Ste, and should have been following a similar path to them. Instead, while Ste was deep into his boxing and gaining focus, I was downstairs partying. Everything was in excess. It was now no longer about trophies and medals, it was all about taking drugs and drinking non-stop.

Then came the chance to stretch the party boundaries abroad in May 2001. Ste and Craig were going for a break to Ayia Napa with Ste's mum, June, her partner Anthony and another mate of mine. We were mates at the time but I want to let it be known we're not any more. The route he took in his life later on, from my side, was unforgiveable.

Ste and Craig had been going on about the trip for a few weeks, but it hadn't registered in my head.

The day before they were getting ready to leave, they were round mine having a quiet one, while I was off my head. They all started saying to each other, 'You ready for tomorrow. I'm buzzing. Can't wait.'

'Where you going?' I asked.

'Ayia Napa. It's gonna be mad.'

'You're fucking joking. I'm coming.'

That night, still off my head, I jumped on to Teletext and in the early hours of the morning I ended up booking this holiday. A few hours before heading out, I called my mum.

'I'm going to Cyprus.'

'What? Why? With who?'

'Just going on holiday. Meeting Ste and Craig out there.'

'You're not getting up to anything, are you? Just be careful.'

'Nooooo. Don't be silly. Just going on holiday, mum. Of course I'll be well behaved.'

I decided I'd take a few tablets with me to keep me buzzing out there.

Because the police were always round my flat, I used to hide my drugs in an old burnt-out derelict pub. In order to get in, I had to climb up this drainpipe, crawl through this burnt-out pub and get under the floorboards, which is where I kept my stash.

When I got to Manchester airport, I was still off my head and went to the toilet. I must have looked a right state. Once I'd locked the door on the cubicle, I shoved the drugs up my arse. Problem was, as the time for departure got closer, I got paranoid and started to realise this was not a good idea. I ended up getting cold feet and flushed them down the toilet.

After landing at Larnaca airport, I suddenly realised I didn't have transfers or a hotel booked. When I was on Teletext, I'd just booked flights. I jumped in a taxi and said, 'Take me to Ayia Napa.' When I got there, I tried calling the lads, but everyone's phone was dead. I was thinking, 'What do I do now?' I had my suitcase with me and saw this bar closing for the night, so decided to rough it and went to sleep under this table.

A few hours later, I woke up and had some breakfast at a nearby café. After finishing my food, I asked the lady who was running the place if I could leave my suitcase with her, as I didn't know where I was going and didn't want to have to pull that around with me all day. She said, 'You can, but I can't be responsible. If it goes, it goes.' 'I'm gonna have to take that risk,' I replied. I went to a shop and bought a six-pack of lager, then walked up and down the streets and beach, looking for my mates. Just as I was about to give up hope, I heard a group of lads on motorbikes popping their horn. It was them.

'No way, Martin! What are you doing here?'

'I told you I was coming. I'm gonna have to sneak into your hotel and stay with yous as I don't have a room.'

'Sound.'

Thankfully my suitcase was still there, so I went and grabbed it then jumped on the back of one of the motorbikes and we headed off to the hotel. It was my first time abroad on holiday without my family. Every night we were getting bladdered, being typical young idiots abroad, just wrecking the place. We had no respect. I was also doing loads of drugs and word got about that we had a decent stash in our hotel room which we'd bought from some lads out there.

Things started going downhill very quickly. I was riding back to the hotel on a motorbike in the early hours when I decided to stop and do a good deed. This young lad was walking down this long street and I stopped and said, 'Where you going?' He told me the name of the hotel and I said, 'That's miles away, mate. Jump on the back and I'll take ya.'

On the way there, we went down a little ramp which had some sand on it and the bike gave way underneath me. I crashed into a telephone pylon, broke my collarbone and I was flat out on my back in agony. The other guy walked off with a bloody nose.

I got up and decided it was a good idea to ride the bike back to my hotel. However, I ended up turning left most of the way home because I couldn't turn right due to my collarbone. Every time I did need to turn right, I had to slow the bike down and move it slowly bit by bit until I was facing the right direction. Then I'd go again. With the accelerator on the right side of the handlebars, every time I twisted it I almost passed out with the pain.

I should have gone to the hospital, but I decided to carry on partying. Later that day, a big group of us went out, including a couple of girls from Salford and two Garage MCs from London who were out there gigging. After a mad session that night, off our heads on drink and Ecstasy, we decided to have a few drinks at the bar by the hotel reception and then went up to the room and continued with the party.

By this stage, it was about 7am. I was that fucked, the only thing I remember was cleaning my trainers. I even said to one of my mates, 'Look how clean I can get your trainers.' I took his laces off, scrubbed them and had them looking brand new.

Then something happened and to this day I still can't tell you where I'd gone or why. I went walking the streets for hours barefoot, no t-shirt, no money, with just my shorts on and a pair of trainer laces around my neck. The condition I was in, that drugged-up and dehydrated, I could have easily died.

I was hallucinating bad. I thought everyone was playing a game, following me down the street and every time I'd turn around to look, I thought they were jumping behind cars. I'd turn thinking, 'They're there,' and then walk over to one of the cars looking for these imaginary people. I must have looked a right state to anyone walking past.

I walked into a shop in a daze and for some reason I thought I'd walked in with a girl. The lady behind the counter said, 'Can I help you?' 'I don't know what she wants,' I said as I pointed to the imaginary girl. Turns out I was pointing to a bunch of necklaces. The second I realised, I ran out.

By now, the sun was coming up and, not having any shoes or socks on, the floor was starting to get really hot and I was running for bits of shade. The first hotel I saw, I jumped into their pool just to cool down. When I came out, I went into the nearest shop and nicked a drink as I was close to fainting.

As the drugs started to wear off, I headed back to the hotel room. I still had no idea why I'd gone walkabout in the first place. When I got back, I headed to the pool. The second I got there, Ste's mum came up to me in a real panic, badly upset.

'They've all been arrested for drugs. The police have raided the apartment. They booted the door in and stormed in with armed response. They're looking for you.'

Just as she was speaking, one of the guys who worked there recognised me and started shouting. I looked over, then did a runner. In the meantime, the police had released all my mates, bar one.

A couple of hours later, I sneaked back to the hotel room, but the door was locked. I knocked, but nobody was in. I knew the patio door was always open and decided to climb the outside of the hotel, to get to the roof. That was always a stupid plan, because it was on the sixth floor. Even more mad, because of my broken collarbone, I had to climb up with one arm. When I got to the roof, I leant over, dangled with one arm and somehow landed on the balcony. I really don't know how I did it. I remember looking down at one point thinking, 'Fucking 'ell.'

When I got into the room, I went looking for my case straight away because that's where the drugs were. I was thinking, 'If the drugs are still in the case, I'll get rid of them and the police will have nothing on me.' But I quickly discovered that my case was gone, which also had my money. I had fuck all now. I laid down on the bed really gutted trying to work out what to do next. I started to fall asleep, but that didn't last very long, as about 15 minutes later one of the cleaners walked in. He turned to one of the other staff and shouted something which had the word 'police' in it. I got up, barged past the cleaner and did a runner.

I'd heard that Cyprus was dead against drugs and we were getting slammed. I was 18 and told by people who were out there working that my family and mates back home wouldn't see me again until I was 30. I couldn't go back to the hotel, so I was ducking and diving to keep out of the way of the police. I slept outside this club called The Castle one night and, in all honesty, I can't remember where I stayed for the other nights because of the drugs and being delirious due to not eating.

After a couple of days, I ended up meeting Craig to get some money and food. This led to my first ever encounter with tuna. When I met Craig, he'd left a bit of his lunch, which was a tuna salad. As knackered and hungry as I was, I thought to myself while shaking my head, 'Why would anyone have a salad when on holiday?' I'm not a massive fish lover, but I ended up cleaning the plate.

Now I was on the run, I was thinking about getting the boat from Cyprus to Egypt and then flying from there somehow back home. Problem was, my passport was in the bike hire shop and because I was off my head I couldn't remember where I'd parked it up. To this day, I don't ever remember getting that passport back, or where I'd parked the bike.

I was desperately low. I didn't know what to do. I saw this church and went to go in, but needed to have a top on. Because of my broken collarbone, it took me about ten minutes to get my t-shirt on. When I got inside, I just prayed. I'm not a religious person, but I thought, if I'm going to ask for help, this is the place to do it. I don't remember the exact words I said, but it was basically asking God to look after me as best as possible over the next few days.

I was in the church for about an hour and probably overstayed my welcome, but I had nowhere else to go. I called my mum and explained what had happened. 'The hotel is surrounded by armed guards. They're watching every move I make and I've also smashed me collarbone.'

She broke down crying and started screaming, 'Martin, what have you done? What have you done?' The way she reacted was as if she'd been told I'd been killed. I started crying and ended up smashing the phone box I was calling from.

My mum almost had a breakdown she was that stressed. A couple of my mates went round to see her and said, 'Try some of this [cannabis].' My mum had never tried drugs before or after this time, but had a couple of puffs. Despite everything that was going on, to this day she maintains it was the best night's sleep of her life.

By now, I started to think about my mate who'd been nicked. If he was inside, he'd need a bit of back-up. I slept rough for another night, then handed myself in. I was in shit street and I knew it.

I phoned my mum again. 'I'm heading back to the hotel and waiting for the police to come and pick me up. I'm handing meself in.' I knew she would have been thinking non-stop about what had happened since the first call, not knowing where I was sleeping and whether I was dead or alive, so at least this was some kind of relief for her.

I went back to the reception at the hotel and you could see the shock on the face of the staff there. When I got to the desk I said, 'I'm handing meself in. Tell the police I'm here.' I didn't need to tell them though, because they'd already called them the second I walked into the hotel. They showed me to an office and I sat there until the police arrived, which was about two minutes later.

When they spotted my collarbone, they took me to the hospital straight away. Immediately after, I was taken to the police cells in Ayia Napa. The first cells of many.

# CHAPTER 11

# COPPING IT

*'He who learns but does not think, is lost! He who thinks but does not learn is in great danger'*

Confucius

WHILE I was in jail in Cyprus, my flat got kicked in by a group of lads with hammers, who were looking for me. I don't know why or who they were, but being in Cyprus saved me from that episode. In the meantime, my flat was taken away from me. The council had been dying to take the flat for ages because of the number of complaints about the parties we were having. So, I decided to stay at Zapper's.

Coming back to St Helens after a couple of months banged up abroad was like I'd walked out of a nightclub and straight back in. I was buzzing. I had a cracking tan from being allowed out for 12 hours a day at the prison compound in Cyprus, had bags more confidence and no intention of trying to make a new start.

I was still young and wanted to pick up where I'd left off. More clubbing, more drugs, loads of fighting. Also, now that I'd served prison time abroad, I was starting to enjoy that reputation. I was looking forward to enjoying that style of life. The only lesson I did learn from Cyprus was that I never wanted to take Ecstasy again. I knew I never wanted to feel that out of control. I started doing a lot more wheeling and dealing with my mates. Whatever money I made was spent on fuelling my lifestyle. More drink and drugs. I was straight back to acting like a complete dickhead and the antics started again.

Between 2000 and 2001, I'd had a ridiculous number of fights at Wigan Pier, Maximes and Cricketers and pissed a lot of people off along the way. There were a number of times I'd get told that firms were looking for me, wanting to fill me in. I'd even started to go out tooled up, just in case.

On this particular night, I'd been causing trouble in Cricketers and had been kicked out. I walked out bladdered and fell asleep in one of my mate's cars. One of the doormen at Cricketers grassed me up to this one firm, letting them know that I was there for the taking. When they arrived, the grass pointed to the car and said, 'He's asleep over there, on his own.' They walked over and were just about to fill me in when one of the henchmen recognised me. His son was my younger cousin. He turned to the others and said, 'You're not touching him. I'll get it sorted and make sure he doesn't come here kicking off again, but this time you're not touching him.'

Unfortunately, that experience didn't stop me from behaving the way I did. Nothing could at that point of my life.

\* \* \* \* \*

The problem when you start to get a reputation in the local area is that you start getting nicked for stuff which the police might otherwise turn a blind eye to, or give you a slap on the wrist. I used to remember being asked by the coppers, 'What's your name?' After I'd said Martin Murray, they'd call it through to the station. You could hear them on the radio saying I had previous and they'd nick me straight away. They saw me as a nuisance, which I was.

Another thing was your background and I'm not just saying this to be bitter. I've seen it happen. My dad was an ex-con, whereas if somebody had a dad who was something like an accountant, they'd get sent home, whereas I'd always be nicked.

It got to the stage that every week me or one of my mates was in court. It became a running joke. Our mindset was, 'We're only in court. It's just a laugh.'

Take Christmas Eve 2001, for example. I got caught taking a piss in town and was immediately thrown into the back of the police Tranny van. It didn't help that my mate then started pissing all over the bonnet.

No surprise really when the police ran over and nicked him as well. We went down to the police station and they gave us a court date, but we didn't show up. That then got me further in the shit. It didn't take them long to find me, though, because they knew I'd be back at my mum's at some point and waited for me to come home.

A couple of weeks later, on 10 January 2002, I was in St Helens Magistrates' Court. I was found guilty of being drunk and disorderly, and fined 60 quid, with a conditional discharge for six months. In addition, for not surrendering myself on time, I was given a further conditional discharge for another six months.

Exactly one week later, on 17 January 2002, I was back in court again. Just before I'd gone to Cyprus, on 7 May 2001, there was a fair in Sherdley Park, St Helens. It's an annual event and was well known for having fights over the years.

This lad pushed over a girl, saw I'd clocked him and that I was going to make a beeline for him. He and his two mates then tried to sneak off behind the back of the fair. I chased after him with my two mates but in the meantime loads of people at the fair started running with us because they knew there was going to be a fight.

I caught up with him and we started having a straightener. Out of nowhere, the police arrived like something from a cowboy movie on a load of horses. They split us up, CS gassed us, arrested us and took us to the police cells.

I had some drugs down my pants and when I got to the front desk at the station, I knew they'd search me and take most of my clothes off. I thought, 'What am I gonna do now? How am I gonna get out of this?'

I'd been CS gassed bad, to the point where all my face was blistering up. I said, 'I need some fresh air.' They took me to this place out back by the police cells. The coppers were watching the other lads I'd been fighting with, so I saw my chance.

I needed enough time to get rid of the drugs, or move them from the front of my pants and then 'cheek' it (get 'em in between my bum cheeks). As I was trying to figure out what to do, my mate Butty came in. He wasn't involved in the fight, but he'd been accidentally CS gassed. His mate had got a claim the year before through the police for the same thing, so he thought, 'I'll make some money from this.'

He came to the police station to let the coppers know, but they said, 'You were involved in the fight,' and nicked him as well.

As he came in the cells, he started kicking off, which transferred all the attention to him. 'I don't fucking believe it! You've CS gassed me by accident and now you've arrested me. This is out of order.'

While Butty was off on one, I was 'cheeking' the drugs. They let us out late that evening, by which stage my face was blistered bad from the gas. First thing I did when I got home was take a shower, which was probably not the cleverest move. There was loads of CS gas still in my hair and the second the water came down on me, it felt like I'd been gassed again.

Only five days after leaving the judge in St Helens, on 22 January 2002, I was in front of a different judge, this time at Warrington Magistrates' Court, relating to an offence on 13 January 2002. A load of us from St Helens used to go to Warrington, as we'd always have a laugh there and usually a fight. There was always some kind of commotion or trouble, which is kind of what made it interesting and fun back then. Now, it would be my worst nightmare.

When we walked into this club, I introduced a few of my mates to some of the lads from Warrington, then nipped to the toilet. When I came out, the whole place was empty. I thought, 'That's weird.' What had happened was two of my mates from opposing firms had ended up having an argument, had a scrap and it spilled outside. I started walking to the entrance, thinking they must have been out front, when one of the doormen pushed me off the top steps. I fell down, managed to gather my feet, turned around from the bottom of the steps and said, 'What was that about, ye dickhead?'

There was a copper there who turned to me and said, 'Oi you. Stop swearing.' The doorman then told me to 'fuck off', and I said, 'Who do you think you're talking to?' I got nicked for, and I quote, 'using threatening/abusive/insulting words or behaviour, with intent to cause fear or provocation of violence'. All that for calling the doorman a prick. Nothing was ever mentioned about me being pushed off the top of the stairs. I'm not saying I'm innocent in everything I've done, because I know I'm not, but things like that are ridiculous.

I got fined £100 and paid costs of £50.

CHAPTER 12

# ALL SAINTS

*'Wrestling and boxing is like ping-pong and rugby.*
*There's no connection'*

Mickey Rourke

WITH all this madness going on, I still made time to see the Grand Rugby Final between Saints and Wigan at Murrayfield, Edinburgh. Like Ayia Napa, it was a spur-of-the-moment thing.

Whenever Saints were in a grand final, a load of coaches would leave from Fingerpost. Me and Zapper went out the night before and woke up a little bit giddy. We saw all the lads were going to the final and were gutted we weren't. We tried to get on the coach but there were no seats available. We decided we'd make our own way and figure it all out when we got there.

We jumped on a train and somehow we managed to get tickets for the game. To this day, I'm not even sure where we got them from or how. We watched the first half, pissed, decked out in all – and I mean all – the cheap tat they were selling outside. Scarves, hats, badges, you name it.

I then ended up losing Zapper at half-time. After trying to find him, I spent the next 20 minutes mooching around looking for our seats, which I never found because I was that bladdered. By complete luck, we bumped into each other at full time, then met a few of the lads from St Helens, who were now getting ready to go back on the coaches.

After a quick one with the lads, we decided to stay on, have some food and drinks, and buy some ale for the way home, so we could be buzzing on the train. The intention was to then head back to Wigan Pier to finish the night off. Happy days.

We jumped on a train from Edinburgh to Glasgow, but then missed the last train from Glasgow to Wigan. Problem was, we were wearing Saints colours, which are red and white, and Rangers had just played Aberdeen, who also wear red and white. We didn't realise there was a massive rivalry between the two teams, though. As we started to walk through the train station, we were getting snarled at by every Glasgow fan. For some reason, they kept calling us sheep shaggers. We kept saying, 'We're Saints. Rugby, not football.'

The police could see we were getting proper grief and said, 'Listen. I'll advise you to take that off now.' He was referring to our tops and all the rugby tat we'd bought. He then said, 'What time's your train?' 'We've missed it. We're here for the night now,' I replied. 'In that case, I definitely advise you to take that gear off, or you'll get yourselves in trouble.' At first, we kept it on thinking we'd be alright, but every person who passed us pretty much had a go at us. We ended up dumping it all in a bin.

As you do, we decided we'd nick a car and drive back home. Me, I don't have a clue about cars. Zapper reckoned he was an expert. I turned to him and said, 'Do you know how to nick a car?'

'Yeah, yeah. I can wire a car easy, mate.'

'Sound. Let's go and find a car and drive it to Wigan Pier. We can get there before it closes.' Seemed like a good plan.

We started walking around looking for any shady streets where we could nick a car. Finally, I pointed and said to Zapper, 'What about that one there? You know how to wire that one?' He replied, 'Yeah, yeah. I can wire that one, no problem.' I picked up a brick, threw it through the window and Zapper jumped inside.

He then turns to me and says, 'Oh no. It's one of them new cars with a diamond lock on it. I can't do it.' I'm not even sure if such a thing exists, but I said, 'Ah no. I don't believe it.'

Now we were on a mission to find a car which didn't have this special lock on it. We walked around for ages until we found an old car. I turned to Zapper and said, 'Surely that won't have a diamond lock on it?' He said, 'No, no.'

Brick goes through the window and in goes Zapper, fiddling around with the lock. After a bit, he turns to me in a panic and says, 'I don't believe it. It's got a diamond lock on it.' I replied, 'How can it have a diamond lock, Zapper? That car is older than both of us put together. You said diamond locks were only on new cars.' Basically, he didn't want to admit that he couldn't hotwire a car.

So there we were in Glasgow, with no money, freezing cold, mooching the streets, trying to kill time before our train came in eight hours. We ended up speaking to this mad Scottish fella. Zapper said he was a bag-head tramp, but I thought he was sound. I'm not sure if he was homeless, but either way, we ended up with him.

We walked into this estate in Glasgow and this guy walked into the back of a chippie and nicked three chicken wings. Zapper's a vegetarian, so I ended up getting a double portion.

Soon after, this guy said, 'Come and stay at me sister's house.'

'Sound mate,' I replied.

Zapper starts nudging me saying, 'He's setting us up. He's setting us up.'

'What you on about? He's alright. He got us chicken wings. Chill out,' I said. We start walking and Zapper says again, 'He's setting us up. They're gonna do us in.' I couldn't be arsed with it all, so in the end I turned to this guy and said, 'Listen mate. We're alright. Thanks for the offer, but you crack on without us.'

It got to the early hours of the morning and we started getting really tired. Only problem was, where were we going to sleep? The train station was now shut, so we kept on walking the streets and in the end, in the middle of Glasgow, we found a burnt-out car with no wheels on it. Our bed for the night.

The temperature had proper dropped. When I woke up and looked over, Zapper was like a little shivering dog. I gave him a nudge, then we made our way to the station. I'd never been so happy to get back to St Helens to a warm house, a bed and some food.

Thing is, if I'd known what lay ahead for me back home, I'd have stayed up in Glasgow for a few more months.

CHAPTER 13

# REGRET

*'There is a higher court than the courts of justice
and that is the court of conscience. It supersedes
all other courts'*

Mahatma Gandhi

TWO weeks after my last court appearance on 8 February 2002, there I am back at St Helens Magistrates' Court. It's sad to say but I was becoming a regular. That fortune teller was spot on. Since December 2001, I'd been in court for five different charges over a six-week period. This time, it was relating to something stupid I did on 11 November.

We used to go to petrol stations and park up round the corner and we'd put a bit of black tape on the number plate to make the letter 'E' into a 'B' or do something with the numbers. We'd then fill up the car with petrol and drive off. We also used to do the same with shops. Walk in, take a load of stuff and drive off. It got to the stage where we didn't need anything and we were just doing it for a laugh.

On this occasion, we went to a shop, nicked a case of lager and then got caught on camera. I was fined 50 quid and had to pay £4.33 compensation, which was basically £12.99 split three ways, for a case of beer.

Not long after, I had a proper scare. Some fella had been done in bad near where I lived and left for dead. Whenever anything went wrong back then, it was always like I'd had something to do with it.

I wasn't even in the area at the time, but someone had told the police it was me. The police suddenly appeared at my house and questioned me. I was half asleep from a heavy night before and didn't have a clue what they were talking about. However, when they started to say, 'It's looking like attempted murder,' I soon became alert.

In the end, they checked the CCTV in town and let me go without charge. Episodes like this should have a been a massive wake-up call, but it wasn't. My next appearance in court didn't come with a fine or a conditional discharge. I fucked up big this time. It was relating to something that had happened on 7 October 2001. When I use the term, 'I'm embarrassed,' I mean it with deep, deep regret. I'm referring to a person I can no longer associate with and an episode I don't enjoy revisiting.

On this day, my mates had all gone out to Cricketers, but I was banned at the time. They then went on to some girl's house party in Bolton, but I'd been barred, because she didn't want me there. She knew, whenever I went out, I'd cause trouble – which was fair enough.

I decided to stay local around St Helens and walk around, going from pub to pub getting pissed on my own until the early hours. I couldn't tell you where I went, I was that drunk.

About six in the morning I went back to my mate's house, where we all used to go after finishing a night out. When I got there, I didn't realise they'd all been taking the drug GHB. They were all out of it. Two of them never made it out of the car and were crashed on the back seat. As I walked into the house, I saw this little bottle of GHB and drank it. What happened next was a blur.

I remember my mum phoning me up in the afternoon asking, 'Where are you?' as I should have been at work for the Sunday shift. 'I'm not going in.'

'Martin, what are you doing? Stop being stupid.' I ended up going over to my mum's and having an argument with her.

After leaving her house, I bumped into a mate of mine in the street and just remember him laughing at me. He wasn't laughing at me because I was funny, but as if to say, 'You're spaced out. What the fuck are you doing to yourself?' I was on a different level. A different planet. I chatted with him for a few minutes and then went walkabout on my own. What happened next makes me very embarrassed.

There was this guy going door to door collecting meter readings. I was that off my head that for some reason I remember thinking, 'He's got money. I want it.' I went over and tried to street-rob him. Nothing physical, though. I just asked him for his money in a threatening way.

He had something in his hand, some kind of a stick which he was using for meter readings, and he came at me with it. I realised I wasn't going to get any money, so I walked away. I then went into this pub, which was usually chocka, but apart from three young lads who were about 15, it was empty.

All I remember is going in, walking round the back where I used to go with my mates, nobody being there and walking through the pub again. Bearing in mind I must have looked a right state, in my head, I thought these young lads were taking the piss out of me. The GHB had affected me bad.

I then walked out the pub entrance, turned left and waited there. I wasn't waiting for anyone, I was just standing there spaced out, off my head on drugs. I don't know how long I waited. Might have been a minute, might have been ten, might have been 20. I don't know. If those lads had turned right or gone straight, they would never have bumped into me, but they'd decided to turn left for whatever reason. As they walked past, I said, 'Are you taking the fucking piss out of me?' I was bang out of order.

'No, no. What are you on about?' they said. I shouted, 'Gimme your phone. Gimme your money.' I still don't know why I was doing this. It made no sense.

I don't think they gave me a phone, but they gave me a couple of quid. They weren't men, these were kids. I wished they could have been grown men, so they could have filled me in. I wish they'd have done that. Not because of the trouble that I was going to get into, but because I was being an absolute prick and a bully, which is something I've always despised.

Next thing, this police car from across the road drove over this green making a beeline for me. I knew the area, so ran off, jumped over a wall and gave them the slip. In the state I was in, I don't know how I did it.

I ran down to a pub called The Primmy (The Primrose) not far from my house. I made a call from the pub to this girl I knew at the time. 'Can I come to yours? I've just fucked up.' She came over and drove me to her place. When I woke up, I had a straighter head on my shoulders and then realised what I'd done. I'd made a big, big mistake. I knew what was going to happen to me.

The police went round my mum's looking for me, but I went and handed myself in. I had an idea of who'd grassed me up, but never went and saw them, because what I'd done was that out of order. For the following seven months, I was in and out of court.

The judge put to me a plea of guilty, I said, 'No, no. Wasn't me.' I don't know who I thought I was kidding. I also did a line-up and got picked out. Again, I denied everything.

It ended up going to the crown court on 20 May 2002. At this point, it was a case of plead guilty and get three years or plead not guilty and get five. I pleaded guilty straight away. When I got sent down to the cells under the courthouse, it then hit me. The screw who opened the door said dead calm, 'Are you Martin Murray?'

'Yeah, yeah,' I replied.

'Have you just been sent down for street robbery?'

'Yeah.' He then exploded. 'I fucking know you have, you fucking prick, because they were my fucking lads you did it to.' They weren't his kids, but I'm guessing he knew them very well.

As he escorted me to the coach heading to HM Prison Lancaster (Lanky) Farms, I started to wonder what kind of reception I'd be in for at that end.

## CHAPTER 14

# CHICKEN RUN

*'Those who do not learn from history are doomed to repeat it'*

George Santayana

O N the coach ride over, I was thinking, 'This is it.' Don't get me wrong, three years isn't a long sentence, but I was just starting to enjoy myself on the outside world and was now depriving myself of my peak years.

We arrived late at night, checked in and were given our clothes, which was jeans, trackies, shirt and jumper. The screw then walked us down the landing to our cells. When we got to my cell I said, 'Cheers mate.'

He growled, 'I'm not your fucking mate. Get in there.'

First night, I looked out of my cell window, took a deep breath and thought, 'Fuck me. I'm in here for at least the next 18 months.'

In those first few days, I had to show my character. I went to prison not giving a fuck, but in the same breath I wanted to keep my head down, do my time and get out, which is easier said than done when you're in with a bunch of young lads full of testosterone, many with attitude problems and violent tendencies. It was wild there. Everyone wanted a fight and at any given second something would kick off.

Compared to the prison in Cyprus, this was completely different. I wouldn't be getting a tan here and the mood was very serious. Every other day you were in your cell for 24 hours, the other days you were in for 23 hours. No cellmates. That didn't bother me, though, as I've never struggled being on my own, but I really started to appreciate the thought of freedom that much more.

The screws did lighten up after a while, which was a bit of a relief, and I managed to pass my time without too much bother. After six weeks, I got moved from Lanky Farms to an open jail at Thorn Cross. It was completely different and I started pissing around. I then got kicked out of there for being too boisterous, probably because I was allowed to interact with people more. I was then moved to Forest Bank, where I was padded up with a lad called Ste Hawksworth and never really moved from my cell. Then I went on to Hindley, where I was on the education block and was padded up with a good lad called Locko (Ian Lochran). Funnily enough, I ended up crossing paths again with Locko in 2005 at another jail. All we used to do at Hindley was sit there and watch films all day in an office. But like the other youth prisons, the moment you stepped out of the office, scores were being settled everywhere. After Hindley, it was back to Thorn Cross for my final stretch.

\* \* \* \* \*

I have to say, I met some real characters in jail and made some good friends, who helped me pass the time a lot easier. Take John Hassall and Jimmy Williams.

Me and Jimmy both ended up working together in the gym as orderlies, where we'd often get shouted at, along with John, for playing football instead of cleaning. We both loved our rugby and ended up building a prison rugby team, playing against Jimmy's old amateur club, Crosfields, who were a good side. We played them twice, in fact. Lost first time and drew the second. Jimmy played stand-off and I played scrum-half. We also played football every week. John was the captain and we lost every game, which was more a reflection on our skills than John's.

A few of the lads knew I boxed, so I asked Chizzy if he could come down to the prison to take a session. He agreed in a heartbeat. Any lad who wanted to take part could come and train. It was all set up in the sports hall and loads of people signed up to it. Chizzy turned up with trainers Kevin and Michael Bacon. They were impressed to see about

20 lads eager to train. He brought loads of boxing gear so everyone could have a go, and got me up front to show some drills he wanted us to practise.

I kept in touch with Chizzy throughout my time in prison. Even though I'd let him down, he never gave up on me and always made time to chat or read the letters I sent him. The most memorable thing I did write to Chizzy in Thorn Cross was that I'd promise to win the ABAs for him when I got out and that one day I'd make him proud.

The first session was so popular that Chizzy ended up coming back on a weekly basis. We had a good bunch of lads and the boxing discipline was helping us behave, but as much as I avoided it I ended up having a few fights with the gloves off.

I'm not trying to glorify jail and say it was great fun. It was sometimes, but it could also be a dangerous place. For some especially, if you didn't know how to fight, you could easily get bullied and your time inside could be a lot worse. You have to remember that these prisons were for youth offenders and were wild. Every day there were always fights in the cells and showers, and tellys being thrown off the landings. It was non-stop.

This one day, there I was minding my own business when this guy from Manchester came over and asked where I was from. When I said St Helens, he said, 'They're all muppets from around there.' I offered him a straightener on the top landing, out of the way from the screws.

The guy was massive and you could see him sizing me up thinking, 'This will be easy.' The other thing was, I was always smiling and joking. That's how I've always been. I've never been one to walk around shouting and frowning at people to intimidate them, so because I didn't have an aggressive front he must have guessed I'd be an easy target to bully. We went upstairs and squared up, then a few seconds later I hit him with a combo which left this lad's face covered in blood. It was all over in a matter of seconds, which in itself was a blessing, because if I'd have gone to town on him, I would have been straight back out of Thorn Cross after only two days and in more trouble.

Thankfully, after a while people could see I could handle myself and left me alone. More importantly, they knew I didn't want to fight.

I just wanted to get on with everybody. In fact, they soon realised I was the biggest joker on the wing.

When a new lad moved to our floor, we had them doing the 'chicken run'. It was like an initiation ceremony. It was one of the funniest things you could see. The wing was like an 'L' shape. You'd have to run from one end of the landing and back, with everyone stood at their cell doors with their pillows ready to whack you. It was hilarious to see these guys sprinting down the wing running either in their boxer shorts or with fuck all on, as we were all cheering them on while smacking them with the pillows. As always, one person had to spoil the fun for everyone. Someone put a heavy object in one of the pillow cases, and this lad from Yorkshire got his head split open and ended up in hospital. That was the end of the chicken run.

It didn't stop us having fun, though. Me and John were like a married couple in Thorn Cross. We were padded opposite to each other for about ten months. When you live in each other's pockets for that amount of time, it's like the equivalent of 15 years outside with anyone else. When we were best mates, we were best mates, but when we fell out it was like a mini divorce. It would become dead awkward because as I'd come out of my pad, he'd come out of his at the same time. We'd then have to walk down together to the canteen and sit there facing each other, without saying a word. This would sometimes last for a few days. But once we'd made things up, we'd be best mates again.

Me and John started up a kangaroo court, which was held in the toilets upstairs. We had a jury and John was the judge, whereas I was always the prosecution. At some point, everyone got prosecuted – apart from me and John, that is. As judge and prosecutor, we were above the law.

Here's an example of one of the cases. We shared toilets, showers and stuff, but everything was kept dead clean between everyone. On this occasion, someone had left a massive crap in the toilet, so we had to try and find out who it was. When we'd worked out the culprit, here's how the court went.

Someone would come in as a witness and say something like, 'I saw you go in there last and when I walked in, the smell was unbelievable. Then what I saw in the toilet was the worst I've ever seen.'

I'd then say to the accused, 'We believe it was you. How do you plead?'

Everyone would be trying to act serious, but we'd all be doubled over laughing. If proven guilty, which they always were, they'd have to do a punishment like running round the landing naked or eating a tin of soup with ten sachets of coffee in it. Kangaroo court was great. It certainly helped pass time and created a good atmosphere. Every prison needs a kangaroo court.

The screws didn't mind us messing about. As long as we respected them, they respected us. Things like kangaroo court and the chicken run were harmless. I ended up making friends with a few of the screws at Thorn Cross and am still in contact with them now. The only screw who did scare me was this woman who looked like a chunky version of Rod Stewart. She had the same haircut and that, but looked like she was on steroids. A lot of steroids. That said, even though she was always tough on a lot of the prisoners, she was always good with me and John. It might have had something to do with the comments we'd leave on the food.

There was a meal book at the end of the servery and me and John would spend about 15 minutes every night after supper writing long reviews about how scrumptious the potatoes were, or how expertly cooked and well presented the glazed onions looked. If you read the reviews, you'd think we'd just been to a Michelin starred restaurant. We used to see the screws reading the comments after and laughing their heads off.

Me and John would then go back to our cell, like the married couple, and have our brew and a roll-up. You'd get two and a half brews out of the flask, so we used to take it in turns each night as to who would have the half a brew extra. The other person would have an extra half a roll-up.

\* \* \* \* \*

The good thing about Thorn Cross was that it was an open jail. That meant I'd have days outside of the prison.

About 12 months into my sentence, I was given three days' home leave. Instead of doing the sensible thing and steering clear of trouble, I got involved in this big fight. This group of lads walked into Cricketers. Turns out they were doormen on a night out. From nowhere, it kicked off into a mass brawl. Proper mad free-for-all. Bottles flying, windows smashing, doors coming off hinges.

We got to the car park and the lads we'd been scrapping with disappeared. The doormen from Cricketers closed the doors behind us and left us to it. It then got a bit stupid. I was with about 40 lads and they went over to the side of a car and started going, 'One, two, three,' then tipped it over. Within no time, all the cars had been smashed up and turned over.

We then left Cricketers and were looking for a taxi. Next minute, all I heard was this big screech of tyres, as this car came flying at us. I jumped back out of the way at the last second as the wing mirror clipped me, but it ploughed straight into three of my mates and they all skittled off over the car. We just licked our wounds and came straight back.

The night after, I went to Maximes and had another massive fight there. Straight after, I was walking home with our Danny, who was covered in blood, when the police pulled up.

'What's gone on, lads?'

'Nothing,' I said. 'He's been hit by someone, but they've run off. He's alright.'

The copper then turns to our Danny, 'What's your name?'

As I'm stood next to him looking at the policeman, our Danny says, 'Wesley.' The second he said Wesley, I wanted to turn around and say, 'What?', but I played a poker face and kept looking forward.

'Wesley what?' the policeman says.

'Snipes.'

'Fuck off. What's your name, lad?'

'No, honestly,' I said. 'That's his name. He gets this all the time. Nobody believes him.' The copper accepted it and drove off.

I turned to our Danny and said, 'Wesley-fucking-Snipes??' 'I don't know why I said it,' he replied. We both cracked up laughing and headed home, although I wouldn't have been laughing if I'd been arrested while on home leave.

* * * * *

Back to Thorn Cross. There's certain dates in a calendar year that stick with you. My birthday and Christmas Day behind bars in Thorn Cross were spent getting stoned with a joint. However, New Year's Eve 2002 was a different story. We'd arranged for a load of stuff to be thrown over the prison wall and had a mad party. Things like vodka, Ecstasy and weed. We got smashed. Proper smashed. The thing about prison, those laughs are always short-lived. The bottom line is, you don't have your freedom. Working when you didn't want to work and being restricted on what you could have were constant reminders.

That said, those reminders obviously didn't affect me enough, because I was back to my mad ways on my release.

## CHAPTER 15

# FIGHT CLUB

*'French fries kill more people than guns and sharks,*
*yet nobody's afraid of French fries'*

Robert Kiyosaki

WHEN I walked out of Thorn Cross prison in August 2003, I'd served 15 months but still had three months to do on tag. I could have done 18 months inside and come out with no restrictions, but when I saw the opportunity to come out three months earlier, I took it.

My mum and Danny were waiting at the gates to pick me up. Neither of them drove at the time, so our neighbour and friend Lee Prior took them. When we got back to my mum's house, my family and all my mates were waiting for me to have a homecoming party. Only problem was, the tag restricted me from going more than about five yards outside the front door, so we had to stay indoors or in the garden. Didn't stop us partying, though. We carried on right through the night and crashed in the afternoon the day after.

One thing I did notice in those first few weeks was how behind I was on the banter. They'd be chatting about stuff that had been happening locally and I wasn't able to contribute. I kept finding myself saying, 'Tell us that story,' whereas before I'd have usually been part of that story.

A good mate of mine called Ian Webster (Webber), really helped me when I came out. He was the project manager on a building site and took me under his wing, getting me a good job. Webber's one of them you could always have a chat with and gave sound advice. He'd been there, done that. The problem was, I didn't have the right head on me.

Having done two stints in prison, I had a reputation. I'd grown a few inches (at last), put on a bit of weight with all the exercise I'd done inside and wanted to take things to the next level.

At the time, I could never see myself with a girlfriend or having a family. I wanted to have kids, but the way I was living, I didn't think I'd live long enough to get that far. I used to try and work out how long it would take me to get a girlfriend, then how long it would be before we decided we'd want kids and then how long it takes to have kids. I knew this was years and years away and I was struggling to look beyond a weekend at that point.

On the fighting front, after being released, it didn't take long for me to get involved in my next massive fight a few weeks later.

We'd gone to Wigan Pier and ended up having a scrap with this group of lads in the car park, who we had history with. I got smashed with this telescopic cosh across my back and it went off from there.

They scarpered and we decided to walk round to Cricketers to finish the night off. Thing is, we kind of knew something was going to happen, so as we were walking we were looking for anything we could use to fight with, as we knew these guys would come back all tooled up.

As we were queuing up outside, I decided to take a piss round the corner from the entrance. All of a sudden, this gang appeared with machetes. This club only had one way in and out, so we ran inside to the reception, where all the doormen were standing.

As we were trying to get in, all the doormen were pushing us back out, while this lot were coming at us. As we turned around, the gang swung at us with machetes and knives and we stepped back. Then we'd have a go at them and they'd step back. This went on about five or six times, like a tide coming in and out. Zapper ended up getting chopped in his leg and one of the doormen got chopped in his hand.

After a few minutes, it finally fizzled out. I think it was because we all started to realise it was already seriously out of hand and someone was going to get killed.

It was scrap after scrap now. About six weeks after being released, I went out one Saturday to Wigan Pier with a couple of my mates and we had this big fight in the chill-out room with a group of lads. There was a fire exit there and I got punched by one of the doormen and I went flying right down a full flight of stairs. Miraculously, I got up and was fine. Just a few bumps and scrapes. We dusted ourselves off and went on an all-night, all-day bender, finishing off at the Pickled Egg pub in St Helens on the Sunday evening.

I knew the police were looking for me, so I cut my tag off and threw it into The Bonk, which was a massive field. Why it was called The Bonk, I have no idea. I was now on the run and sleeping here, there and everywhere.

On the car front, my lack of judgement with second-hand motors hadn't changed much after coming out of prison. Digger's dad, Mushy, used to sell cars. He's a top man, Mushy, but that day he sold me and Mozez a dodgy Ford Ezzy (Escort). Neither of us had passed our test at this time.

Straight after getting the Ezzy, we drove straight to St Helens and pulled up into a car park before going for a walk around town. When we came back, the car wouldn't open. We ended up having to rip the sunroof off to get in, but the second we jumped through, the alarm went off. Some security guy came over and we explained our issue with the doors not opening. He took a look at us, as if to say, 'You both look as dodgy as fuck,' but he let us go.

The day after, my dad called and said, 'I need to take your mum to Matalan. Can I take your car?' 'Yeah. No problem. Take the Ezzy,' I replied.

They went shopping, came out with a load of bags and went over to the car. My dad tried opening the door, but it wouldn't move. 'Shit. What we going to do?' my dad says. 'Dek. You're gonna have to climb in through the sunroof,' my mum replies.

As my dad was trying to get in, he got stuck in the sunroof, with my mum pissing herself as his little legs were dangling and kicking and while the alarm was blaring. People were stopping to look, wondering if my dad was actually thieving the car, while my mum couldn't even explain the problem with the locks because she was laughing so hard.

Funnily enough, he never borrowed the Ezzy again.

* * * * *

A few weeks later, on 9 November 2003, I was about to dig myself a deeper hole. Me, Zapper, Garvey and another lad had just come back from a bit of shopping in Liverpool and had been on it all day. We came back to our local pub to have a few more, then around midnight we left and went over to this chippie called Pizza Heaven.

We ordered some chips and they came back frozen. Zapper then said, 'I'm not fucking having them,' and threw his bottle of WKD behind the counter.

Problem is, the bottle landed in the chip fryer, exploded and started a fire.

I shouted at him, 'What the fuck have you done that for?'

We then walked outside and it started to kick off. I turned round to the bloke who owned the place and said, pointing to my mates, 'This is going to end up bad. Try and calm yours down and I'll take mine away.'

They had more people than we did and probably thought they could take us, so didn't back down. It turned into a mental mass brawl. Next thing, the police arrived and we were all up against the shutters of a shop being cuffed. We were taken to Copy Lane police station in Liverpool, because St Helens station was having a refurbishment. I was charged with affray … as Danny Murray. But on the way out, I signed my release form as 'M. Murray'. I completely forgot. I had to sign it in three places and straight after I'd done it, I thought, 'Fuck. They've got me here.' I was expecting them to turn to me and say, 'Do you think we're that stupid?' but instead they let me out.

They gave me a court date, but I couldn't go because I was down as being our Danny. There was me thinking I was clever, but this would come back to bite me in 2005 with some stiff consequences. In the meantime, I went on the run.

A few weeks later, I was involved in this mad fight in Wigan. There was me, Zapper, Garvey and our Danny. We got in this taxi and headed to this club, which was in a cul-de-sac. Our Danny was that out of it that we leant him up against a wall and he fell asleep. We left him there and headed into the club.

Not long after getting inside, I got into this argument with someone over something stupid, like a spilled drink. I then went to the bar to get some beers when suddenly – wallop. I'd just been snippered from the side by some lad.

I dropped down on one knee and the drinks went flying. I got up, went at the lad who'd hit me, but then the doormen kicked me and my mates out of the fire exit. They also kicked out the other lads we were fighting with and we all ended up in this car park at the back of this club. We knew we were heavily outnumbered and started looking around for anything to arm ourselves with, finding these flimsy curtain-rail-type bits of metal.

Next thing the club emptied and poured out into the car park. It was us three versus the lot. Every time someone went for us, we were whipping them with these bits of metal, but having to straighten them after as they kept bending. Any other time, it would have looked funny.

We ended up rolling around on the floor and having a big rumble. Zapper got stabbed in the leg, while I ended up getting bottled over my head and glassed in my back. While all this was going on, we started to get backed up and I said, 'Wake our Danny up.' All our Danny remembers that night was us standing in front of him saying, 'Fucking wake up. They're having us.'

Somehow we managed to get to this tiny little taxi rank around the corner and jumped straight in a cab, with this gang still running after us. Another close call, but again, we learnt nothing from the episode.

# CHAPTER 16

# MOST WANTED

*'Opportunity knocks only once. You never know if
you'll get another opportunity'*

Leon Spinks

I'D been begging Chizzy to let me in the gym for weeks, but he'd
banned me because I was giving it a bad name. I kept asking Birchy
to speak with him to allow me to train for the ABAs, but he refused
to even talk to me.

Even though he banned me, there was no way I could train at any
other gym. I couldn't picture myself training with anyone else. My
heart, my body, everything was with him at that gym. I was desperate
to fight in the ABAs, but when he banned me it was like a good excuse
to go on the piss and get smashed.

My head was so far in the wrong direction that I even started
planning robberies. We started scoping post offices, cash in Transits,
banks, looking at what time the cash carriers came, what tools we'd
take with us, then looked at the best escape routes and where we'd stash
the cash. That sort of stuff. I came that close to following through.
We're talking a matter of days.

Then came that call. Without a doubt, it kept me away from a
major sentence.

Chizzy had changed his mind. There I was, sitting in my sister's
flat smoking a joint, still buzzing from a non-stop weekend bender,
when the phone went. It was Ste. 'Do you want to fight in the ABAs?
It's next Sunday.' That woke me up.

I came off the phone and thought to myself, 'Right then. You're stoned, pissed, out of shape, overweight and on the run. You can do this.'

After coming off the phone to Ste, the day after I was at the gym. When I walked in, Chizzy says, 'You've only got one fucking chance at this, you. No more fucking about.' Nobody did motivational speeches like Chizzy. The four-day training camp went well, although I almost messed things up the night before the weigh-in.

My mate called me to say he'd seen a load of metal ground pipe collars on a building site and that it was easy pickings, because the builders had left for the night. We went over and spent hours grabbing all these collars, then loaded up the van to the limit and drove off.

The morning after I weighed in for the ABAs, instead of focusing on my weight, I was thinking, 'Imagine if I get nicked for doing that?' I wouldn't have taken part in the ABAs. What a dickhead.

Somehow, I weighed in bang on the welterweight limit of 69kg. More than anything I was mentally prepared, more than I'd been for anything in a very long time. However, I have to say, without the support from loved ones, it would have never happened.

During the ABA tournament, I stayed at my grandparents' house and they proper looked after me. Cooking, cleaning, the lot. I knew if there was any chance of me not getting caught whilst being on the run, it would be with them. I was there for about six weeks and all I did was eat, train and stay low.

Chizzy used to pick me up in the morning, then I'd train and he'd take me back. He always made sure I went from door to door and didn't go astray during those journeys, which is more than can be said of his driving during the competition.

After beating Shaun Farmer, Louis Kempster, then Brian Rose, I was up against Callum Johnson in the semis down in Portsmouth. I asked Chizzy if two of my mates could come and he said, 'Yeah. No problem.' Then he said, 'Who are they?' 'Zapper and Garvey,' I replied. 'Errrr … yeah … they can come. As long as they don't fuck about,' he warned while pulling one of his frowny faces. I knew he wasn't so fussed about Garvey, because he was quiet, but he hated me hanging around with Zapper, because he knew that when we were together, we'd always be up to no good.

We went down on the Thursday as the weigh-in was on Friday. I was fighting on Saturday. We all jumped into the boogie bus and headed down to Portsmouth. Throughout all our trips, Chizzy would always get lost. These were the days before sat navs, so he had a stack of maps and never knew how to read them.

Chizzy also had this knack, whenever he stopped to ask for directions, to choose a person who was foreign and didn't have a clue. This only made him more mad, which in turn meant he'd be even more short-tempered with us.

First petrol station on the way down to Portsmouth, Chizzy filled up. He didn't realise at the time but he'd left the petrol cap by the pump. He was always doing stuff like that. We'd be driving somewhere and he'd suddenly shout, 'Shit. I've left the fucking chip pan on.' Next thing he'd spin the car around and drive home.

About 20 minutes later, he says, 'This petrol's going down quick. What's happening there?' About another ten minutes later, he says, 'We'll have to fill up again.'

We pulled up to the station and the second he opened the petrol flap, he started shouting, 'I – don't – fucking – believe – it. I've lost the cap.' He ended up putting a rag in it, but the way the petrol was flying out was ridiculous. We filled up four more times and it took us 12 hours to get to Portsmouth. Journey from hell. Classic Chizzy.

After checking in and getting something to eat, we went to our rooms. I had one to myself, whereas Zapper and Garvey were sharing and decided to go out for a few pints. On the way back to the hotel, they got their hands on a bottle of whisky to keep the party going. There was a strict no-smoking policy in the room, but they decided to cover the smoke detector with a sock and have a cig out the window. Things started going wrong pretty quickly. Apart from setting the alarm off, Garvey redecorated the bed in sick.

In the morning I woke up and Zapper says, still pissed, 'You won't believe what happened last night.' As he started to tell me, Chizzy was standing there with a face that was fuming. The hotel staff started saying to Zapper, 'You're getting fined for smoking in the room. If you don't pay, we'll call the police.' Chizzy's turned to me and said, 'Fuck's sake. I don't believe this.'

The hotel staff repeated themselves to Zapper and Garvey, 'If you don't pay, we'll call the police.' 'Call them. I don't give a shit,' Zapper says. Chizzy heard him and walked over to Zapper and said, 'What did you say then?' Honest to God, I reckon Zapper actually shit his pants. I'm not joking. Have you ever seen someone when they really swallow it? Proper make the gulping noise and start stuttering. Chizzy shouted again, 'Come on. What did you say?' Zapper was trying to speak, but nothing was coming out of his mouth. 'Pay the fucking fine,' Chizzy says. And Zapper did.

The day after, I fought Callum Johnson and won. That was my toughest fight of the competition without a doubt and I ended up having a real ding-dong for three rounds with Callum. Either way, I'd made it to the finals.

Probably the hardest fights I had during the ABAs weren't part of the competition. You'll also be glad to hear, for once, they weren't on the street. I've been asked if I've ever had my nose broken or jaw broken and the answer is yes.

My jaw [break] happened at Maximes nightclub around the year 2000 and I'd had my nose broken a few times in street fights, usually off my head. But the first time I actually remember having my nose broken was sparring a Serbian called Geard Ajetovic during these ABAs. He'd fought in the Sydney 2000 Olympics and had also won European gold and world silver as a junior. He was a top fighter.

What happened was, we were sparring at our gym in Clock Face, St Helens and there were these two Serbians. Chizzy says to me, 'Get some sparring with these lads. They're both top boxers. It will help you with the ABAs.' 'Sound,' I replied.

I got in with this first Serb and pretty much did what I wanted. I remember thinking, 'I thought these Serbs were meant to be good.' A couple of days after, I went in with Geard and thought it would be just as easy. What a wake-up call. He fucking poleaxed me. He was so natural, leading me on to shots, and the difference in class was evident.

We sparred another time at St Aloysius Gym, Huyton and I was switched on. The spar was more in my favour. I gave him a shiner and he kept saying it was a result of the cold air. Never heard that one before. Shortly after, we sparred for the third time at the 051 gym in

Liverpool. The gym was part of a big complex that had a nightclub called Club 051 and Geard was a doorman there. Me and Chizzy just rolled up and Geard was in there with a load of his doormen mates watching. We were doing four two-minute rounds and he poleaxed me again. After two rounds, Chizzy said, 'Come on, Martin. That's enough now.' 'No fucking way Chizz. We've come here to do four and that's what we're doing. I'd rather take my licks than quit.'

Well – did he give it to me? Proper smashed my nose in. He hit me straight on with three big back hands and flattened it. It doesn't look bad from the outside, but from the inside it's bent inwards to this very day. Either way, those savage spars with Geard certainly prepared me for the ABAs and probably helped strengthen me mentally and physically throughout the competition.

So here I was, on 27 March 2004 at the Wembley Conference Centre in London for the national ABA finals, up against Stephen Briggs. It was a national title and my gateway into the England team. Most importantly, I wanted to win the ABAs because I wanted to give the trophy to Chizzy as a token of appreciation for him believing in me. I always wanted to do that for him, so the pressure of winning was big on that front.

I don't remember a great deal about the fight itself, apart from boxing confidently, but what I do distinctly remember was Chizzy shouting the second the final bell went, 'He's done it! The lad's done it!'

Having my hand raised was surreal. I never thought it could happen with all the shit that was going on at the time. It was such a great feeling. I'd won the schoolboys [championship] and that was a buzz, but this was different. To say you're the best in Britain for your category gives you a great sense of achievement.

Perhaps not something to boast about, but I did also wonder how many other boxers in Britain had won the ABAs while on the run.

\* \* \* \* \*

With this pending case looming over my head, I knew the police would catch up with me at some point, but I was determined to do something with my boxing before that time came. Problem was, there was still a big part of me that was finding it hard to behave and I was in denial about it. I just thought trouble was looking for me, but looking back, I was putting myself in a position that would encourage bad things to happen.

A couple of weeks after winning the ABAs, I got nicked for something stupid, but enough to get me in court again. About ten of us had been on a heavy session the night before and when we woke up, we thought it would be a good idea to go to Silverdale, in the Lake District. My mate Dennis Foster has a son called DJ, who was only two at the time, and he was on a caravan break with his grandparents up there. A few of us decided to jump in the van and go up there to give DJ an Easter egg.

The second we hit the road we were back on it and by the time we got there, we were all drunk. Just to make sure we had enough supplies for the return journey, we all went into this shop near where DJ was staying. We each grabbed a few crates of beer, then walked off laughing. We didn't even do a runner because we were that bladdered.

Straight after, we decided to go for a couple at this little pub in a tiny village in Silverdale. As we were having a drink, the windows started to rattle and you could hear a chopper was directly above the pub. Didn't think anything of it.

Next minute, honestly, it was like a SWAT team came in. Coppers burst in from the front and the back at the same time and nicked us. Outside, they blocked the road off from both ends, with a queue of police cars parked up with their lights flashing. The locals had never seen anything like this before and the police were treating it as a massive thing. As they threw us into the back of a van, all the neighbours were clapping. It looked like a scene out of *Heartbeat*.

We woke up on Easter Sunday in Lancaster cells. Everyone got a slap on the wrist, apart from me, because I had previous. Five days later, on 15 April 2004, I was up in front of the judge at Lancaster Magistrates' Court. I got fined £75 and had to pay costs of £43 for the beer we nicked.

My mate gave me a call to say that our story was headline news in the Silverdale paper the week after. The locals are probably still talking about it to this day.

CHAPTER 17

# INTERNATIONAL CALL

*'Martin was a ferocious trainer. He was always
at the front of the running queue and was one of
the hardest working in the team. He was on the
verge of becoming an England regular. It was a
shame he fell back into the old routine'*

Tony Bellew, 2016

O N the boxing front, I was still buzzing from winning the
ABAs. Even better, that win had earned me the chance to try
out for the England squad, something I'd dreamt of for years.
From day one, I loved every moment. The camaraderie, the training
camps and, believe it or not, the strict discipline. I'll always remember
one of the first training camps in Sheffield when the head coach, Terry
Edwards, turned to me and said, 'John Chisnall has said so much about
you. Come on. Show me what he's been saying is true.' I worked my
arse off for that session. Gave it 110 per cent. Terry liked what he saw
and gave me the chance. I'll always be grateful to him for that.

A few weeks after walking out of the court in Lancaster, I was off to
Ireland representing a North West select team. I was up against a lad
called Scott Fitzgerald and thankfully won the bout with no bother.

The day after, on 8 May 2004, me, Chizzy and legendary Salisbury
boxing coach Alan Lynch were watching the first Pacquiao vs Marquez
fight in the hotel room and he told me, 'It's all here for you, Martin.
You just gotta stay focused and keep training hard. Put all the graft in

now and you'll do well.' He was referring to my future in the amateurs and the pros.

There were some good boxers in that North West team, including Tony Bellew, who like myself had also won the ABAs that year. I'd got to know Tony during the ABAs, but that trip in Ireland is when I really got to know him well and we shared some great memories.

The tournament in Ireland was multi-nations and Tony was expecting to fight a very good Irish international. Instead these two Greek guys rocked up. Turns out they were the number one and two for Greece in his category. But there was a problem, because they said they couldn't fight each other. Tony said, 'That's alright, I'll fight 'em both.'

He got in with the first guy, who looked the more athletic of the pair, and hit him with this massive left hook. The guy was asleep before he hit the floor. I mean proper snoring. The next day he fought the number two, who had a big gut and this massive tache. As Tony said after, 'He had a chest full of hair and I barely had a hair on my bollocks.' Tony came out first round and hit him with a jab and the Greek guy's eyes opened up as if to say, 'What the bleedin' 'ell has this man got in his gloves?' A couple of shots later, he went down and that was the end of him. Two fights in two days and two knockouts in two days for Tony. We went out and had a good pint after.

A few weeks later, I was off to Cyprus for a competition with big Pricey (David Price), Nathan Brough, Kevin Bacon, Chizzy and a few others. I'd not long been in Cyprus, but on the wrong side of the bars. I'm sure the guys in passport control didn't need to know that or the fact I was on the run in their country.

In the end, it was only me and Nathan who boxed because when the other heavyweights saw the size of Pricey, they all pulled out. Pricey ended up having a holiday and later said, 'I was supporting Martin and Nathan, while I was supporting bottles of lager in my right hand.'

I fought a Serb first and beat him comfortably, but then came up against this Russian southpaw, who was a good kid, and he beat me fair and square. After me and Nathan got our fights out of the way, we had a few days to ourselves. Apparently, when they booked the original planes, they couldn't get a return flight the day after the competition finished, so we ended up with a few days extra. It turned into a lads' outing and we helped Pricey in supporting those bottles of lager. It's one of the few trips where I'd managed to steer clear of trouble, although it did get very close on one occasion.

There's a lot of squaddies in Cyprus and one Saturday night, after a few beers, as were walking down this road minding our own business, out of nowhere, this squaddie appeared in front of us. He wasn't a massive lad and he knew we were boxers. He picked Nathan Brough out and says to him:

'Do you wanna fight?'

Nathan looks at him and says, 'What? Fight *me?*'

'Have a fight with me now. Fifty euros to the winner.'

Nathan looked at him confused, but I said straight away, 'I'll fucking have the fight for 50 euros. Let's go now. Come on.' The fellow was like, 'No, no, no. I'm gonna be straight with ya, mate. You look like a lunatic and (pointing at Pricey) your mate is way too fucking big. I'll fight him,' as he pointed at Nathan. Me and Pricey started laughing. Intent on wanting to put it on Nathan, the squaddie says, 'Come back to the club and we'll have a fight.'

We ended up going to this nightclub and one of the bouncers, who was a Cypriot boxer, knew us and managed to calm it down. In the end, nothing happened, thankfully. Lucky for that guy, because Nathan would have put him out cold.

My final international competition was in December 2004, as part of an England vs USA squad. All the best boxers in Britain were on the team, including Frankie Gavin, Pricey, Nathan, Tony and Amir Khan, fresh from winning his silver medal at the Olympics in Athens. I was only supposed to fight once, but a couple of days before the fight we found out that Perko (Neil Perkins) was injured and I was asked if I'd be willing to step in and take his place to fight in London. Turns out I was fighting against future pro middleweight world champion Danny Jacobs, then five days later we'd be doing it all again at the Liverpool Olympia.

On the day of the fight we fought four tough, close rounds, but then I lost 19-17, which was really hard to swallow. I then ended up having this massive bullshit argument with Chizzy on the train home the next day, which was not even related to boxing. Being stubborn, I didn't go to the gym the whole week or speak to Chizzy. I tried to keep fit by doing my own thing, but ate loads of crap.

The day before the weigh-in, he called up and asked if I was still fighting. I loved Chizzy to bits, but that was hardly a professional way of going about things. Then again, my life was far from professional either at that time. So there I was, the day of the weigh-in at the Britannia Adelphi Hotel in Liverpool, fully clothed in the sauna with a bin bag on. My weight was shot. I knew this fight was not going to be easy.

Where Jacobs had stayed sharp and in good shape from the first fight, I'd deteriorated. In the third round, I realised that I was getting my head pinged off, so decided to start throwing bombs. Just as I was thinking nothing was going my way, I dropped him. I thought, 'I've done it! He's gone,' but Jacobs got up and started shaking his head, as if to say, 'Not today mate.' He then went on the back foot and beat me 23-12.

A few weeks later, I fought in the box-offs. I had three fights over three days and won the lot against the top four in the UK. What a great experience and what an end to an incredible year. I'd gone from having a week's notice to enter the ABAs and winning them, to fighting for the England squad alongside some of the world's best fighters. And let's not forget to mention making headline news in the Silverdale rag.

Without Chizzy constantly on my back, I'd have never even entered the ABAs. I'd also like to say a special thank you to Terry Edwards for taking a chance on me, as I never saw him after that last tournament. I'd like to be able to tell him that my past is what messed up my amateur future at that point. I was like a time bomb ticking away. I'd like to explain that I genuinely did want to progress as an international fighter if I'd had the chance back then, instead of underachieving as I did. I'd like to take this opportunity to tell him that.

I wish I could have repaid him better than I did.

# CHAPTER 18

# F WING

*'You've good power in both hands, lad, and good technique. You've got a good head on your shoulders. Don't be going back out there and getting yourself into trouble again. Let your hands make money for you. Don't let them bring you back into prison'*

Jimmy Christian, 2005

I'D just received funding from Sport England and was finally starting to get paid for boxing. After winning the ABAs in 2004 and having represented the England squad, I was tipped as having a good chance of winning the ABAs for a second time the following year.

Unfortunately, what had happened on 9 November 2003 at Pizza Heaven was coming back to haunt me. I was at the gym but felt like I was training for nothing as I knew I was going to be in jail again soon. I said to Chizzy, 'This is pointless. There's nothing I can do. Between being on the run and the court case for Pizza Heaven, I'm fucked.'

In 2004, there were headlines in the papers of me being crowned ABA champion. This time round, as the 2005 tournament was getting underway, nobody knew where I was. Most people thought I couldn't be arsed to turn up. The *Liverpool Echo* said, 'In the absence of England number one Neil Perkins, still ruled out after breaking his wrist in December, and number two Martin Murray, the AWOL St Helens battler, the 69kg division is wide open.' That tournament was there for the taking, but instead, in February 2005, I was nicked and was on remand in Walton prison, awaiting trial.

On 4 March 2005, I was in front of a judge. By now, this was my tenth court appearance. Me and Zapper were standing in crown court and should have been trying to make a good impression, but instead we were wearing trackies and laughing while the judge was giving us what for.

The problem was, once I'd started laughing, I couldn't stop. As the judge said, 'Do you think this is funny, Mr Murray?' I laughed even more. It was more a nervous laugh now.

There were four of us in court, but as usual, with my prior form, I was the only one who got sentenced. I ended up getting a 15-month prison sentence for affray and cutting off my tag, not to mention breaking all the conditions that came with being on licence. All of a sudden, my dream of being a professional boxer was starting to vanish.

\* \* \* \* \*

Walton was different to any prison I'd been to before. When I did my 15-month stretch in 2002, it was at youth offender institutions. There were fights all the time and it was wild, but it was mainly fist fights. Straighteners. Here, it was all adults and the rules for fighting were more severe. Some of the prisoners had committed serious crimes and had long sentences hanging over them. It was a good motivation looking at them to keep my head down, serve my time and get out as quickly as possible.

When I first arrived I was moved around to a few different wings, but in the end I settled on F Wing, which was good as there were a couple of lads there who I knew from St Helens. I've always been respectful to people and generally get on well with everyone. The screws picked up on this and soon after settling down I was given a job as a cleaner, then later on gym orderly, which were two of the better jobs you could get.

I was also lucky to get a lot of boxing training done in Walton, but that wasn't all my own doing. There were some key people who helped me along the way such as John Wilson (Willo), who had arrived about five months before me. I used to go down and get my food and he was on the servery. I knew straight away he was a sound bloke. Not long after we met, he started padding me.

After a few sessions, it was obvious that if I was going to train properly I'd need some equipment. As you can guess, there wasn't a sports shop in the prison, so we improvised and made our own gear. The hand wraps we made from ripping up the bed sheets, but the pads took a lot more work.

The pillows back then were like a solid black foam brick. Willo would put a plastic plate on top of the pillow and cut round it with a plastic knife. He then got a couple of rolls of duct tape from Alex Hagan, one of the main screws on our wing, to hold it all together. He even invented some hand straps for the pads, using the cardboard from the toilet rolls.

I want to give a mention to Alex. You'll never find a fairer or more respectful man. He knew that the prisoners had made some bad decisions in life and wasn't there to give them a hard time. He helped to guide them as much as he could without being too heavy handed, and as a young lad that was a great help to me. Some of the screws didn't agree with the boxing, but Alex used to say, 'It's better you're punching pads than punching each other.'

Pad work with Willo was always in his cell. He used to share it with a lad I knew from St Helens called Big Butty, who was happy to let us use the cell for boxing. Funnily enough, Big Butty was mates with Butty from back home. Small world.

It was only one bunk in each cell, so we used to move the cupboards to the side and everything off the floor to make as much space as possible. Willo kept saying, 'You've got some power there, lad,' and nicknamed me Martin 'The Power' Murray. Although it's still down as my fighting name now, I don't really use it any more. Either way, Willo came up with it.

When we started off it was just me and him, but within a couple of weeks there were about ten people crammed in, sitting on the bunk watching us go through our routines. Unfortunately, Willo got shipped out to another prison after only a few weeks. I was gutted as he'd managed to get my head focused. Thankfully, someone else came along who picked up where Willo left off.

One day, Alex introduced me to Jimmy Christian, who was 50 years old at the time. Jimmy used to box and had done a bit of coaching. 'Would ya train me?' I asked. 'Of course I will,' he replied. We sat down for about half an hour and I told Jimmy about what I'd done in my amateur days and the boxing club I trained at. He could tell I was serious and got cracking with me straight away.

Without fail, Jimmy padded me every day. I trained like fuck in there and it didn't take me long to hit 14 stone of solid muscle. It was the biggest I'd ever been before and probably the fittest at that time of my life.

I never felt like I was fully able to repay Jimmy's kindness inside, but I was able to give him something of value to me, which I knew he'd appreciate. I had my England shorts sent to me while I was still in Walton and signed them to him. They had my ABA badge on them and he was made up. It was the least I could do.

\* \* \* \* \*

There were loads of top lads on our wing, including Warren Cox and a lad called Clint Tinsley, who was from St Helens. I knew him before going inside. I also met a couple of lads called Stav (Steve Larrisey) and Sandsy (Dave Sands), who were padded up next door to me. Both good lads from Birkenhead, who turned out to be lifelong friends.

Stav used to work on the servery, which meant he was able to fuel the food train for us. He used to have breakfast with the officers and if there was anything left, like some bacon or sausages, he'd sneak it out and give it to the lads.

When he couldn't fuel the food train, I'd return the favour and make Stav and Sandsy some hot dog butties. Although it took a while to get the hang of cooking them, I got there in the end.

Some of the beds had old springs on them. If you took a couple of them, you could wire them up to a plug with the negative and the earth, then plug it in. You'd then place the springs into a flask of water, pop the hot dogs in and the springs would work like a heating element in a kettle.

I'll be honest, though, I wasn't the best electrician in the world. The likes of Jimmy Christian could wire up the springs with his eyes closed.

First time I tried it, I blew the leccy for the full landing. I thought, 'Fuck me. What have I done?'

Like myself, Stav and Sandsy loved their sport. Sandsy especially liked his football and used to take the piss out of me whenever I played. I'll be the first to say I was shit, but he used to say I looked and played like one of those Australian football players, because during the summer I'd walk around in a vest and was always tackling people hard. Probably true, to be fair.

Boxing was also very popular and we even managed to organise an epic match behind bars. It was between a lad named Lee Murphy from Wigan, who we called The Wigan Warrior, and Alan 'The Hitman' Sandalls. I was interviewing them before the fight, using an aerosol can as the microphone, asking them how their training camps had gone and any predictions for the fight. Then we all went upstairs on the fifth floor landing showers and had two sets of fans to cheer them on. If we'd been caught, we'd have all lost our cleaning and kitchen jobs.

As the referee, I squared them up, then explained the rules. They only had a glove each, because we only had one set. I turned to them and said, 'This is just boxing, lads. Keep it clean.' It started almost immediately and The Hitman punched The Wigan Warrior smack on the nose. The Warrior has now stepped back and said, 'My nose! My nose!', in his thick Wigan accent. In the meantime, The Hitman was saying, 'My shoulder, my shoulder,' as he'd dislocated it throwing the punch.

All the screws were on the second floor, but as The Hitman was in agony screaming about his shoulder, they all started running upstairs to check what had happened. We all legged it before they arrived and nobody was any the wiser. One of the quickest and funniest fights I'd ever seen. We tried to get a rematch, but it never happened.

Not long after that fight, I had a conversation with Sandsy about how I thought boxing could be my way to make a living and escape from my life of crime. Sandsy had his head screwed on, had his own business and knew how to invest. He started explaining to me about getting into property, securing a house, how much I'd need for a deposit and all that sort of thing. I said at the time, 'When I get out I'm going to have a proper go at it.' He replied, 'Do you think you can earn proper money? Do you think you'll get to the point where you can earn 30 grand in one fight?' I said, 'Yeah. I do.' Sandsy nodded with a smile and said, 'Then go for it, mate. I'll come to your every fight.' And he did. Although he wished he almost hadn't in Argentina in 2013. More about that later.

\* \* \* \* \*

As much as I tried to steer clear of it in Walton, I did end up having a couple of fights. One I regret and one I don't. One of my mates at the time wrote to me and let me know that there was a lad inside who'd kidnapped his brother. I do a lot for my friends and if someone does something to them, it's like a personal insult to me.

Chizzy told me a few years earlier, 'Martin, let me tell you. I don't care whether it's in six weeks, six months or 20 years, sooner or later, you'll find out that certain people are not your mates.' He was so right. As crazy as it sounds, I was willing to put myself in a compromising position in prison which could have possibly got me an extended sentence. It turned out later the guy who'd asked me was no mate of mine.

Anyway, I found out which wing this lad was on and saw him one day on a visit. I kind of befriended him on the visit, knowing I needed to get him over to the wing to fill him in, because I couldn't have done it there, otherwise I'd have got in trouble. I told him, 'Come over to our wing. It's full of St Helens lads and you'll have a laugh.' When he came over, I ended up giving him a hiding. I'd love to see him now, just to be able to apologise. I'm not proud of what I did. I was out of order.

The other fight was with some lad over dirty washing. Each landing would have a cleaning day and I was in charge of laundry for our wing. For example, landing one was on Monday, two on Tuesday etc., with Sunday off. I used to do what I could washing-wise, but some of the lads would sometimes ask if I could do extra stuff for them in exchange for a bit of burn. One day this lad came down and asked if I could do some for him. I was honest and told him I was snowed under. I wasn't trying to be difficult. If I could have helped him, I would have. He saw it differently and went and slagged me off to everyone. I decided to have a word.

He'd just got his dinner and had his tray in his hands, when we got into an argument. He was a big lad and got up close to me looking down and said, 'You don't know who you're messing with.' I ended up punching him up and down the landing and his dinner ended up all over the walls and all over us. By the time we'd finished, we both needed some washing done.

Thankfully, one of the screws saw what happened and that I didn't start it. The last thing I needed was being sent down the block because of that prick. Apart from that, I kept my nose clean, which was probably a good thing as Walton prison had a reputation for being extremely violent.

The prison officers came round in the morning and would ask if you wanted a razor blade for shaving. You were marked down on a form as having a razor and would have to return it later. Occasionally, one would slip through the net and pretty much every time it was made into something nasty. Prisoners would take their toothbrush, heat it up so the plastic would melt and stick the razor blade in it. Sometimes, people would put a matchstick in between two razors on the toothbrush, so that when they slashed someone the cut would have no skin on top of it and you couldn't stitch it.

If you were a bit wise, you'd be OK, but if you didn't play by the rules there was no ifs or buts about it, you were getting hurt. For example, if someone asked for something and couldn't pay it back or you started giving someone cheek, their time would come sooner or later. In addition to getting slashed, people would get sugary hot water thrown on them and when it hit, their face would start melting.

As I'd done for most of my life up to that point, I was still wheeling and dealing and had my own round of selling burn. For example, if you gave someone half an ounce of burn, they'd owe you an ounce back the week after. If they owed you too much burn, then they'd give you credit from their canteen account. I had a good round going.

Access to drugs was easy, but I was only ever into them when I was partying, so never felt the need. Unfortunately, there were loads of smackheads in there who were reliant on the stuff. There's many ways to get drugs in and that will always be an issue in prisons.

Compared to the guys who were doing ten- and 15-year stretches, I was only in for a short time. However, I was in there long enough for the sights, sounds and smells to start making an impression on me. More the sounds than anything. Certain ones really got into my head. The banging of the doors and gates, and the jingling of keys especially.

Once, I was in my cell early in the morning and starting to wake up. Kind of in that daydreaming phase, I heard the gates bang and I thought it was the back gate of my mum's house at home, because that was always banging. Then I woke up and realised I was still in Walton. Yet another reminder that my freedom had been taken away.

Unfortunately, the worst reminder came a few months into my sentence, and that was something which I'd never fully get over.

# CHAPTER 19

# DOUBLE BLOW

*'Saying goodbye doesn't mean anything. It's the time*
*we spent together that matters, not how we left it'*

Trey Parker

THERE'S certain things I really regret in my life. One's the street robbery. I'll never be able to shake that guilt. Something else which I've never been able to fully get over was being behind bars when I was needed on the outside.

On 27 March 2004, I won the ABAs. It was probably the highlight of my life at that point. Exactly one year later, on 27 March 2005, I was in Walton behind bars and couldn't have been much lower.

I was in my cell when a screw came over and said, 'You're wanted down the office.' I went down and they said, 'Your uncle Steven's been on the phone. Your grandmother's died.' I thought it was my uncle Ste, my dad's brother, and as we didn't speak to my dad's mum, Audrey, I wasn't too bothered. She was never there for my dad when he was a kid and was never there for us when we were kids, when she could have been. That made us all resent her even more.

The screw then passed me the phone.

'Martin. It's me, Ste.' This was not the Ste I was thinking about. This was my auntie Pam's fella, from my mum's side of the family. 'You alright mate,' I said. 'Your mother's died. She had a massive heart attack while putting the washing outside.' That's when I realised it was my mother, Theresa, my mum's mum. I hope I never have one of them phone calls again. I burst out crying straight away. Being behind bars made it even harder. I was desperate to go to the funeral and I wanted to be there for my mum to comfort her, but they said it was immediate family only. I told them she was like a mum to me, but they weren't having any of it.

What a lovely woman she was. I'd always been very close to her and my father, and they'd always been close to their grandkids. When we were little, whatever they did, they always made us feel like it was never a problem for them.

We used to joke about her name, Theresa Greenhalgh, which with a St Helens accent sounds like 'trees are green'. I'd have loved for her to still be around now. Not just to see how my life has turned, but so I could have appreciated her more. I wish I could have spent time with her as a level-headed person, instead of someone who'd been off the rails for about five years. Thankfully, I'll always have those weeks when I was on the run to cherish. During that time, we spent a lot of quality time together and I'll never forget everything she did for me.

It turned out to be a very tough year for my father, because he'd lost his soulmate and was just about to have more bad news, as his best mate Chizzy was very ill. I wish I could have also been there for him to offer support. If I was feeling bad, God knows how he felt.

Chizzy had cancer for years, but it went bad when I got sent down. We were very close before, but after I won the ABAs we became even closer. I think he was made up, knowing that I'd given it a proper go and the result that came with me giving my best. There wasn't a prouder man on the planet when I gave him that ABA trophy.

I used to phone him all the time when I was in Walton, but in the second week of August he deteriorated rapidly. I'd been chatting every day with my mum and Chizzy's missus, Carol, and they both said, 'He's only got a few days to live.' Chizzy had decided to go back to his house for the last few days, so he could die there. I went to the phone at the end of the landing and gave him a call straight away.

One thing about Chizzy, he had a big heart, but he never told me he loved me. As we were having this chat, I broke down. Proper crying. He was crying as well. I think we both knew it was the last time we were going to speak with each other. Then he said it. 'Martin, I love you.' It gets me upset just thinking about it. He meant so much to me.

When you know you're going to lose someone like that and can't be with them, that's hard. To not be able to say that final goodbye was even worse.

I went back to my cell and wrote him this big long letter, which soon got soaked because I was non-stop crying as I was writing it. The letter was basically thanking him for everything and also that what he'd said about friends and fakers was right and that I should have listened more. I sent the letter straight away, but I'm not sure if he received it.

The day after, 16 August 2005, I spoke with my mum. Despite really fighting it, in the end the cancer got him. I was absolutely gutted. I went back to my cell and just sat there staring into nothing.

Jimmy Christian came by. He could tell something was up and gently said, 'You look a bit lost, mate. You alright?' I told him what had happened and he sat down next to me and had a little one-to-one chat. 'Do him proud when you get out, Martin. Don't get involved in stupid shit any more. Make a new start. Do it for him and do it for yourself.'

I heard that Chizzy got a good send-off. The church in St Helens town centre was absolutely heaving and hundreds were spilled outside. They played a recording of Chizzy singing one of his favourite songs, Frank Sinatra's 'My Way'. Apparently, there wasn't a dry eye in the house.

Chizzy was quite a tough character, but he was always doing good things for the community and trying to guide people to make the right choices. Judging by the number of people who turned up for his funeral, he obviously made a big impact on a large number of people.

His grave is opposite my mother's. Two great people close to each other. RIP. Gone, but never, ever forgotten.

\* \* \* \* \*

When I was in Walton, my mum had been to see another fortune teller. She'd never met this one before and she said to her, 'You have a son who is in Liverpool at the moment. Not sure where exactly, but in that area.' The teller never mentioned anything about prison, but went on to say, 'He's going to turn his life around. You might not think it now, but he will. And possibly, he's going to travel abroad with his career. I see a trip overseas.' My mum was desperate to believe her, but just couldn't see it.

I came out of Walton prison in October 2005, after serving eight of the 15-month sentence. My time definitely taught me that I needed to sort myself out. The problem was, I had little responsibility in my life at that point and part of me still couldn't understand why I needed to behave myself.

In the end, it turned out to be one person who helped flip my life around and make me realise there was more to it than just partying and scrapping.

HE CAME running out of the toilet in Panama Jacks, [handwritten: JOES] where he'd been fighting with a load of rugby lads. I didn't even know that but you could tell something had happened, because he said, 'Come on, we're going.' He always seemed to be in the middle of fighting. This is one of the main reasons I couldn't be doing with getting with him at the time. Back then, there always seemed to be trouble around him and I just couldn't be bothered with it. I didn't know him well enough to say, 'Let's work through it.' Why would I want to get involved with something like that?

*Day after, I'd be like, 'What was up with you last night?', and he'd say, 'What?'*

*'What do you think? Again. You were fighting last night.'*

*Then he'd reply, 'Why you being like this with me?'*

*It was as if it was normal to him and his mates, but it wasn't to me. I wasn't used to going out and seeing people fighting. It was like a different world. Not one I liked. He couldn't see that at first.*

*But, something kept drawing me back to him …*

**Gemma Murray, 2016**

CHAPTER 20

# A PROPER GEM

*'She's been a saviour to him. Nothing more*
*certain. He'd have been forever in a life of crime*
*if he didn't meet her.'*

Buller – Martin's Father, 2016

BOUT two weeks after being released from Walton, Digger called me.

'I'll meet you in Breeze Bar about eight o'clock tonight.'

'Listen, I'm not going,' I said.

'If you do change your mind, I'll be there at eight.'

Not a single part of me wanted to. I'd been out the night before, still felt a bit rough and just didn't fancy it.

However, later that day, even though I couldn't be arsed, I decided that getting out of the house would be better than moping about. When I arrived, Digger wasn't there.

In fact, nobody was. The place was empty. I didn't have my phone with me to call him as I'd left it at home on charge and started thinking whether to stay or go back.

Next thing, a mate of mine called Danny Woodward walks in and says, 'What you up to?' 'Waiting for Digger, but it looks like he's not turning up,' I replied. Danny had just nipped out of the bar next door for a minute and spotted me. 'Listen, I'm in Panama Jacks with this girl on a date and she's with a mate. She's lovely. Why don't you come over and get chatting to her?' 'Sound,' I said.

I'd been fighting in Panama's a few weeks earlier and as I got to the entrance, the doorman said, 'No trouble tonight,' 'OK mate,' I replied. Thankfully, I didn't cause any trouble and we went on to a few other bars.

The girl was called Gemma and the first thing that struck me about her was how beautiful her eyes and teeth were, but also how shy she was. From the get-go, we had a laugh. In fact, I'd never got on with a girl so well before, that quickly. I knew that this was the type of person I wanted to be around.

The day after, I was chatting to a mate called Mike Gill, who I'd always catch up with on a Sunday down the pub, and he asked, 'What d'ya get up to last night?' I replied, 'I met my future wife.' Mike almost fell off his stool laughing.

Me and Gemma exchanged numbers, but our first date was a long way away. When I used to text her and didn't hear anything back for a couple of days, I'd delete her number. I thought she was taking the piss out of me, but it wasn't that at all.

Gemma didn't know me before that first time, but some of her friends had heard of me. Not in a good way, though. They were saying, 'He's a bad boy. He's in and out of jail. Be careful.'

I just thought her friends were being dead negative, but then I'd go ahead and confirm their suspicions.

Not long after first meeting Gemma, I met her at Panama Jacks. Not a date, just her mates and my mates out in town. I went to the toilet and this big Kiwi rugby player walks past me full of attitude, dropped his shoulder and barged me. I said, 'What d'ya do that for, ye prick?' He fronted me and it went off.

After having this massive free-for-all in the toilet, slipping around on the floors covered in piss, I walked out the toilet and said to Gemma, 'Come on, we're going. Now.' She had no idea what had happened and didn't ask any questions, but you could tell she wasn't impressed.

I didn't give up, though. I'd purposely go out just so I could hopefully bump into her. When I did see her out, it was back to the texts again. 'It was good to see you,' and I'd save her number again. I'd text her, but she didn't text back straight away, so I'd delete it again. It used to piss me off and became a bit of a running joke.

On nights when I wasn't going out, if she'd text and say, 'I'm going out tonight, hopefully I'll be able to see you', I'd be straight on the phone to my mates saying, 'Fancy a night out tonight, lads!'

Believe it or not, it took around four months to organise our first proper date. I wanted it to be just me and her, but she said she was bringing her best mate Kellie, so I brought my mate Mozez along. I was sober, proper nervous and really wanted to make a good impression.

We met at a pub, went to a couple of other places and then went to this nightclub in St Helens called Nexus. They sat down and me and Mozez went to the bar. Next minute, this lad who I knew through boxing barged into me off his head. I turned to him and said, 'Watch what you're doing, mate.' Before I could even finish my sentence, he headbutted me.

Next thing, we were rolling around on the floor. The doormen who stepped in knew me, so they left me alone and kicked this other lad out. I thought, 'I'm not done yet.' I felt like I'd had the proper piss taken out of me.

I ran around the back entrance waiting for him, as that's where the doormen where throwing him out from. As he came out, I went to town on him. Then, all I remember was somebody putting me in a chokehold from behind. I tried to pull him off, but I couldn't. One of his mates choked me out cold.

Next thing, I was being woken up by this copper. As I looked at him I thought, 'Shit. I'm on licence here. I'm on tag. If I get nicked now, I'm remanded.'

'What happened?' the copper says.

'I've just been choked out. I don't know what's happened.'

'What's your name?'

I kept referring back to the choke, saying, 'I just don't remember what happened,' basically trying to put off giving my details. Just by chance, another copper came over and said, 'Fucking you again.' I turned around to the first copper and said, 'See – he knows me!' He turned to the other guy and said, 'You know him?' 'Yeah,' he replied. He told me to fuck off and I scarpered.

I then text Gemma saying I was off to Mozez's sister's house and asked her to come over, which thankfully she did. When she arrived, she said, 'Oh my God. What happened to your eye? I've never seen a lump like that before.' I was dead straight with her and told her what had happened. You could say, the first date with Gemma didn't really go to plan.

A couple of days later, I was at Wigan ABC. Ray Jennings (Mike's dad) sometimes used to train me there. That Monday evening, I walked in with this massive black eye and he said, 'What the fuck have you been doing?' 'I was in a bit of an altercation. Wasn't my fault.' Ray shook his head and then absolutely tortured me with a gruelling session. Great.

If a black eye was my only worry at that point, my life would have been so much easier. The rest of the year wasn't going to finish very well for me.

CHAPTER 21

# COSTLY TEXT

*'There is a place where the sidewalk ends'*

Shel Silverstein

MY FIRST date with Gemma didn't go as planned and neither did the first meeting with her family.

I'd been round Digger's on an all-night bender when Gemma and her mate came over. We were in the garden having a few drinks when she said, 'Do you want to come round to my house? Nobody's in.'

'I'm not coming. I've been up all night drinking,' I replied.

'Just come over. Nobody will be there.'

Nobody there! I was sat downstairs while she was getting ready and the whole house came back. Gemma's mum, Liz and stepdad, Pete, both her nans, an auntie and her four-year-old cousin, who was running around like mad.

I was sat on this couch, quiet as a mouse, feeling proper rough, and they've said all perky, 'Who are you?'

'I'm with your Gemma.'

'What's your name?' Liz says.

'Martin.'

'Ah. You're the one from St Helens she keeps talking about. Do you wanna drink?'

'No thanks.'

'Do you want anything to eat?'

'No thanks.'

'Do you want a carrot?'

Very random, that one. 'No. I don't want a carrot, thank you.' I still wind Liz up about that now.

I wish I'd have met Gemma years before. She made me see sense. Made me feel what I was getting up to was not normal behaviour.

Unfortunately, getting back to normality was not an overnight process. The first few months after I met her, my life was still one crazy event after the next. Not long after we started going out, I ended up getting involved in a scuffle which would have me in court at a later date. As with the Pizza Heaven episode, I never started any of this.

I was out with a few of my mates on Bombie night, 2005. Me, Digger and another four or five of us went to a club in Preston called the Sidewalk. One lad decided he wanted to come, but I wasn't keen because he was bladdered. He said, 'I'll be fine, mate. Come on.' I went and picked him up, but the second he got in the back of the car, I thought to myself, 'Why did I do that? Look at the state of him.' He was far from fine.

We got to the club looking like a right bunch of scallies, all wearing trackies and trainers. You couldn't wear jackets in this club and because my trackies had no zips, I put my money in one of my trainers.

When we got in, I went to the bar, then I bent down to get the money out of my shoe to pay for some drinks. By the time I stood up, this lad, the one that was bladdered, had kicked off and was getting dragged everywhere by loads of doormen, filling him in. I jumped in the middle of it and we all ended up spilling outside.

The CCTV footage shows me talking to this one doorman. I was saying, 'What the fuck went on in there?' He was with about five big meatheads and was speaking to us like dickheads. I said, 'Listen, mate. We don't want any trouble, we just want our jackets and want to leave.' He replied, 'Fuck off, you're not having them.'

I then explained, 'My jacket has my phone in it, I need it.' 'You're not having it, ye prick,' he replies.

I was really angry and threw a right hand, but he must have seen it coming as he stepped back a bit and rolled the punch. He then said, 'Haaaa! What was that, you knobhead?'

The CCTV shows me and my mate bouncing up and down in front of the door entrance, getting ready to have it with them. What it didn't show was six doormen tucked away in the entrance, geeing each other up saying, 'What shall we do, lads? Shall we get 'em?' They then charged at us.

The guy who'd slipped my punch ran at me and walked straight into a one-two, dropping to the floor. I then dropped his mate and then another one and it turned into a free-for-all.

While all this was going on, Digger had got himself in a position with this one doorman, who wanted to have it with him. As the doorman walked over to Digger with the intention of levelling him, Digger did this Ali-style shuffle and the doorman looked at him thinking, 'Who's this?' and backed off. I nicknamed him the 'Sidewalk Shuffler' for a while after that.

If that wasn't impressive enough, Digger then went back into the club on his own. I don't know what he was thinking. When he got inside, he realised he was fucked if the doormen spotted him. He needed to get out again and went over to this girl and said, 'If I give you 50 quid, will you walk out with me as a couple?' She agreed.

Digger used to do this thing where whenever we'd be queueing up for a taxi, he'd disappear. I'd be looking for him, then next thing, a taxi would go past and he'd be waving at me with a big smile on his face as he went past.

Back to the club. A few minutes later, out walks Digger with this girl and some hat which he'd found on the way out. He walked straight past the doormen, then straight past me with that stupid smile and wave, just as I was getting nicked. As the police arrived, they CS gassed us and before we knew it we were in the back of their van. I was charged and given conditional bail. I'd committed affray on my licence again, so I was expecting a long sentence. Certainly longer than Walton.

Two months later, I was up in Preston court. The second they said, 'The bench is going to retire,' I knew I was going to be remanded. I turned to the court usher and asked, 'Can I go to the toilet, please?' He replied, 'No problem.' That was it. I was gone. I did a runner straight out of the courthouse, jumped on the first train back to St Helens and went straight to our Katie's house.

It didn't take the police long to work out where I was. One policeman in particular made it his mission to arrest me, but our Katie did a great cover-up job. Every week was the same story.

Copper knocks on the door and our Katie opens, while I'm upstairs.

'Is he here?' the policeman asks.

'No.'

'When's the last time you've seen him?'

'I work at Pontins, so never see him.'

'What I find funny about coming to this house is that you all live under the same roof, but none of you happen to see each other.'

'I know. It's crazy, isn't it?'

* * * * *

Just over a month later, I got myself into even deeper shit. Me and my mate had just been kicked out of Wigan Pier and got chatting to these two girls in the car park. They were in a car and we said, 'Where you going?' 'Pleasure Rooms in Liverpool,' they replied. We said, 'OK. We're coming with you.' Just to clarify – we weren't on the pull.

I went back home and got changed into jeans because we were wearing trackies. We went to Pleasure Rooms, had a top night and went back to their house for a party. They then dropped us off the day after and that was that.

A week later, me and this same mate went to a party. I turned to him and said, 'Do you want to go to Pleasure Rooms?' We managed to convince some lad at the party, who we didn't even know, to drive us over. Coincidentally, we bumped into the same two girls. 'Can't believe you guys are here!' they said. Again, we had a top night and then went back to their house and stayed up all night partying.

About two in the afternoon the day after, the lad who'd driven us over said, 'I have to be back at work later, so I'm going now.' Me and my mate were getting ready to leave when the girls said, 'Don't worry. We'll take yous back later.' 'Sound,' I replied.

We got back on it again but then, after about an hour, the girls started falling asleep. I asked one of them, 'Can you take us home?' By now she was tired and replied, 'Fuck off. Make your own way home. We're getting some sleep now.'

There we were stranded in this house in the middle of Liverpool thinking, 'What we gonna do now?' That's when I spotted her car keys on top of the telly. I turned to my mate and jingled them in front of him. He smiled and nodded at me as if to say, 'Yeah. Come on.' We jumped in the car bladdered and drove off.

Soon after, this girl realised what I'd done and called me. 'Why did you take my car?' she says.

'Because you said you'd take us home and you've not.'

'I'm sorry. Bring the car home and I'll take yous straight away.'

'OK. I'm turning around now.' I wasn't, though. I was buying myself some time because I knew they were going to call the police or there would be a firm of lads waiting for us when we returned the car.

Five minutes later, she calls again. 'Where are ya?' 'Ten minutes away,' I replied.

About 15 minutes later, they realised I wasn't coming back and I received another call. It was the police this time. 'Listen. Just turn round now and take it back to the owner.' I turned my phone off.

Me and my mate went to the pub round ours and as we were parking up I crashed the car into a wall. We went into the Oddy's pub in Parr for a few drinks and then went on to the Bull's Head further down the road and had a few more.

About 11 o'clock, everyone started leaving, including my mate. I said, 'Where you all going?' They said, 'We're going home.' I called Digger and said, 'Where are you?' 'I'm around Warrington,' he replied. 'I'll come and see you,' I said. I should have never been behind a wheel in that state.

We got to Warrington, had a few more drinks and about 1am everyone started to leave. We were still up for it, so I said, 'You up for Pleasure Rooms?' Digger agreed and I was back there again, less than a day later, but this time in a stolen car.

We got to the front doors and the doormen took one look at how bladdered we were and said, 'Not tonight, lads.' We turned around, walked off and then couldn't remember where we'd parked the car. It took us an hour to find it.

Digger says to this very day, 'I should have never let you drive home that night.' I was falling asleep at the wheel, while Digger was slapping me hard around the face, shouting, 'Wake up, you dickhead, wake up.' When I dropped him outside of his house, he was fuming.

I drove home and got on to my mum's estate, parked up round the side in case the police came and then woke up the morning after, asleep on the steering wheel. This girl started calling again asking for her car. I got this kid from our estate, who dropped it off in a car park in St Helens and left the keys on top of one of the wheels for her.

She got her car back, but it was the damage that she was now angry about. She wanted 500 quid from me or she was phoning the police. I told her I wasn't going to pay up and I then stupidly sent a text saying, 'I know where you live.' That text would cost me later.

In fact, she had my phone number with a whole string of texts to refer back to. I was fucked.

# CHAPTER 22

# MAYHEM IN MALIA

*'Man on the run*
*Playing for fun*
*Wind me up*
*Leave me undone'*

Dash Berlin

WITHIN five to six months of meeting Gemma, I'd developed deep feelings for her and was hoping we could get serious as a couple. Unfortunately, I had to tell her that I was leaving the country and going on the run for three months as I wasn't ready to go back to prison. I also decided to tell her how I felt. 'I need to leave. Not because I want to, but because I have to go. I just wanted to say – I think I love you.' Sounds cheesy, but it was like that Elvis Presley record, 'Always on my mind.' And she was.

When I packed my bags for Crete in May 2006, I knew it was going to be my last massive blowout. I knew I was going back to prison when I returned and I'll be honest when I say, I went out to Malia and did not give a fuck. I really didn't. After all the shit I'd done and been through in my life, this was probably the most dangerous, self-destructive and at times depressing episode of my life. But it was also one of the best.

Four weeks after running out of the courtroom in Preston, me and Davo paid for a two-week package holiday with no intention of coming back after that time. We went out with a couple of grand each and smashed that money in no time.

After the two weeks were up, we had to leave this really nice hotel and ended up living in an apartment above Maccy's for a month. I love a Maccy's, but this one, like the flat, was proper hanging.

Me and Davo found jobs working for a guy called Manos. You know the kind of thing – standing out front, handing flyers to passers-by, offering three-for-ones. Because we had free ale, we'd be out front absolutely hammered all the time.

After a few weeks, Davo changed jobs and started doing PR at a club called Orgasmic. The job came with an apartment above the club and they took ten euros a day out of his wages for him to live there. Once the month was up at Maccy's, we went and lived over there.

I won't lie, money was tight out there. Any cash we had, from the get-go, we split straight down the middle. I also need to say a big thanks to Robbo and Mozez, who used to give my mum a few hundred quid every couple of weeks to send over to us, just to keep us going.

Manos took a shine to me. He said I was his PR and security all rolled into one. If anybody was kicking off, giving any of the girls shit or being a nuisance in the bar, I'd sort them out. I'm still in touch with him now. However, I don't know how he put up with my shit on occasions.

As I said before, boxing in the ring was never an issue with me, it was fighting outside of it which always got me in trouble. I'd had a fight at this club called Bananas the week before and Manos had given me strict instructions not to fight in there again. Problem was this guy from Swansea was being a real prick and wanted a fight with me.

By now, it was about five or six in the morning and I couldn't be arsed fighting. More importantly, out of respect for Manos, I promised him I wouldn't fight in Bananas. As it was starting to get light, I knew it was home time for me. I left Bananas and started walking home, not intent on fighting. Next minute, I hear this moped riding next to me. It was the Welsh lad. He also had some girl on the back who he'd picked up at Bananas.

He pulled up beside me and parked up the moped. I was thinking, 'Fucking hell. What do I have to do to catch a break here?' He started saying, 'What the fuck's up with you?' obviously trying to impress the girl. I replied, 'What the fuck's up with me? What the fuck's up with you?'

Before he got off the bike to make the first move, I cracked him off it.

While this was going on, a load of people were arriving in coaches for their holiday, looking at us with that expression of, 'What's going on here?' Somehow, next thing, I was arguing with all the bin men who were clearing the street up and loads of locals. I started getting paranoid that it was all about to kick off big style. I ran back to the apartment and woke Davo up.

'Davo. Davo. Listen. We're gonna have to go. I've had loads of bother with the locals. Quick. Get your shit together. It's about to kick off.' Davo, still half asleep, says, 'Don't worry mate. We'll get some tools. Anybody who walks through that door will get it.' Then I repeated it again and he suddenly woke up.

We started throwing all our stuff into two suitcases, ran outside, borrowed two scooters (without permission) and drove to our mate's apartment in town, with us pulling our suitcases along at 30 miles an hour alongside the scooters. We then got a taxi and headed to the airport.

When we arrived, we looked at the flights available. Flights to Ibiza – there weren't any. Flights to Magaluf – no flights. Flights to Zante – same. We stayed there for a couple of hours, then sat outside in the baking sun rough as fuck, thinking what to do. We decided we didn't want to leave. We were going to take it on the chin and go back to the strip in Malia.

It didn't take long for things to kick off again. The day after, we were watching England play in the football World Cup in this pub, when this guy I knew pulled up on his moped and said, 'Jump on a minute.' I said, 'Why?' He replied, 'I just want to take you somewhere.' I jumped on and thought nothing of it. We went round to this bike place where he worked, then he went in the office and came running out swinging a baseball bat at me in the middle of the Malia strip.

I said, 'What the fuck are you doing?' It turned out the Welsh lad I'd had a fight with was a mate of his. So there we were in front of this bike shop, at a crossroads, getting ready to have a fight. This guy started saying, 'I need this bat because you're bigger than me.' His boss owned the shop, came out and threatened to have me killed, but thankfully

Manos sorted the whole thing out. Good old Manos. He was always looking out for me like a crazy son. He might not know the value of what he did for me when I was out in Crete on many occasions, but I'll never forget.

There was a big mix of people working PR from all over the UK. We didn't make a massive number of friends with the locals, but the ones we did were really sound.

There was one Greek guy called George, who worked at Bananas. Cracking bloke. Really nice fella who I'm still in touch with to this day. He treated me and Davo with respect and helped us out on a number of occasions when we didn't have a penny to our names.

Unfortunately, I couldn't stop getting into fights. It was like I'd never left St Helens. Every pub, club or bar I went to, I'd end up having a scrap, although it wasn't always my fault.

There was this really nasty gang of lads in Malia, who weren't from Crete. This one night, they walked into this club called Sugar and started molesting a group of girls that were with us. Hands all over them, touching them inappropriately. About a week before, I'd been fighting in Sugar and they don't like you fighting in their clubs in Malia because it's bad for business. Not that I can imagine fighting helps to promote business in any other clubs around the world.

My right hand was knackered from fighting and I could have done without the hassle, but I said to this gang, 'What you doing? Fucking get off. These girls are with us.' The biggest of the group grabbed my wrist dead tight and was staring at me really intensely. I was thinking, 'The second he lets go of this hand, he's getting it.'

The instant his hand came off my wrist, I banged him, then banged his mate. His mates ended up scarpering. The doorman then came over and kicked me out. By now it was about six in the morning and just getting light. As I came out the front of the nightclub, I stood there for a moment and let my eyes adjust to the sun. That's when I looked left and saw the gang walking away up this hill. There was six of them now.

One turned around and saw I'd been kicked out. He nudged the others and they all looked around at the same time. I thought, 'Fucking 'ell. Here we go again.' I could have run, but they would have got me the day after, or the day after that, so I decided to deal with it at that moment. I waited at the bottom of the hill for them to come down and was bouncing on my feet ready. I steamed into them and then remember falling into these mopeds and getting pelted every time I was trying to get up.

They knocked me out, made a right mess of me and left me for dead. I was black and blue all over, my face was swollen badly and I had a long cut on my back. I don't know if they'd gone at me with a knife and didn't get me proper, or I'd got the cut falling over the mopeds, but I was left with a long slice up my back. Davo was in the club at the time and when he came out with some other lads, they carried me about 100 yards round the corner, in front of Subway (the sandwich shop). When I came to, I knew I'd been in a bad fight.

I went home to sleep and woke up sore as fuck. I knew I was in the shit with this gang now, so I went to see Manos. I explained what had happened and he shouted at me, 'What have I told you? Do not fight with that gang. They're crazy.' I said, 'It's happened now. There's nothing I can do.' He said, 'Don't worry. I'll sort it out. Just don't fight with them again.'

Not long after leaving Manos, I was on my way to work when the big guy who'd grabbed my hand in the bar went past me on a bike. He was wearing shorts and a vest and looked like Deebo in the film *Friday*. He stopped, put the bike to one side and said in this deep voice, 'You.' He then did the gesture of the knife across the throat. We squared up and I said, 'If you want to go, let's go.' He then pedalled off, but kept doing the knife across the throat.

When I got to work, a few members of this gang started walking past me, sizing me up. I turned to Manos and said, 'It's going to go off here in a minute.' He told me to jump on the back of his scooter and we went to this bar in the middle of nowhere. The fellow who owned the place apparently had a bit of weight with the locals.

As I walked in, one of the gang who'd done me in was there. His hand was in plaster. Turns out he'd broke it on my face. This guy had told the guy who owned the bar that he was giving leaflets out down the strip and that I'd taken them off him, threw them on the floor and said to everyone, 'Don't go there, it's shit.' I turned to Manos and the owner of this bar and said, 'He's talking shit. That's not what happened.' Now everybody was shouting away in Greek and this gang member was still going on at me.

At the time, some lad had gone missing out there. He was never found and there were 'Missing' posters all over the lamp posts trying to jog people's memories. This guy from the gang said to me, 'See that poster. Easy for you to disappear like that. Easy.' I'd have had it out with him right there, but knew that would have been a one-way ticket off the island, most likely in a coffin.

I came away with a stern warning and as time went on, it kind of blew over.

\* \* \* \* \*

Just as I was starting to get a little homesick, I had a few lovely surprises from some familiar faces back home – although some hadn't always been friendly.

Just before leaving St Helens to come to Malia, we were having some trouble with some lads from Haydock. We'd done some stuff to them and they'd retaliated. This was the gang who got us with the machetes outside Cricketers that time. One day, there I was working in front of Manos's bar when they suddenly appeared. I thought we were going to go straight into a brawl but we managed to sort things out, which was good. In fact, we partied with them for the week and it turned out they were all top lads. It was also nice to put all the problems we had with them to bed.

I bumped into a few other people from back home while I was over there; a good mate of mine, Appy, his wife Diane and an old mate, Shane Meadows, who I used to party with years ago. They were proper familiar faces, so it was really good to see them.

Randomly, I bumped into Matthew Macklin. Boxing was on every Friday night in the bar opposite where I worked, so I wasn't much use to Manos then, as I'd be trying to PR but was watching the boxing at the same time. This one Friday, I'd watched Macklin beat Marcin Piatkowski in four rounds, then a couple of days later I've seen him walking down the strip with a black eye from the fight. I recognised him but he didn't know me, and we just had a little chat about boxing. At the time, he was getting ready to fight Jamie Moore. I would never have thought it back then but Macklin would end up being my manager and Jamie would end up a top mate and one of my trainers.

Macklin wasn't the only boxer I bumped into. Over the coming weeks, I ended up bumping into my old mate Lee Jennings and his brother Ste and a few of the lads from Golden Gloves ABC, including Ste Mullin and Ryan Hill. Funnily enough, I ended up having a boxing match in Malia. Very random.

One day, this guy walked past the bar and recognised me straight away. Turns out he was the Cypriot boxing coach and we'd crossed paths at the Ireland and Cyprus boxing competitions in 2004.

After a bit of a chat, he says, 'Do you want a fight? A boxing match.'

'Yeah. Why not. When is it?' I replied.

'Next couple of weeks, there's a tournament on the beach. You'll get paid as well.'

'Yeah. I'll have a bit of that.'

The coach was in talks with this local boxing promoter about putting on this eight-man tournament. However, that was K1 (mixed martial arts) rules. I said I wasn't going to fight K1, so they agreed to have me as a one-off for boxing.

I knuckled down to training with good intentions and found a tiny weights gym in Malia and managed to do a bit of shadow boxing. Problem was the guy who ran it told me, 'We don't like that in here,' so I ended up leaving and did a couple of runs instead. Then I thought, 'Fuck it. It is what it is.' I'd been drinking and smoking every day for about six weeks, so there was no way I was ever going to get really fit.

Instead, I decided to make the party even bigger and managed to get Digger over to join us for a week. I'd been calling him for ages, usually in the early hours when I was pissed up. 'Get out here, mate. You'll love it!'

This particular day, around four in the morning, I left him a voicemail with the usual crap, but also said, 'I've got some news. I need your help.' Because it was the early hours, he didn't answer, so I ended up calling him later that day.

'Dig. I've got this fight on the beach.'

'What kind of fight?'

'Like a proper boxing match.'

'I'm coming over. I'll do your corner.'

Me and Davo were made up that Digger was coming over and rented a convertible jeep for the week. As we picked him up from the airport and drove off, Digger says, 'What's the plan for the day then, lads?'

'Go back to the apartment, then we'll hit the bars,' I replied.

'Apartment, eh?' says Digger, sounding impressed.

When we got back, Digger's jaw dropped. 'What the fuck is this? Apartment?!' Me and Davo were pissing ourselves as we explained to Digger that the old thin stinky mattress on the floor was his. The shower was in the corner in open view and there were fans all over, blowing the smelly air.

Digger says, shaking his head, 'Seriously lads. This is the worst room I've ever seen in me life. I can't stay in here. It's hanging.' 'Come on, mate. It will be old school,' I said, while still laughing my head off. Digger walked over to the balcony, looked at the mattress again, then dragged it over to the balcony. 'That's where I'm sleeping. I can't take the smell in there.'

After a couple of days, Digger settled in and was loving the Malia vibe, although he did get a bit concerned one night when we went to this club and one of the gang members walked in. One of them pulled out this big Rambo knife, stuck it in the floor and started dancing around it. 'What the fuck is that about?' he said. I told him the story but said not to worry because I'd smoothed it out with them, which is more than can be said for the rest of the evening between me and Digger.

Ever since I've known Digger, we've always had stupid arguments and in the morning we're best mates again. We were at a bar and some people I knew came up to me to have a chat. I'd been talking to them for a while and he couldn't deal with it. Next minute, he ran over and clotheslined me (held his arm out WWE-style at neck height) and I went flying. I got up, we had a big argument and we had to get pulled off each other. We then went our separate ways for the night.

I must have had a good night because I crashed out down an alleyway. As luck would have it, or not, out of all the alleyways in Malia, Digger chooses to take a piss down this one at five in the morning. He left me there and couldn't wait to tell me in the morning. 'I noticed this massive pile of bin bags about six feet high. Next thing, I saw this body in among the bags. I was worried someone had been killed, then saw it was you asleep. I was pissing myself.' Being the good mate he is, he left me there until I woke up about three hours later. I was known for being able to fall asleep anywhere. I once fell asleep standing up, while taking a piss against some bins. It was one of the first few times I took Gemma out. Bet she was dead impressed with that.

A couple of days later was fight night. They'd set up a proper ring down on Pleasure beach and all the local workers and English people turned up to support me. It was absolutely packed. Even the people from the local apartments were cheering me on from the balconies. My hand was fucked from all the street fighting I was doing over there in the bars and clubs, but I still went ahead.

As Digger was warming me up on the pads, some lads came over and asked if he could teach them how to box. Just as Digger was about to say he'd never trained anyone in his life, I said, 'He's a professional boxing coach. It won't be cheap.' Digger didn't let on, but I could tell by his look he wanted to burst out laughing.

Next thing, we got the nod that we'd be up next. For some reason, I entered the ring wearing this big Mexican sombrero. I don't even remember where I got it from. I told Digger, 'I'm walking in there smoking a joint and drinking Smirnoff Ice in the corner between rounds.' He said, 'What? No way. I'm not going in your corner if you're doing that. No smoking and you'll have water or nothing.' 'OK mate,' I replied.

The fight was pretty easy, bearing in mind I'd been on a six-week bender. It was only three two-minute rounds, so I just moved around picking and landing my shots when I wanted. I stuck to my deal of drinking water in between rounds, while Digger and Davo were sinking the Smirnoff Ices one after the other in the corner, in between telling me, 'Get stuck in, Mart. Go on, mate.'

The second I was announced the winner, the crowd went mad. Everybody was calling me the champion of Malia, like that meant anything. Me, Davo and Digger were walking down the strip with these massive Mexican hats, like local heroes. Everywhere I went, people were coming out of bars giving us bottles of champagne. It was mad. We had a big party that night, right the way through to the morning. Even though I'd been done for 200 euros of my purse, at that point I didn't worry about it. I had money in my pocket and was living it up.

\* \* \* \* \*

A couple of weeks later, the boxing promoter calls. 'I've got another fight for you.'

However, the lad who I'd boxed said, 'I want to meet with you.' That was strange because he didn't come from Malia. Anyway, I met with him and he said, 'Don't take this fight. They're flying someone in from the Cypriot team who's fit.'

Everyone who had seen me win would have been betting money for me to do the same again. I was the favourite. The promoter was going to put all the money against me, so they'd cash in. I said, 'Yeah, I'll do it,' but I had no intention of fighting again.

Then the lad I'd already fought against also wanted me to fight him again, but for me to take a dive and then we'd split the money. I laughed and said, 'That's not happening. No way.' I went to the boxing promoter and said, 'I need to borrow some money. Two hundred euros. I want to train properly.' I had no intention of training, but made him think I was up for another fight. This was money he owed me from the first fight, so I didn't feel at all bad.

Me and Davo ended up having a right laugh with that cash. We'd proper roughed it over there at times. If we got a good wage between us, the day after it'd be gone. We'd have a big day eating stuff like a mixed grill or a T-bone steak, and if we had a shit wage we'd have something like a gyros wrap. But with 200 euros in hand, we decided to really enjoy ourselves.

The money lasted about three days and when it ran out we decided that we'd had enough of Malia and booked some tickets for home. During those days, we stayed low and the day we were flying out we sneaked out of our room and saw these girls from Greenock, Scotland and said our goodbyes to them, then headed off.

What we hadn't realised was that word had got around that we were going. The promoter got wind we were heading off and came down to the airport with another fella. He pulled out this knife and went for

Davo but before he could do anything, Davo turned it around, which then cut the promoter's hand. Davo then chucked the knife in the bin.

The promoter was now shouting to anyone who would listen, 'They've got drugs in their case. They've got drugs in their case. Check, check.' He was trying to delay our flight, so he could keep us on the island and get us filled in at a later date. He was just a shithouse. After all the fighting I'd done in Malia, the last thing I wanted to do was to get nicked on the spot because of this guy.

Before we knew it, the police came running over. They then took us to this questioning room, where the promoter's talking to the police in Greek, trying to give his side of the story. I've turned to the police and said, 'Speak in English, we don't know what you're saying. In fact, get me the British Embassy.' The police started umming and ahhing.

In the meantime, the promoter was still going on about drugs, when I said to the police, 'We've got no drugs but if you check those cameras you'll see he's walked in with a knife. All we want to do is get our flight and go home without any hassle.' The second the knife was mentioned, the promoter shit it and got out of there fast.

Funnily enough, I bumped into him a few years later, when I was watching Jamie Moore fight against Ryan Rhodes. First thing he did was apologise.

\* \* \* \* \*

As I said before, I had some great laughs in Malia, but there was a flip side to the coin. I was very anxious the whole time I was out there. About once a week, in between the partying or at the end of a late night of drinking, I used to go out for big, long walks on my own to gather my thoughts. I didn't know where my life was heading at that stage apart from knowing I was walking straight back into a prison sentence when I got home.

I'd met Gemma and in an ideal world wanted to get things going with her again when I got back. I used to watch the series *Prison Break* (the irony) before I went to Malia. Gemma used to watch it back home and I'd always call her up the day after each episode, every week, to have a chat about it. In all honesty, I didn't give a shit about the programme. That was my way of kicking off our chat, then we'd be on the phone for about an hour. It was like she restored my sanity when we'd chat because the second I'd come off the phone, I was wild again. I started to wonder whether she'd met someone while I was away and whether she'd wait for me when I went to prison. I was basically thinking, 'Is it even worth me keeping in touch with her, because it's all going to end up a mess.'

Same with boxing. There was no guarantee I had a future in boxing. Everything was a big question mark in my life. No matter how much I drank or how many walks I went for, there never seemed to be any solutions or any positives. I was in no man's land. I was on self-destruct in a major way. That's why I was always drunk and always fighting. I'm serious when I say I'm lucky that I managed to stay alive with the way I was living and thinking in Malia.

As the plane landed in the UK, mentally, I was all over the place.

# CHAPTER 23

# PRISON BREAK

*'If I had some idea of a finish line, don't you think I would have crossed it years ago?'*

Richard M. DeVos

TWO weeks after getting back from Malia, I went on a shopping spree with Mozez. As we were checking some new gear out, I noticed this fella was looking at me funny. I remember thinking, 'What's he staring at?' He walked off and I thought nothing of it.

I went to the changing room to try some stuff on, when there was a heavy-handed knock on my door. It turned out the guy staring at me was a copper and he was with four others. Mozez wanted to shout over to make me aware when they walked in, but with nowhere to escape that would have just given me away, so he kept quiet hoping they'd just walk out. That never happened, unfortunately.

I was nicked, frogmarched out of there and taken straight to Preston court cells. The incident from the nightclub in Preston on 5 November 2005 had finally caught up with me. Funnily enough, the shop I was nicked in, like the nightclub in Preston, was also called Sidewalk. Not a lucky name for me.

On 18 August 2006, I was back in court. I knew I was going to jail but I thought they were going to throw the book at me. Bearing in mind I was up for affray, on licence for affray and had been on the run for over four months, I was certain I was looking at the maximum they could dish out for the offences.

One of the other lads who had been involved was sentenced to two months while I was on the run. The judge had said that one of the doormen came at him and he reacted in self-defence. Then when it came to me, because they couldn't find the CCTV footage, they could only give me the same sentence they'd given to him, which was two months. I thought to myself, 'This is it. When I come out, I'm getting my life together because I'm never going to get as lucky as this again.'

I was expecting up to a three-year sentence, which was a strong possibility with my track record. If I'd have got a sentence that long, I doubt very much I would have been with Gemma and who knows what I'd have come out like. In fact, because I was expecting a long sentence, I told her not to wait for me and to get on with her life, as she didn't need this shit. I can't explain how relieved I was when the judge said 60 days.

I went to Preston prison and kept myself to myself. There were no jobs. I basically spent the next 30 days behind my door. It was the shortest sentence I'd done, but it felt like the longest because I was so excited about getting out and turning my life around.

All I thought about during those 30 days was getting out, settling down with Gemma and getting back to my boxing. However, it took us a few days to reconnect. I was upset because she never wrote to me, but that wasn't her fault. She'd never known anyone in jail before and didn't know what to do. This wasn't her way of life.

The thing with me, if I genuinely care for someone, I can never stay mad with them for long. It only took a couple of days for me to see sense and I decided it was best to have a chat with Gemma.

I was half expecting her to be the same shy person and pick up where we'd left off, but she gave it to me straight and said some stuff which I needed to hear. 'I think things will need to be different, Martin. You can't keep fighting like nothing's changed. I can't carry on like this. If you don't change now, you'll carry on like this for the rest of your life, in and out of jail.'

She was right. By the time I'd met Gemma, it's embarrassing to say, I'd had hundreds of street fights. I was going out most nights of the week, sometimes having two or three fights each night. I didn't want to go back to my old life or jail again but if I didn't change, that's exactly what would happen. Most importantly, I didn't want to lose Gemma.

Thankfully, over the next few months, me and Gemma worked things out and in December 2006 decided to go serious as a couple. She turned out to be a massive part of the transformation which lay ahead for me. That said, not everything went as smoothly as I would have wanted, especially around her family.

In early 2007, me, Gemma, Liz and Pete went to the rugby. They're mad Warrington fans and we went to see St Helens v Warrington at the Halliwell Jones stadium. They didn't know anything about me, so there I was trying to be this respectable person.

We went to this pub called The Lord Rodney, just outside the stadium, which is where all the fans went. I used to have some drugs on me at the time and when we got into this pub, straight away this lad called Brains spots me. It was at a time when I had a reputation previously for using drugs and he comes over while I'm standing with Liz, Pete and Gemma, and says, 'Fucking 'ell. It's shit in here. Have you got 'owt?', meaning if I had any tackle.

My head almost fell off my shoulders with embarrassment. I panicked and shouted, 'What are you doing swearing? This is my girlfriend and her family. Be respectful. Go on, go away. You're doing me head in.' I ended up losing it a little bit and ushered him on.

After a couple of minutes I walked up to him and said, 'Are you for fucking real? You can't assume you can talk like that in anyone's company. Have you got 'owt? Have you got fucking 'owt? In front of my girlfriend and her family.'

When I went back over to Gemma, she said, 'What's up with you?' 'We've got to go now,' I replied. 'It's alright. Calm down,' she said. 'Yeah, yeah,' I said all nervous. After the game, we went back in the Rodney for a drink and then jumped into a taxi to go to Liz and Pete's.

Pete jumped in front and the rest of us in the back. The taxi driver turned around all upbeat and said, 'You alright?' directing it to me. I looked up, realised I recognised the driver and thought, 'Here we go.' He then said, 'What you up to?'

The driver used to do the doors around Warrington and knew my face. I replied, 'Nothing. Been to the game.' I was trying to keep the answers to a minimum.

'Seen 'owt of Digger?'

'No, no. Not seen him.'

'Have you been back in jail lately?'

Honest to God, I could have died there and then.

Fair play to Liz and Pete. They didn't say a word or create an atmosphere. When we got back to their house, Liz did something which I've always loved and respected her for, especially as I was feeling a right twat. As I got out of the car, she could see I was embarrassed and said, 'Martin, listen. We're not bothered about what you've done in your past, as long as you look after our Gemma. That's all I want.'

It made me feel so much better and it's all I've ever done since meeting her.

\* \* \* \* \*

On the boxing front, I saw my chance to start anew and went for it. The Friday I came out of Preston jail, I went out with the lads on the weekend, then on the Monday I went to see John Lyon at Wigan gym. 'I need to do something with my life. I want to dedicate myself properly now. John, I want to turn pro.'

John had been in the game a long time and had heard all the bullshit before. He took a breath and then said, 'Calm down. You need to get some amateur bouts behind you and prove to me that you can stay on the straight and narrow if this is what you really want to do. It's alright saying this, but I need you to prove it. Words are easy. Does that sound fair?' I nodded.

I'd just like to say why I didn't decide to carry on training with Kevin and Michael Bacon. The truth is, I needed a fresh start. I have no doubt whatsoever that they would have done a cracking job with me but after Chizzy died, I couldn't bring myself to go back to the old gym without him being there. It just wouldn't feel right. I'd like to give a special mention to Kevin. He was always there for me throughout my amateur days, even when he knew I was off the rails. He never judged me, just tried to help and guide whenever possible. To this day he remains a good friend and I still enjoy doing a gruelling pad session with him.

Back to the boxing. That Monday, I cracked on with John at Wigan ABC. We then started to go to the JJB gym in St Helens and did a bit of one to one. Within a few days, I could feel that everything was starting to come together nicely.

Even though everything was going well on the boxing front, unfortunately, my past was about to rear its ugly head again.

Barely two months after coming out of Preston prison, I was back in front of a judge at Liverpool Magistrates' Court on 13 November 2006. This was relating to when I nicked that girl's car after a night out in Wigan Pier in December 2005.

I was really anxious going into the courtroom as I knew this was a messy case and I'd fucked up badly. The list of stuff the judge started to read out was the longest I'd ever had compared to any other court appearance.

'You're charged with taking a motor vehicle without consent; using a vehicle while uninsured; using threatening, abusive or insulting words or behaviour to cause harassment, alarm and distress; failing to surrender to custody as soon as practicable, after appointed time.'

After hearing all them convictions, not to mention my prior form, I was certain that I was going back to prison. I was willing to accept whatever was thrown at me, but decided to tell the judge where my head was now.

'I'm not denying anything I've done, but I'm really trying to change my life. I've been in the gym every day since coming out of Preston and am trying to really knuckle down with my boxing training. I'm looking to turn professional soon. I understand what I did was wrong and I'll never do it again. Just give me a chance. Please.'

After quizzing me for a bit, he gave me 200 hours of community service, a tag to wear for three months, a six-month driving ban and a £100 fine. The second I realised there was no prison term to be served, I let out a massive sigh of relief. Either it was my genuine plea and the judge could sense something different this time, or perhaps I was just lucky. Either way, I wasn't going back to prison again.

Although I wasn't in a position to bargain, the hours of the tag were way too short. I'd have never been able to go to the gym. I asked if the judge could extend them to help with training and, fair play, he did.

\* \* \* \* \*

My first fight back into amateur boxing was against Tom Doran. I went and fought him on his home show and stopped him. I then had another four fights and won them. The final contest was in Holland in early 2007, which came with a funny conversation for John. He received this phone call from a guy in the police who was in charge of boxing.

'I've got a bout for Martin. Is he available?'

'Should be. Who's it for?' John replied.

'Martin would represent the UK police association team. It's against the police association in Holland.'

'He's got a tag on. He can't go abroad.'

'Don't worry about that. If he's willing to fight, we'll sort that out.' And they did. They had my tag taken off, legally, which was the first time in a long time, and a few weeks later I was in Holland captaining a small team that included my old mate Lee Jennings and Natasha Jonas, who was just starting out back then. A nice little group made the trip over, including my dad, Dennis and Garvey, which was a nice last memory for me to have as an amateur.

We all fought in this massive arena and I was up against a 75kg fighter, who was in all honesty an easy match. I dropped him with a body shot and nearly stopped him, but he managed to hang on in there to the final bell.

I didn't go into the competition knowing it was going to be my last, but the thought of exactly when I should turn pro had been at the back of my mind for a couple of months. I started to weigh up how long it would take for me to fight in the ABAs again and get back in the England squad. I was also approaching 25 years of age.

When I got back to England, my mind was made up. After over 80 successful amateur fights, I knew the time to get cracking was now. If I messed up this time, there was no turning back.

CHAPTER 24

# SERIOUS BUSINESS

*'It was jail, dying or boxing and I chose boxing'*

Martin Murray

THERE were a number of lads in a pub I used to go to, where Chizzy once said to me, 'You can easily stick your finger out here and say, "He could have been a good 'un. And him and him and him." I didn't want to be that guy supping a pint in the pub in a couple of years' time, scrapping on the street and pissing away a career. As my mate Dennis told me, 'Instead of twatting people on the streets, you can twat them in the ring and make money.'

The next step for me was to get a promoter. I'd not long come out of jail and couldn't go to a big promoter because I wasn't coming off any good form. My last big win was at the ABAs in 2004, so I was a gamble to anyone at that point.

Thankfully, I was surrounded by good people who helped guide me. At Wigan Boxing Club, John Lyon ran the seniors, while Damian Jones and his dad Richard looked after the juniors. Richard was a bigwig for the British Boxing Board of Control (BBBofC) at the time. He knew Steve Wood and he was offering what I wanted – local shows and regular fights.

At the time, Steve's best fighter was Jamie Moore, who trained at Oliver Harrison's gym in Salford. Richard really rated Oliver as a trainer and I really liked Jamie Moore's fighting style. Seemed like a sensible move. I'll be honest, I went to a couple of other gyms before going to Oliver's, but after the first session with him I knew I didn't need to look elsewhere. Me and Oliver clicked from day one. I liked the way he did pads, gave instructions to fighters in the ring and the way he understood them and their feelings, especially mine.

It was also important for me to start afresh. I could have gone to gyms in Liverpool where I knew people, but I didn't want that. I wanted to go to a gym in a new area where I didn't really know anyone and Oliver's gym ticked that box.

The only tough part about training was getting there. When I first started going up to Oliver's gym, I hadn't passed my driving test, which was my own fault really. Getting a three-year, a 12-month then a six-month ban before even applying for my licence might have had something to do with it. Driving when I was banned also didn't help. Either way, I couldn't get behind the wheel of a car.

Richard drove me the first couple of times, but wasn't able to drive me up all the time, so Teddy Noonan took over. Despite not paying me a great wage as a kid, I'll never forget what Teddy did for me back then. He knew getting to and from the gym as quickly as I could was important. He never made a fuss and always made it feel like it was a massive pleasure for him to do so. It was almost as if I was doing him a favour.

Teddy passed away in 2016. From the time I was getting ready to turn pro, we had some proper laughs, especially with Mad Benny. When he was wheelchair-bound, I used to pick him up, spend a few hours down the pub with him having a right laugh, then I'd drive him home. Not because I was paying him back for his kindness but because he was a good mate who I genuinely enjoyed spending time around. RIP mate. Miss you. Thanks for all the laughs.

Someone else I'd like to mention is my first ever professional sponsor, Adam Cotham. A couple of months before my debut, he gave me £500. It was at a time when I had next to nothing, apart from a bad reputation. I'm still mates with Adam to this day and will never forget the faith he showed in me at a time when many didn't want to have anything to do with me.

That said, if he'd seen me on holiday a few weeks later, he might have reconsidered the offer.

# CHAPTER 25

# NEW CHAPTER

*'The universe is not short on wake-up calls. We're just*
*quick to hit the snooze button'*

Brené Brown

FIRST holiday I ever went on was with my family to Magaluf when I was 14. At the time, we stayed at a family resort. Ten years later, a couple of months before my pro debut, and I'm back in Magaluf on a lads' holiday. Different hotel this time.

One day I said to the lads, 'I wonder if that hotel I stayed at all them years ago is still there. Who fancies going over for an afternoon?'

The day after, we decided to check it out and stay for a few beers by the pool. The main difference now was that it had turned into a Club 18-30-type set-up. The place was packed but there were two distinct groups of lads on this day. A younger lot in the pool and an older lot lounging around it. It was the young ones who were being really loud and acting like idiots. There I was, lying back on this lounger, while one of my mates in the pool suddenly finds this young lad standing in front of him, shadow boxing.

My mate looked over at me as if to say, 'Look at this dickhead.'

I was in a different place in my life now. Me and Gemma were looking to start a family and I was getting ready for my pro debut, so the last thing I needed was to get involved in a brawl. I've mouthed to my mate, 'Fuck him off,' basically meaning, 'Get rid of him.' As I've said that, the lad in the pool has seen what I've just said and looked at me and said, 'What lad?' I took a deep breath and thought, 'Here we go.'

He jumps out of the pool and comes bouncing over to my lounger. I sat up and he shouted, 'What did you say?' I replied calmly, 'Listen mate. We're both on holiday. You lot have a good time and we'll have a good time and there doesn't need to be any trouble.'

He started mouthing off, saying, 'You think I'm a dickhead? Eh?' I repeated myself, trying to calm things, but he didn't want to listen. I could tell he was getting ready to kick off, so I stood up from the lounger and ended up grabbing him by the throat and almost throttling him. As I let him go and pushed him away, he starting shouting more abuse. Then out of the corner of my eye, I've seen one of his mates running at me. I stepped back and hit him with a left hook and he hit the floor. I was fuming now, simply because I didn't want to fight. I shouted at the lad from the pool and said, 'See what you've done? There was no need for this.'

Security then arrived and tried to nick us, so we all ended up doing a runner. We got round the corner of the hotel and I looked at my hand, which was swelling up badly and really throbbing. A couple of months before, my mate had an emergency operation after punching somebody and almost lost his hand. I thought, 'Before my boxing career's even started, I've fucked it up.' That episode acted as a wake-up call.

\* \* \* \* \*

Three weeks before my pro debut, I was in St Helens Magistrates' Court, but thankfully it was a bit of a nothing event. I'd breached the conditions of my community service because I was training all the time at Oliver's. I explained to the judge, 'I've turned professional about four weeks ago. It's my routine now. I need to train at these hours.' The judge replied, 'Can anyone verify this for you?' My then manager was present and the judge got him down to swear on the Bible and all that. Everything I'd said my manager was able to back up.

The judge was happy with what was said and my community service slate was wiped clean. He continued to say that I had a suspended sentence and if I got done for anything in the next two years, I'd definitely be going to jail.

That was the last time I was ever in trouble with the law. It was one chapter finishing for me and an exciting new one starting.

## CHAPTER 26

# BUNDLE OF JOY

*'Plan your work and work your plan'*

Salvador Sanchez

I MADE my pro debut against Jamie Ambler in Wigan on 22 September 2007, precisely 23 days after walking out of St Helens Magistrates' Court. Michael Gomez was meant to be topping that bill but a couple of weeks before he got the call to fight Amir Khan, so pulled out. Steve Wood was going to cancel the show but because I'd already sold about 500 tickets, he went ahead. I more or less topped the bill on my first show, even though it was just a small-hall affair.

It was a same-day weigh-in and I was told it would be at 12 stone. I came in at 11st 13lbs, then Jamie Ambler weighed in at 13 and a half stone. Hardly ideal, but I'd sold that many tickets, I didn't care. I just wanted to get in the ring and get my professional career off to a good start.

Come fight night, I was calm. That was until I looked through the doors where I'd be walking out towards the ring and saw my supporters being led by Craig Lyon (not the boxer) chanting my name and getting the place going. Little did I know it, but that first fight was the birth of the Barmy Army. Craig was soon called 'The General' because he got everyone going with the songs. Over the next few years, the Barmy Army would double, then triple in size, including divisions in St Helens, Warrington, London and even Wales later on. I'll always be very grateful for their support.

When my name was announced for the ring walk, the place erupted. After the referee's instructions, Oliver said, 'I've looked at this guy. You don't want to go in there trying to knock him out and end up in a messy fight. Just box to my instructions.' That's exactly what I did and won on points over six rounds. Ambler was a journeyman weighing in at near the cruiserweight limit. If I'd have gone for the knockout, it could have made it a scrappy affair and I may have damaged my hands in the process.

The Ambler fight was the first and last professional fight my mum came to watch. She couldn't bear seeing me get hit and nearly passed out every time I did. My dad, on the other hand, has come to all of my pro fights, although my mum had to have a chat with him after this one.

Here's the thing. I've always offered my dad ringside seats for my fights and he's rarely taken them. The reason being, like my mum, he always gets really bad nerves and prefers to sit with his mates. For the Ambler fight, my dad had one too many beers and my mum flipped. 'Dek, you can't get drunk at Martin's fights. What if someone takes a photo of you and says, "Look at the state of him. That's Martin Murray's dad."'

That was that. After Ambler, he straightened up his act. However, my mum wasn't exactly a great support to him in the build-up to my next fights. The thing is, my dad's a stresshead and my mum is a wind-up merchant. I take after her. She would hear about my next opponent and say to my dad, 'This boxer he's fighting next, he's a big lad.' Or, 'Have you seen the record of this lad? He's had a few knockouts.' My dad would shout, 'Stop saying that to me, Carol! Why do I want to know about any of that, eh? That's it. I've had enough. I'm going upstairs.'

Five weeks after the Ambler fight, I was up against Phil Callaghan on the undercard of the Jamie Moore vs Andrew Facey rematch. During the build-up for this fight, Oliver knew what I had in mind. I wanted to knock Callaghan out. He said, 'Just go in and do what you have to do.'

I hit him with a peach of a right hand in the first round and his eye ballooned instantly. It was horrible. I could see it getting bigger and bigger in front of me. Only thing was, when I threw the shot, I instantly felt my hand go, so I kept popping him in the eye until the referee came over and stopped it.

I had to go up to the gym a couple of days after for some pictures with Jamie and Mark Thompson. Oliver said, 'Have you had your hand checked out?' I said, 'No, no, not yet,' but I knew it was bad because it was throbbing. Oliver says, 'That's the reason why I prefer for you to do what I ask, instead of trying to please the crowd. You'll be off training for weeks now. Who's going to pay your wages? The crowd won't.'

I went on the Monday to get it seen to and it turned out I'd broken my thumb. Apparently the break almost went right across the whole thumb, so it was pretty serious. I was put in plaster and couldn't use the hand for a couple of months.

With time to kill, I ended up going to Vegas to watch Ricky Hatton fight Floyd Mayweather in December 2007, which was a trip that turned around and bit me on the arse. There I was on a plane with a few of the lads and a load of Ricky Hatton fans having a good time and this immigration form appeared. One of the questions asked if I had a criminal record. I thought, 'If I tick "yes" now, they're going to send me back,' so I ticked 'no'. In hindsight, if I'd have known about the form, I wouldn't have booked the trip in the first place.

Despite that, I had a cracking time out there and had an unexpected surprise while out at the local shopping mall. I was out with my manager, his lad and a mate called Trevor Standish Sr.

All of a sudden, this big group of bodyguards appeared, with some tiny little blonde woman standing in between them. Trev says, 'Must be someone famous.' I took a good look and said, 'It's Pamela Anderson, mate! Let's get a picture.' 'Yeah, yeah, let's go,' Trev says. I'm not the kind of person who gets starstruck, but for Pamela Anderson, I made an exception.

I walked over and said in my strong St Helens accent, 'Scuse me, Pam luv.' All the bodyguards turned. 'Would you mind if me and me mate have a picture with ya?' 'Yeah, no problem,' she replied. She was really nice and polite. Sadly, Trev died at the time this book was being written. Lovely fella who'd lived a colourful life and we just got on from the get-go. I'm sure he'd have had a giggle if he'd read this story. RIP mate.

* * * * *

Four months later, on 16 February 2008, I was back in the ring against Dean Walker. I won the fight on points and went on to win the next four over the next few months. Although I now had a 6-0 record, I came away from those fights deflated simply because my opponents weren't great.

I know they were there to pad out my record, but that's not the way I wanted to do things. I wanted fighters who'd give me a real test. Looking back, though, everything happens for a reason as I got my future fights off the back of them and for that I have to be grateful.

As I was getting ready to fight my seventh opponent, on 11 August 2008, one of the most incredible things was about to happen in mine and Gemma's lives. The arrival of our first baby, Archie.

I've often been asked, 'Was it a smooth birth?' 'Was it balls,' is the answer. Because this was our first baby, Gemma wanted to go to parenting classes in the weeks before. I kept saying, 'Don't worry, everything will come natural. You don't need to go to them classes.' Not that she took a blind bit of notice of what I said.

I ended up going along to this class about how they deliver babies and all that stuff. At the end, the lady asked, 'Any questions?' I'm quite a squeamish person, so I put my hand up and asked, 'Is it messy?' I could hear a few people giggling while I was deadpan faced. She replies, 'Nooo. It's not messy at all. Everything you see on films and the telly is just for the cameras. It's not like that in a real birth.' LIAR!!

So there I am in the delivery room with Gemma and her mum Liz. We'd arrived late evening and it was at the time of the Beijing Olympics. I was desperate to see the boxing, but it was only on for about two minutes. Liz loves her horses and we ended up sitting there all night, watching showjumping. Gemma had gas, which was probably a good thing as the labour, like the showjumping, went on for a while.

Just as our Archie was about to come out and I'm thinking we might be seeing some light at the end of the tunnel, the nurse says, 'His umbilical cord is wrapped around his neck, he's swallowed his own poo and his head is facing the wrong way.' Not a great combination.

Trying to be useful, I started to get involved with the whole delivery thing, getting caught up in the moment and all that. I stood up, looked down to where the baby was about to come out , saw all this blood and went faint. Next to me was a little trolley with all kinds of instruments and utensil things on. I thought, 'If I fall over now, I'm gonna go straight into that and cut my head open.' I pushed the trolley away and the nurse said, 'You look a bit pale. You've gone a funny colour. Sit down.'

Everybody started crowding around me now, making sure I was OK. In the meantime, Gemma was there with her legs up in stirrups and shouted, 'Hello. Over here!' The midwife went over and was now getting Gemma to do the final pushes. I'd been on Red Bull all night and had another quick swig before standing right up close to Gemma and cheering her on. 'Come on, Gem! Come on luv!'

Gemma doesn't swear much, but she turned to me and snapped, 'Get that fucking Red Bull breath out of my face. NOW.'

They ended up getting that sucker plunger thing that grips the baby by the head to pull him out. While they were getting ready to do that, bang, the doors flew open and this team of doctors and nurses came flying into the room. I'm thinking, 'Shit. What's going on here?' They pulled him out with the plunger and put him on the bed. He didn't move for ages. Seemed like the longest seconds of our lives. Then, all of a sudden, he came to life.

At first, because he'd swallowed his poo and was covered in sludge and blood, he looked like a little scrunched-up alien. Once they'd cleaned him up, he looked lovely. Our Archie. Our first child. I can't describe how happy I was to be a dad and that me and Gemma had started our own family.

Having Archie gave me that extra bit of focus in my life. It was like a switch in my head had clicked on.

# CHAPTER 27

# EYE ON THE PRIZE

*'And the winner, by split decision …'*

Ring announcer, Prizefighter, 22 November 2008

JUST under 12 months after my debut, I fought against Carl Wild on 14 September 2008. It was my eighth fight. Again, he was a couple of weight categories above me, but I went in there and chopped away at his body relentlessly. The difference with Wild was that he had a go back. He liked a fight and that's where the openings came. This was my second stoppage since turning pro and I'd managed to get the media talking at last.

Four weeks later, I was up against Joseph Sovijus from Slovakia. He came out swinging, so I tucked up tight. I saw he had a lazy jab, so I waited for the next time he threw it and hit him with a peach of a right hand, followed by a left hook straight after it. That was it. He was gone. First-round stoppage.

Although I was an undefeated fighter with a 9-0 record, by now fewer and fewer people were buying tickets to see me because I had only fought journeymen. Then, bingo. The opportunity for Prizefighter came up on 22 November 2008.

When word got around I was taking part, everyone wanted tickets off me again. In fact, the second it was announced, St Helens threw their full support behind me. Pubs were advertising me fighting live on Sky and Fingerpost especially did me proud with posters all over the place. Very humbling, because I'd only been boxing professionally for 13 months by this stage.

A big part of me wanted to win it just to put St Helens boxing back on the map.

We trained hard like we always do, but the big difference was that Oliver had to get sparring partners who were going to go all out for three rounds. We'd spar one person for three rounds, then have ten minutes' rest. Then we'd spar someone else with a different style for another three rounds, then another ten-minute break. Then the same again with someone else. We were basically trying to prepare ourselves for how the night could unfold.

The only thing I thought would slow me down during the training camp was our Archie, as he had colic. Somehow, miraculously, it didn't have an effect on me. I used to wake up in the morning and say to Gemma all enthusiastic, 'He slept straight through last night. Didn't make a sound.' Gemma would then say, looking absolutely shattered, 'You joking? I've been up all night with him in the bathroom, so you could have a sleep.'

Prizefighter was a chance for me to get TV exposure and this is where it really started to happen, especially as I went into the competition as the bookies' favourite. That said, there had only ever been three Prizefighter competitions before and the favourite had never won.

Fight one was against undefeated Joe Rea. He'd fought seven times in the US and was trained by Micky Ward, but we didn't get sucked in by any of the media hype. It was an easy win. The second fight was a bit scrappy. Danny Butler's style was very awkward. He'd rush at you and try and smother you with little pitter-patter shots. I wanted a proper fight but it just never ignited. I got the win, though, and that's all that counted.

Then it was Cello Renda. He was the dangerman in the competition and had a reputation for being able to bang a bit. Renda had been on first and stopped his opponent in the second round, which gave him a longer break. I was on last and all of my fights had gone the distance, which meant I had the least amount of time to recover. We went into the final with identical odds of 4-1 to win.

Round one went off at a furious pace but I had it under control, boxed well and beat him to the punch. With about 30 seconds to go, I hit him with a couple of jabs and a one-two. He went down and took the eight count. As I went in to finish him off, he threw a massive left hook which came out of nowhere. It hit me clean on the chin and I don't know how it didn't take me out. Thankfully, the bell went seconds later. Oliver gave me a bit of a bollocking when I got back to the corner and told me to 'keep boxing' and get back to what I was good at.

Second round, I went out there and had it with him, which was probably the wrong tactic as my boxing had won me the first round. I reckon he won that second round and the last one was even as we both bit down on our gumshields and had a good old shoot-out. It was a close fight. I saw it 10-8 first round to me, 10-9 second round to him and last round even. Looks like the judges also saw it close, as I won a split decision.

In the meantime, our Katie's nerves had got the better of her. She'd been on edge for all three fights but the second my hand was lifted in the final, she had to run to the toilet and was sick all over the place.

The competition came with a cash prize but at the time I wasn't thinking about the money, just winning the fight. When I went in the corner for the last round against Renda, Oliver said to me, 'Do this for Archie.'

We'd had our Archie three months earlier and were struggling for money. Only a few weeks before he was born, Steve Wood ran a competition through his VIP companies at Robin Park, Wigan for all his fighters. It was kind of like a fun sports day, but fitness-based. There was loads of stuff like what distance you could do on a rowing machine in a minute, how many push-ups you could do and a few other exercises involving weights. That sort of stuff. I came second in it and got 300 quid. Me and Gemma were buzzing because we could now get our Archie a pram.

When I was announced as the Prizefighter winner, I was busy celebrating. Then someone said, 'You've won the 25 grand.' I was like, 'Fucking get in!' Twenty five bags. Buzzing.

A couple of months before, Gemma unfortunately lost her nan and she'd very kindly left us a bit of money. Between that and the Prizefighter cash, it acted as our get-up for the mortgage on our first house. Things were starting to move in the right direction.

# CHAPTER 28

# BELTING WIN

*'First time I went to Oliver's and saw him skipping
and training, I'd never seen anything like it. He was
an animal in the gym. I still say it now. There were no
easy spars with Martin. It didn't matter who you were
— you were getting a hiding'*

Tony Dodson, 2016

AT the time, we were renting a house in Wigan. The intention
was to take myself a little bit out of the area. Most of my time
now was spent either training on my own, with Gemma or
with our Arch. After a while, people realised how I wanted to live. It
was like when I stopped taking drugs. I'd be out and people would say,
'D'ya want a bit of this?' After I'd refused a few times, they'd get the
idea and stop asking.

As I started to leave that life, I also realised I wanted to help people
on the other side of the fence, using my life story and boxing to guide
them. I wanted to help those people who might have taken drugs,
got involved in street fighting or had been drinking to excess, simply
because that used to be me. It was early days but I knew somewhere in
the future I'd be doing more of that kind of thing.

Not long after Prizefighter, I was invited to a sportsmen's dinner.
I was on the top table with Scott Quigg and Nigel Benn, answering
questions from the audience, although I don't think me or Scott had
any questions fired our way. It was more about getting us on the map.

I had my picture taken with Benn and the second it was done, he said, 'I've been watching you on telly.' For one of my childhood heroes to say that was something else. They say don't meet your heroes because they'll always let you down, but he was the complete opposite.

We ended up chatting all night and I think the comedian was a little pissed off because I was sat one side of him and Benn on the other. All we did was lean back behind him and chat. In the end, Benn turned to the comedian and said, 'Swap seats, mate,' so we could sit next to each other.

Benn gave me some great advice. 'Get your first house paid off. When you've done that through boxing, you'll know that all this time you've been getting up at the crack of dawn doing this training, the sacrifices, the spars, you can always look back and say it was worth it.' I wanted to do that anyway, but the way he put it made me so much more motivated.

* * * * *

Four months later, on 6 March 2009, I fought on the undercard of Jamie Moore's European title fight against Michele Piccirillo. I was up against a guy called Mikheil Khutsishvili and, even better, I was fighting live on Sky.

The camp went really well, training and sparring alongside Jamie. Before meeting him, I'd been able to hold my own against most sparring partners. I thought it would be like that with Jamie when we first started sparring. What a wake-up call. He proper took me to school. I thought, 'Wow. What he does, I need to incorporate into some of my style.' The spars we had over the next couple of years you'd pay to watch. We pushed ourselves to the limit during those sessions, although it was Oliver who came off worse on one occasion.

We used to do our hill sprints not far from the gym. On the way there, Oliver was riding a BMX and as we approached these restriction barriers, which are intentionally there to stop bikes passing down the path, you could see Oliver measuring up the gap, confident he'd make it through. Next thing, you heard this almighty metal 'clunk', followed by Oliver flying over the handlebars like a stuntman in the movies.

Me and Jamie have never laughed so hard in our lives. Then we had a moment where we looked at each other and thought, 'Shit. He's hurt himself here,' because he was lying there lifeless. We sprinted straight over and as we stood above him about to give him a nudge, he went, 'Ahhhh. Gotcha!' We were literally crying with laughter.

The fight itself against Khutsishvili was easy. He threw a few big hooks but I completely outclassed him. After four rounds, his corner pulled him out. Jamie went one better and stopped Piccirillo in three to become the new European light-middleweight champion. I was really made up for him after all the hard work he'd put in for this fight.

\* \* \* \* \*

Around this time, another opportunity came my family's way. It was never something we intended to do long term, but when it came knocking we decided to give it a go.

One of our good friends, Mike Allinder, who was well respected in the community, used to run The Roundhouse pub in Fingerpost, but after about two years he decided he'd had enough. It was shut down, then re-opened, but started to get overrun by the locals and became known as a pub with a bad reputation. The pub went through loads of landlords really quickly and one day the people from the brewery asked for me and my mum to go and meet him.

They said, 'We want you to run it for us. You're probably the only people in the area who can. Would you consider it?' We agreed and made a proper go of it, although I did have a few fall-outs.

Before we had the pub, some of my mates would go behind the bar, completely disrespect the landlord and pull their own pints. When we got it, that all changed. I wanted the pub to be a place for the lads, but I also wanted it to be a place for the local community. I had a strict no drugs or scrapping policy. 'If you're going to do some gear, go outside. There's loads of regulars in here who don't want to go into the toilets and see lads crammed into a cubicle sniffing. Also, I don't want any fighting inside the pub.'

Thankfully, it started to run exactly how we wanted it and we ended up having some great times over the next three years.

\* \* \* \* \*

A month after the Khutsishvili fight, I was up against Kevin Concepcion. He'd fought 15 times with only one loss. I'd seen a lot of him on Sky and said to Steve, 'Get me him. I'll beat him.' At the time, I'd had 13 fights and lost none, so it was a decent match-up. On the day of the fight, I wished Kevin luck, as you do, but I knew with all the luck in the world he was never going to beat me.

I went out there, settled down and with about 40 seconds left in the first round he took a heavy knockdown. I had him on the ropes and hit him with a big right hand, followed by a left hook to the body. Fair play to him for getting up. Twenty seconds later, he was down again. Second round I caught him with a really heavy left hook to the chin and he was down once more. The bell rang for the end of the round and then, at the start of the third, the doctor took a look at him and the fight was waved off.

Beating Concepcion was seen as a step-up and there was now talk of me fighting for the British title soon. The only issue I had at this point was that I didn't have a promoter. Just want to point out, if the deal had been right with Steve Wood, I wouldn't have left him as he's a lovely bloke and has done an incredible amount for boxing in the North West of England. It was purely a business move.

While I was on the lookout for a new manager, Oliver put on a show as a one-off against Thomas Awimbono on 25 July 2009. He had a good record and had taken Bradley Pryce 12 rounds in his previous fight for the Commonwealth title. I went out there and outboxed him. It was a dull fight as he wasn't really giving it back and just surviving. I genuinely remember thinking halfway through the fight, 'Fucking 'ell. This is boring.' The main thing for me was that I got the win but also that I did an eight-round fight, as I was desperate to clock up some more pro mileage.

After the Awimbono fight, I signed with Hatton Promotions. My first fight under them was against George Aduashvili on 25 September 2009. I put him down in the first with a jab to the stomach. After he made the count, I hit him with some big overhand rights then caught him with a peach of a left hook to the body as the bell went, and I heard a big sound come out of him as he sank down to the canvas. Job done.

Six in the morning the day after the fight, I was up doing sprints around St Helens. I was champing at the bit. I went home thinking, 'This is it. Time to take it up a level.'

Two months later, I was up against Sergey Khomitsky, or 'marble head' as he later became known. At the time he'd been beaten five times in 28 fights, but only stopped once, by Gennady Golovkin. We had a DVD of him knocking someone out, so we knew he could punch a bit. But that didn't matter. I had the mentality that if I wanted to achieve my goals, I needed to be beating guys like this.

First round, as he landed, you could tell he had power. Second round I caught him with the right hand and put him down. Same again in the fourth. He was tough as old boots. He caught me in the seventh with a shot and it wobbled me a bit. I was on the ropes and tried to grab hold of him, but as I did he stepped back and I kind of slipped down his legs. I didn't go down because he hit me and put me over, I'd just fallen. It was ruled a knockdown but I knew I was well in front and ended up winning the contest on points. Khomitsky was a good learning curve.

Three months later, I ended up fighting Shalva Jomardashvili on 19 February 2010. Jomardashvili threw it on me from the first bell and I mean threw it on me. Twenty of his 26 wins had come by stoppage and it made sense why. Although I won the fight four rounds to two, it was a hard night's work.

Three months later, I was up against Lee Noble. I was actually meant to be fighting for the Commonwealth middleweight title against Francis Cheka from Tanzania, who Macklin and Smigga had fought. I'd been taking training up to the next level as this was for my first proper title, but the day before the weigh-in we were told Cheka didn't have his visa.

Thankfully, it didn't turn out to be a drama as Lee Noble stepped in with two days' notice. Fair play to Lee. The only drama that did happen was with the Barmy Army on the way up to the fight.

On the way to the Ponds Forge Arena in Sheffield, the coach pulled into a layby as everyone was starting to complain there was a smell of smoke, but not the one you associate with cigarettes. By the time everyone had been rushed off, the coach engine caught fire. Apparently it was like the scene out of the Jolly Boys' Outing from *Only Fools and Horses*.

In the meantime, the ladies needed to use the loo and thought it would be safe to go down the embankment. As they went down this verge, it turned out to be like a marsh and they were ankle deep in cold mud. In the end, the police escorted everyone down the motorway on foot.

As everyone's walking, my dad's brother, our Dave, drove past, spotted him and his mate and pulled over in the hard shoulder. Next thing, Dean Hillman's dad, Kenny, was driving past and spotted Gemma, our Katie and Danny walking along and told them to jump in. Lucky for them, they all made it to the venue in time.

The fight, on the other hand, was nowhere near as colourful. Lee had a go but I knew I was a couple of levels above him. I peppered him from the opening bell and he started talking to me in the third round, saying, 'Is that all you got?' I replied, 'There's five rounds still to go, ye prick.' He didn't come out for the fourth.

\* \* \* \* \*

I feel I need to say something about Steve Wood and his dad at this point. When I parted company with Steve, it was kind of done over the phone and not the way I think either of us wanted really.

Steve's dad was a lovely bloke and always used to pop up to the gym, but when I parted company with Steve I didn't see his dad any more. I then found out about 12 months after that his dad had passed away. I knew how close Steve was to him.

I wrote a card out to the family and then went down to his offices. I hadn't seen Steve for a bit, so felt a bit awkward. I handed the card over and said, 'I've only just found out and am gutted for you, mate.' It kind of broke the ice. There was a mutual respect between us.

One was business and the other was more important – family values.

\* \* \* \* \*

A couple of months after the Noble fight, I was up against Peter Mitrevski Jr of Australia for the vacant Commonwealth middleweight title. I'd already prepared for this once, so I was hungry to get in there and do the business. He'd only been stopped once in 30 outings, so we knew he was tough. We knew we needed to take it up another level in training.

I wanted to stop him, but it didn't happen. He stayed on his feet for 12 rounds but I completely outboxed him. After the fight, Mitrevski said, 'I know you're going places.'

I'm still good mates with him. He's a Liverpool fan and I got him tickets for a game when he came over recently to the UK. He had a coffee at my house first and then he went and saw the match. He's a good lad.

The day after the fight, we had a great celebration at The Round-house with friends, family and the Barmy Army. Everyone was wearing the belt and having photos. Great memories.

My first belt. Little did I know, but my next five contests would all be title fights.

* * * * *

If there's something that can totally take your mind off boxing, it's the arrival of a new-born baby. At 4am on 9 September 2010, our beautiful little girl, Amelia, was born. There were a few difficulties with the birth but nothing compared to Archie.

I was now a father of two and even hungrier to get those bigger fights to secure the future for them. Two months after my daughter's birth, on 26 November 2010, I fought Brazilian fighter Carlos Nascimento for the WBA intercontinental middleweight title. We had our game plan and were just too sharp with our counters, picking him off. Third round, I let rip with a combo and the referee jumped in and stopped it.

That was a good win for me, as Nascimento was a big, powerful bloke who had a high knockout record. His nickname was 'The Butcher', which made plenty of sense, as he came out throwing bombs from the first bell.

After Prizefighter, I'd started to move up the British rankings, but after this win I was slowly starting to get on the world rankings radar. Not top ten yet, but a move in the right direction.

# CHAPTER 29

# BEST OF BRITISH

*'He wrote in one of his letters in prison that he'd make
John proud. And God he's done just that'*

Carol Thompson (Chizzy's missus), 2016

THE year 2011 turned out to be a dream. First up was another Brazilian called John Anderson Carvalho on the undercard of the Amir Khan vs Paul McCloskey bill. I was defending my WBA intercontinental belt.

In the meantime, Matthew Macklin was supposed to fight Khoren Gevor, but it fell through and we were then approached to take Gevor's place. We accepted but Macklin didn't and rightly so as he had got the opportunity to fight Felix Sturm for the WBA world middleweight title.

We were training hard anyway, thinking we'd be fighting Macklin, so we just took it up another level for Carvalho. Golovkin had done him in two rounds in 2009 and I kind of knew that me and Golovkin would end up crossing paths at some point because I knew he was being avoided and I don't shy away from challenges.

My intention was to go in and stop Carvalho early on to make a bit of a statement and that's exactly what happened. In the fourth round, I finished him with a perfectly placed left hook to the body.

Now ranked in the top ten by the WBA, from here on there was only one target and that was a world title shot. I'd always wanted the

British title and I knew it was coming up for grabs soon. When the fight against Nick Blackwell was announced for 18 June 2011, the timing was perfect. Macklin was taking on Sturm in his backyard the week after, so I knew a good performance could maybe get me a fight with the winner.

The ring entrance was great. The Barmy Army were singing songs, as always, at the top of their voices and Dean and Digger were carrying my belts into the ring.

Blackwell was just a young kid, really. He was 20 years old, had fought eight times and won them all, but I was on a different level to him. In addition to fighting for the British title, I also put my Commonwealth and WBA intercontinental titles on the line.

Blackwell was game but I just kept chipping away. Down to his body, then mixing it to the head. A lot of the time, he threw panic punches, punches he didn't need to throw. While he was throwing these big hooks and combos, I'd give him a little chop downstairs. After the fifth round, he retired. He eventually went on to win the British title a few years later and I'd always been behind him, sending him messages of support in the rest of his fights. Unfortunately, his last fight as a professional [against Chris Eubank Jr] had a bad ending, when he ended up with a blood clot on his brain. It devastated the boxing community, including myself. I decided to auction the gloves from our contest towards his fund. I still keep in touch with him regularly and hope he can still be involved in boxing in some form.

Up to this point of my life, this was my career highlight and for one main reason. When I started out pro, one of my ambitions was to be able to dedicate the British title to Chizzy. Ever since he died in 2005, I'd gone round and seen him on my own at the cemetery and still do to this very day.

Soon after the fight, I visited his grave with the belt. I kept my promise to him.

# CHAPTER 30

# SHOW BUSINESS

*'Somewhere along the line, you're going to need to take the initiative in Germany and box the rounds, because if the judges have any doubt, they'll give it to Sturm'*

Jamie Moore before the Sturm fight, 2011

I WAS ranked fourth in the world by the WBA going into the Blackwell fight, so I knew an impressive win could take me closer to a world title shot. I just wasn't expecting it to be as sudden as it turned out.

The week after I beat Blackwell, Macklin fought Felix Sturm and was unlucky to lose on a split decision. He tried to get a rematch but it never happened. Straight after that fight, we knew there was a chance I could fight Sturm and, sure enough, we were offered the fight, but the deal wasn't great. The terms of the contract were shocking.

After I'd paid my sanctioning fees, percentages to my manager and trainer, and let's not forget the taxman, I would come away with around 50 grand. Although the money was shit, the purse would allow me to pay most of the mortgage on the house. Money wasn't the deciding factor, though. It was an opportunity for me to reach the ultimate goal of becoming world champion. From their side, they saw it as a good fight against an undefeated opponent but one they would win.

I flew over to Germany about three months before the fight for what was my first big press conference. Sturm was a massive name who'd had about 15 world title fights at this point and had held the

WBA world middleweight crown since as far back as 2003. There I was, this regular lad from St Helens, walking into 'The Felix Sturm Show'. I barely spoke, mainly because we hardly had any questions thrown our way. It worked for me, though, as I sat back and took it all in.

We also did this promo video, which was surreal. Me and Sturm were in this big metal warehouse, surrounded by fire and burning iron, with this massive camera crew hanging over us. I even had my own little trailer, which said 'Martin Murray' on it. Inside, there was a big spread of food and drink. Really smart. I was loving it and thinking, 'If this is what being world champion is about, this is where I want to be.'

The director passed me this long list of stuff to say while I was standing in a ring with my shorts and wraps on, covered in dirt and grease. I had a quick read and saw it was dead cheesy. I knew the lads were going to rip me for it. Stuff like, 'I'm going to send you to hell. You're going to burn.' I turned to the director, laughed, then said, half thinking he was winding me up, 'Are you serious? Do you really want me to say that?' He replied, 'Ja, ja. This is good. Germans like this. We're not going to use it all. Don't worry.' I was supposed to be really serious when saying it but I couldn't stop laughing. I lost count of how many times we had to retake.

Despite Sturm being on the set, the only time we were together was for the ring scene. They covered the ropes in petrol and set them alight, while me and Sturm did this take for the next couple of hours. They had us shadow boxing and covered us in dirt, as if we'd done our training camps in this big warehouse. The more serious they tried to make it, the more I started cracking up.

However, when we finally stood head to head in the middle of the ring, I looked at him thinking, 'You're getting it.' There were no fits of laughter then.

* * * * *

I'd done 12 rounds before when I fought for the Commonwealth title but I knew this was going to be at another level, so we did a 15-week training camp. Looking back, it definitely should've been shorter as I ended up overtraining.

First thing Oliver did on hearing Sturm was the confirmed opponent was to watch a few of his fights on video. 'I think you can stop him, Martin. Nine or ten rounds,' he said.

The tactics were to wear Sturm down with workrate. Stand in front of him poker face, work the head and body and not give him anything. Jab for jab and little shots straight through his tight guard. We knew Sturm had a good jab and we wanted to take that away and pepper him non-stop, then explode with some big shots. Having just had a hard fight with Macklin, the intention was to put it on him and take him back to the place he'd just been.

I sparred with Rocky Fielding, Brian Rose and Tony Dodson for this one, but also got Khomitsky over because we knew he was tough and he'd sparred Sturm.

However, he did come with some issues. The problem was his English. He didn't know any. He was staying at this hotel in Salford round the corner from the gym and I used to go and pick him up in the morning. The conversation on the drive over would go something like this.

'Y'alright mate.'

'Yes.'

'What you up to?'

'No English.'

Every morning, we'd have this awkward silence. The ride to the gym wasn't that long but it felt like forever. After arriving, we'd then punch holes in each other for about an hour and I'd drop him off to his hotel.

The conversation on the way back was the same thing.

'Y'alright mate.'

'Yes.'

'Good session that.'

'No English.'

Final sparring session was ten rounds, followed by a couple of rounds on the pads. We were flying.

Me and Jamie also went through some stuff on the pads, which was helpful because he'd been Sturm's sparring partner a few years earlier. That's when I knew Jamie was going to make a great trainer. Straight away, he picked up on things that could work. Subtle things that make a massive difference.

* * * * *

We left for Germany a week before the fight and I was nervous from the moment we landed. Really bad. Not nervous for facing Sturm but for the size of the event.

Audi were one of the main sponsors and when we came out of the airport, we had a big fleet of stretched A8 limos waiting, with our own personal driver. I was trying to act like this was a normal thing when coming off a plane, but I'd never had this kind of treatment before.

As we were driving to the hotel, there were massive billboards throughout the city with me and Sturm on them. As a kid from St Helens, that's something I'll never forget.

A couple of days before, my physio at the time, Rob Harris, was giving me a rub down when my manager walked in and said, 'I've just got back from the rules meeting. Here's your gloves.'

They were a pair of Paffen Sport gloves, which are known for being padded, as opposed to say, for example, Reyes, which are punchers' gloves. I said, 'Is he wearing these as well?' Then came the reply, 'No. He's got Grants.' I said, 'What? He's got Grants and I've got these big puffy things? No fucking way I'm wearing them while he has punchers' gloves.' I then got told there were no Grants gloves available for me, which I knew was bullshit. My bottom line was, 'I'm not getting in the ring unless I have the same gloves.' In the end, a pair got sent over from the UK. Unnecessary hassle. The same thing would happen when I went to Germany a few years later to fight Arthur Abraham.

On the day of the weigh-in, I was really nervous but champing at the bit. I just wanted to get in the ring by this stage. Thankfully the Barmy Army gave me great support, which helped take my mind off things. Mind you, how they managed to get to the weigh-in is incredible in itself.

It was their first international trip. In fact, for many of the lads from Fingerpost and Parr, it was the first time they'd used a passport, as it was their first ever journey out of the UK. The staff on Ryanair must have thought, 'Oh God', as they started to rock up. They pretty much took over Manchester airport, shit-faced. The number of supporters was much bigger than the allocation of boxing tickets, but they didn't care. They just wanted to be over there to share in the moment and the atmosphere, even if they couldn't get into the arena.

When they got on the plane, they were climbing over seats, standing in the aisles, making it impossible for the trolley dollies to get up and down. When the plane landed, the German police came on board, and gave them a stiff talking to, basically telling them that if they were like this on the return journey, they'd need to find a different flight. Great start.

The weigh-in itself was pretty quick. Jumped on the scales, did a little interview with Sky and then went back to the hotel and carbed up. I still wasn't able to relax though and didn't have much appetite on the day.

Come fight night, all that changed. The second I got into the changing rooms, the nerves disappeared. I was buzzing. I was now loosening up to music, throwing punches, ready to go. By the time I was getting ready to walk out of the changing room, I was prepared for anything Sturm had to offer.

I was accompanied into the ring by the British Army, who'd been flown in especially for the fight. I got a hostile reception from the Germans, but I expected that. If anything, it fired me up.

After the ref gave us our instructions, I walked back to the corner and Oliver said, 'All about the jab. Straight down the middle. Straight through the guard.' When the bell went, I wanted to have a little look at him, just move around the ring and see what he was bringing to the table, as I didn't want to fall flat on my face. From my side, it was a slow start.

Sturm had a good jab, with not much power, but fast and with a good bit of zap to it, certainly better than anybody I'd been in with before. I'd say that Khomitsky was the hardest puncher I'd been in with at that point, but Sturm was without doubt the sharpest.

I was talking to him throughout the fight. Stuff like, 'Come on, old man.' With my gumshield in and my thick St Helens accent, he probably didn't understand anyway. I kept popping out little shots. Jab, one-two. Double jab, right hand. Every chance I got, I kept popping him, working inside, bringing the shots up and round the side of his tight guard.

There were times I was in close and I hit him with three sharp left hooks on the bounce. No way was I losing this one. About round four or five, he was probably thinking he was in a harder fight than he'd anticipated. We'd watched his fight where he'd been stopped by Javier Castillejo and we wanted to make him revisit that, make him feel old.

Walking into the eighth round I felt confident as I was really starting to warm into the fight. I started thinking of Gemma and the kids, and also having a little talk with Chizzy. It gave me a massive boost. With about 45 seconds to go, I tagged Sturm with a right hand, which had him badly rocked.

Me and Oliver learned something from that fight. Just how good I am with my hands down. We hadn't trained to fight in that style at any point, it just came to me. I started throwing shots at him from all angles and rocked him. Obviously didn't finish him off, but buzzed him for a bit.

Round 10 was a good one from a boxing perspective, but with a strange end. I was letting combinations go and tagged him a couple of times nicely. My range, timing, distance and defence was bang on and by this stage in the fight, that became really clear. With about 30 seconds of the round left, I saw something from the corner of my eye on the canvas. I was focused on the fight, but I remember thinking at the time, 'That's strange. A handbag in a boxing ring.' What happened was, Dean's dad was ringside and was getting so pissed off with Sturm's complaining about low blows, that in the end he threw some random woman's handbag into the ring. One of the officials ended up pulling it away.

Round 11, I started to unload combos on him and went toe to toe, but the better work was coming from me. Then in round 12 he started putting it on me, knowing he needed a big round. He was looking for big shots while I was still unloading combos. Sturm did however catch me with a big right hand, with less than ten seconds to go. He started unloading on me, good shots, but certainly didn't put me in any danger, but most likely, that's what won him the round. As the final bell went, I felt confident I'd won, but always knew it was going to be tough getting a points decision away from home.

When the scores were announced, 115-113 to me, 116-112 to Sturm and 114-114 even, I wasn't shocked with the result being a draw. Just disappointed.

After I'd showered up, we did the post-fight conference. Like before, I hardly got asked a question. It seemed that the only time I ever spoke to Sturm was during the fight. Certainly not before or after it.

My work for that weekend, however, was far from over.

# CHAPTER 31

# HITCHED-HIKE

*'A man in love is incomplete until he has married. Then he's finished'*

Zsa Zsa Gabor

THE Sturm fight was the only one Gemma missed, but she had good reason. About 15 months before it was even announced, we'd booked our wedding date on a Caribbean cruise, obviously not knowing I'd be involved in a big fight on that very same day.

Loads of our family and friends had already booked to come with us, so there was no way we could cancel. I said to Gemma, 'You'll have to go without me, then after the fight, I'll catch up with you a few days into the cruise.' I spoke to Thomas Cook and explained the situation. They checked with the captain of the ship, to make sure it was OK that we re-joined later in the holiday and thankfully it was.

They all flew out the day of the fight, which meant there was no way Gemma could speak to me all day. By the time everyone got to the boat port, they were really excited, because they'd been told that they would be able to watch the fight on Sky Sports, either on the ship or at a nearby bar.

As Gemma touched down in Barbados and cleared customs, it was roughly the time I was fighting. They were running all over trying to find a place to watch it, but the problem was, when they got there, nobody had Sky Sports.

The only option they had was to find wi-fi so they could stream the fight from a website address they'd been given. The search for bars now became a hunt for anyone who had internet access. They found a small group of students who were about 16 years old and on their laptops. Gemma pounced on them and said, 'Can you stream this? Can you stream it?' They were all hovering over their shoulders waiting in anticipation, but again, it was a no go.

In the end, Dean rang Gemma just as the final round had finished. 'It was amazing, Gemma, but it's now gone to a split decision. Here come the scores.' There was a small silence, then Dean shouts, 'He's got it, he's got it!' Gemma's now turned to everyone and screamed, 'He's got it!' and everyone was going mad jumping up and down celebrating. But it was only the score from the first judge. So when Dean said, 'The second judge scored it for Sturm,' Gemma was there screaming, 'He hasn't got it. He hasn't got it.' Then in the end, Dean let her know it was a draw and everyone went 'Nooooooooooo.'

Back to Mannheim. When the draw had been announced, I had this bitter-sweet feeling. The biggest thing for me was not getting beat before the wedding. I was gutted I didn't win, but happy it didn't spoil my wedding. If I'd have got bombed out in a couple of rounds or something like that, it would have ripped into the whole wedding experience and that wouldn't have been ideal.

Now, my journey to meet Gemma and the kids started. Originally, we were all supposed to be flying out of Manchester to Barbados, but with the change in plans, me, my dad and mates Garvey, Martin Hayes, Lee Atherton and Peter Foster all bought extra flights from Frankfurt to Amsterdam, then Amsterdam to Bonaire, where we would then get a plane to take us to the final destination, Curaçao. That's where the ship was docked.

The flight to Amsterdam wasn't leaving until Monday morning, so I left my hotel on the Sunday and stayed at the one my dad and mates were staying at for the night. That evening, we went to this pub in Mannheim and just as we were starting to relax, these big bikers came in. Straight away, they were snarling at us. They knew who we were.

We stayed for a few drinks and then realised there was a real bad atmosphere building up as they started sizing us up. It was getting to the point where it was either going to kick off, or we were going to have to make a quick exit. In the end, we did neither. They came over and we all ended up having the craic. Thank God for that. I'd done enough fighting that weekend.

We got up on the Monday morning and went to Frankfurt airport. Our flight to Amsterdam wasn't for a few hours, so we all went to the VIP lounge and just chilled. For the record, I'm shit scared of flying.

Next leg was from Amsterdam to Bonaire. We got there at night time and had about eight hours to kill. We guessed it would be like Manchester, with bars and loads of stuff to do, so the intention was to stay at the airport. Wrong guess. It was like a dimly lit small hut and there were three airport security guards sitting at a small table playing cards and smoking cigarettes.

In the end, we asked them where the nearest hotel was and booked into there. We put our heads down, got a few hours' sleep, had some breakfast, then headed back to get our next plane.

The final leg the morning after was on a little cattle plane with propellers, from Bonaire to Curaçao. It looked like something out of an Indiana Jones movie. I was sat next to my dad and turned to him and said, 'Dad, can you smell diesel?' 'Martin, I can. It stinks,' he replies. My dad is also shit scared of flying. In fact, apart from my mum, we all hate it. Me, my dad, Katie, Danny and Ricky all get through it by having a few drinks to calm our nerves.

So, you can imagine how me and my dad were feeling as the cattle plane took off, creaking and bouncing up and down. After about ten minutes, my dad looked out of the window and turned to me and said, 'Look at the wing. Fucking 'ell.' It was leaking oil all over it. Not what I needed to see. After the roughest landing I've ever had in my life, we took a taxi to the port and finally got to the ship. As we arrived, they were all waiting for us wearing Martin Murray t-shirts. They had a big banner with my name on it and loads of Union Jacks hanging over the side. I hadn't seen Gemma and the kids for well over a week by this stage, so it was an emotional moment, a feeling I'll never forget. Boxing creates those kind of moments.

\* \* \* \* \*

The wedding itself was amazing, but as always it had to come with some mini dramas.

Being one step ahead of the game, Gemma didn't want me to be in the wedding photos with a face full of bruises, so she gave me some Arnica cream to take straight after the fight. Thing is, my face looked fine, whereas the top of my head was almost black as I'd had my chin down with a nice tight guard for the whole fight. My head wasn't an issue. My hair on the other hand ...

In the morning, I went for a sauna with the lads and then went to get my hair cut at the salon where the girls had had theirs done. Garvey was waiting outside with Lee and I said, 'If they mess this up, it's not gonna be funny.'

As I got in the salon, I said to the guy, 'Do you know how to cut men's hair?' He said, 'Yeah, yeah.' Well, it looked like someone had used a knife and fork to cut it. I went ballistic and walked out. Garvey and Lee were pissing themselves. Very mature. Very supportive. Luckily, Julie, one of our friends who's a hairdresser, got hold of an electric hair shaver and managed to sort it out for me.

The wedding service was done by the captain of the ship, whilst out at sea on the way to Jamaica. Seeing Gemma walking up the aisle with Arch and Amelia is something I'll never forget. The surroundings, the people, it was a very special moment.

About ten days later, after an incredible honeymoon, we headed back to the UK. I couldn't wait to carry on where I'd left off in boxing for the new year.

CHAPTER 32

# PERSONAL PRIDE

*'You gotta try your luck at least once a day,
because you could be going around lucky all
day and not even know it'*

Jimmy Dean

STRAIGHT after the Sturm fight, the intention was to strike while the iron was hot and get another world-level fight. Even though many people, including lots of Germans, thought I should have got the decision, I dropped out of the top ten of all the major sanctioning bodies straight after. Weird. I was hoping to get the rematch straight away but it never happened. When they did come back years later with an offer, it was even worse than the one they'd given me in 2011.

Golden Boy Promotions offered me the opportunity to fight against Julio Cesar Chavez Jr in El Paso. At the time, as well as being world champion, he was a big name and it would have been a massive fight for me. Unfortunately, it never happened because I was denied my visa due to my criminal record. To add insult to injury, I then got a big bill from my solicitors for trying to get the visa.

You can imagine how deflated I was when my next fight was going to be a ten-rounder against Karim Achour. Massive step down. I'd gone from topping the bill, fighting for a world title in front of a crowd of 20,000 people at the SAP Arena in Mannheim, to fighting on the undercard at the Manchester Velodrome in front of about 3,000 people.

It wasn't great.

The fight itself was nothing special. I won it on points and it was another 'W' on the record, but it didn't excite me. I felt like I was at a crossroads in my career.

\* \* \* \* \*

I had a few weeks off after the Achour fight and decided to organise a night out. I called Jamie first and said, 'Do you fancy a night in Liverpool with the lads?'

'Yeah. Count me in, mate,' replied Jamie.

'I've found this hotel for us, it's only half a mile out from the centre.'

'Sound.'

Alex Matvienko and Jonny Rocco came down in the car with us and we were going to meet Rocky and Johnney Roye down in Liverpool. There was no more room at our hotel, so I booked Matvienko and Rocco this other place online.

It was cheap compared to the other hotels in the city, but there wasn't much difference distance-wise to the city centre from the place we were staying at.

Jamie's put on his sat nav, so we can drop Matvienko and Rocco off at their digs first. As we started to get closer, Jamie says with a bit of a giggle, 'This is just a street, mate. I bet ya it's a bedsit.' 'Nooo. I booked a hotel,' I says. Next thing, the sat nav goes, 'You've arrived at your destination,' and Jamie's absolutely pissing himself.

There we were in front of this house, which looked like an old air raid shelter. It was on this terraced street, with loads of stray dogs running around and neighbours shouting at each other. Matvienko goes, 'Fuck that. I ain't staying here. No way.' I couldn't stop laughing. Me and Jamie managed to convince them, saying, 'Come on. Just have a look inside. Might not be that bad.'

We knocked on the door and this woman comes out and shows us up these stairs to the room. 'Right. Here's the fucking rules. No shouting or loud music after midnight and keep everything tidy. You can't come back drunk or bring any girls back, either. Got it?' Matvienko nods his head going, 'Right, OK.' The second we walked out, he said, 'Get my stuff, we're leaving. Now.'

They ended up booking a hotel in the middle of Liverpool, calling a taxi and sneaking out the bedsit without even telling the landlady. Later that night, Rocco completely forgot where they were staying because he was that bladdered and ended up sleeping rough at Lime Street station. All in all, a good night.

\* \* \* \* \*

A few weeks later, me and Gemma decided to have a night out, but just ourselves.

We'd been out around Warrington and at the end of the night went over to the taxi rank. There was a massive queue, so we decided to go to a different taxi rank on the other side of town, by Warrington Central train station.

As we walked into the cab rank, there was this couple in front of us on this bench. He was asleep and she was awake. In the meantime, Gemma pops off to use the loo in the office, while I asked the guy behind the desk to order us a taxi.

The taxi arrived really quickly, so I thought it was for the couple in front. I turned to them and said:

'Your taxi's arrived.'

'No, no. It's not ours,' the lady replies.

'What do you mean? You were here before us and we've only just come. It's your taxi.'

'We're not getting a taxi.'

'What you doing, then?'

'Our train's not until eight in the morning. We're staying here until then.'

This was their story. The couple were from Africa and had come to the UK for a better life. He and his missus lived in Manchester, but sold aftershaves and perfumes in the toilet of this bar in Warrington. The reason they didn't get a taxi was because they didn't have much money and couldn't afford one on what they earned from the bar. They used to do this every night. They finished at 3am and then to save some cash they sat at the taxi rank freezing until the first train came along at eight in the morning.

I didn't know their story at this point, I just didn't want to see this couple out in the cold. I said, 'No. Come on, you're staying at our house.'

At this point, Gemma came out of the toilet, while this lady is explaining to her fella that they're staying with us for the night. Gemma walks over and says to me, 'What's happening?' 'These are coming back with us. Their train doesn't come until eight in the morning. Can't have 'em waiting here in the cold until then.' Gemma just nodded with a nervous smile and said, 'Right, right.' I could tell she was dying to have a go at me.

We all got in the taxi, drove to our house and the first thing I did was phone them a taxi for the morning, so they could get to the train station. I then set them up downstairs – turned the fire on, gave them a quilt, made them both a brew and said goodnight.

When I got upstairs, Gemma said in a high-pitched whisper at a hundred miles an hour, 'Martin, what are you doing?? They could be murderers as far as you know.' 'You can't leave 'em outside, they'll freeze,' I replied. 'I know Martin, but you don't know who they are.' Thankfully, they were no bother.

I set my alarm to make sure they made the taxi alright and then saw them out later that morning.

As the taxi left I thought, 'Shit. I've brought them here, but now they've had to spend money to get a taxi to the station.' A couple of weeks later, I went back and gave him some money to make sure they didn't go short.

The bar has since closed down and I've not seen them for a while. I just hope they're doing well, whatever they're up to.

\* \* \* \* \*

Five months after the Achour fight, we were asked if I'd like to fight Jorge Navarro for the interim WBA world middleweight title. Navarro was unbeaten at the time and had a record of 12 wins, with ten knockouts. The 30th anniversary of the Falklands War was coming up and Sergio Martínez was looking for an Englishman to fight in Argentina. I'd been told that if I beat Navarro, I could end up fighting him straight after. This one I had more motivation to get out of bed for.

We were chief support for Ricky Hatton's comeback fight against Vyacheslav Senchenko on 24 November 2012, so there'd be lots of press coverage. Towards the end of the first round, I went out there and hit him with a double jab, straight right. Nothing in it, really. Just caught him at the right time and right place, and he went over. Halfway through the sixth round, I dropped him again with the same combination. Seconds after making the eight count, I was on him and it was all over soon after.

The biggest surprise of the night was not the result, but what happened in the changing room after. Matvienko was cutting my hand wraps off and I was chatting with Oliver when the door creaked open. Everyone's first reaction as they looked over was, 'Who's this old guy? He must be lost. He's come to the wrong changing room.' Matvienko suddenly says, 'Fuck me. It's Roberto Duran.' I thought he was joking, but then we suddenly realised it was actually him. The room went really quiet for a moment as we all thought, 'Has he really just walked in here on purpose?' He'd come over to watch Ricky fight, so I still wasn't totally sure if he was in the right place.

He then comes over and extends his hand and says, 'Congratulations. Good fight. Navarro is a strong fighter. Well done.' What an honour. We then did a few photos and he left. Very surreal.

After showering, we went to watch Ricky fight Senchenko. On the way to our seats, we walked past Gordon Ramsay and he shouted, 'Martin Murray!' I thought, 'Fucking 'ell. They're all here tonight.' I shook his hand and had some banter. I was close to asking him when he was inviting me to his restaurant. Next time maybe, Gordon.

* * * * *

I've often been asked what it's like to win an interim world title and although I was delighted when I won it, the answer is an interim belt isn't a world title. It did, however, get me a step closer to fighting for one and helped move me back to being number one contender.

FOR ME, they are unforgettable memories. It must be remembered that our fight took place in a football stadium where there was a stand for 40,000 people and on the grass we enabled another 8,000. Everything was sold in advance. HBO came to Argentina with all its team and there were more than 900 accredited journalists from many countries. The fight was rebroadcast to innumerable countries and my company was also co-promoter of the event.

Having just beat Julio Cesar Chavez Jr in a memorable fight with a historic last round, I was considered the number three P4P after Mayweather and Pacquiao. The fight against Martin was like that great celebration at home. I remember Martin coming undefeated and just winning the WBA interim [world title]. He was hungry, he was bigger and stronger than me. I was not so hungry, I had hit the ceiling, it was difficult to get higher after recovering my title in Las Vegas on HBO PPV against Chavez. I was inside my bubble. Martin was the guest at my party and almost destroyed the party!

Martin was very competitive. It was as competitive as I was when I had my first chance to win against a great champion like Paul Williams or Kelly Pavlik. Murray had no other way, he had to give it all, it was his chance. He was a very tough opponent who made his role to perfection and the fight was very hard. Murray was a great opponent.

And as a person? One is in life just as it is in the ring. Martin is noble, he is strong, he is brave, he is real. That was the day we faced. I can only say that you will have my respect and my friendship forever. It is an honour for me to have received this invitation to participate in this book, just as it was an honour to have been competing for 36 minutes. After only 36 minutes of being locked in a ring of 6x6 metres, I can say that there is a link forever.

*Thank you very much,*
**Sergio Gabriel Martínez 2017**

# CHAPTER 33

# ARGY-BARGY

*'Latins are tenderly enthusiastic. In Brazil they throw flowers at you. In Argentina they throw themselves'*

Marlene Dietrich

A FEW weeks after the Navarro fight, in December 2012, we flew over to Argentina for the Martínez press conference. At the time, he was like a God out there and I am sure he still is. They even had a channel on telly dedicated to him, playing all his fights back to back. I went out there thinking I could be in for a cold reception, but I couldn't have been more wrong.

The media were trying to build up the whole Falklands War bit and that Argentinians hate the British and vice versa, but that had nothing to do with me or Martínez. Of course, there was sporting rivalry but we weren't politicians and there was no hate between me and the Argentinians. They were really nice people and couldn't do enough to make me feel welcome.

We had a round-the-clock bodyguard called Big Juan. I couldn't even go for a piss without having him being by my side. Seriously. He'd check the toilet first, then stand outside the cubicle.

As opposed to Sturm, who hardly ever crossed paths with me, the first thing Martínez did when he walked into the press room was walk over and shake my hand. Very humble man. He put an Argentinian football top on and I put an England one on, which added to the banter.

I didn't see him then for a couple of days, but when I did it was a top night. Their national paper was hosting the Olimpia de Oro sports awards and he invited us to attend. It was the equivalent to *Sports Personality of The Year* 2012 in Argentina and he'd just won it. He beat Lionel Messi, which was a huge achievement. And for him to invite us along was a big gesture of goodwill.

Like myself, Martínez is a family man and they were the first people we were introduced to. It was great to meet his family, even though they didn't speak much English and I don't speak much Spanish. We sat down, had a meal and watched all these stars get their awards. You'd have thought I was up for one as there was constantly a camera on me, but it was just because they kept referring to the upcoming fight and every time there was a mention, I'd be live on telly.

Straight after Martínez received his award he shot off, simply because he got mobbed. We stayed on. The awards ceremony was in this big nightclub and now the awards were done, they moved all the tables away. We went over to the bar and the fella whose club it was came straight up to me and said, 'Are you staying?' I replied, 'Yeah. We'll have a couple of drinks.' He was made up. 'Brilliant, brilliant! Anything you want, you can have it,' he said.

He took me, Ricky Hatton and a couple of others to the end of the bar, with a line of security guards in front of us. The fella who ran the club said, 'The VIP area is now set up for you.' I'd had VIP treatment before, but this was ridiculous. I felt like royalty.

\* \* \* \* \*

The first Monday of January 2013 was work time. The fight was set for 27 April 2013, so it was almost one long training camp leading up from the time we first headed over.

I had a really bad elbow going into this camp. We tried loads of stuff to get it sorted. We even tried strapping it up before the spars to stop the arm extending, which didn't work because it didn't allow me to find my range. I just had to crack on.

Me and Oliver had worked on some good tactics on getting past a southpaw. Although I'd never really struggled with southpaws, I knew that Martínez was special, so we made some adjustments. The intention was every time he'd come forward, I'd step back and make him fall short to dishearten him and make him waste energy. We also wanted to get over his southpaw jab and rough him up, cut the ring off and keep the pressure on. Basically, dogging him. As the days were ticking down to fight night in Buenos Aires, countdown for something else was up. Or should I say someone. Me and Gemma were expecting our third child, but after Archie's antics and Amelia's middle-of-the-night arrival, we didn't know what to expect with this one.

The ideal birth for any boxer before a fight would be this. Go training, come home, wife goes into labour, has the baby after a couple of hours, job done. Well, on 23 March 2013 at 3.40 in the afternoon, that's exactly what happened. Baby Aisla came into our lives with a smile on her face and has been a little joker ever since. More worryingly, she seems to have my sense of humour.

* * * * *

We went out ten days before the Martínez fight and again it turned out to be an unbelievable experience. We flew to Amsterdam and from there to Buenos Aires, Argentina. After stepping off the plane, it was VIP again all the way. Our new bodyguards, Cristián, Sebastián and Martín, got our cases, we skipped passport control and then we went outside to find our vehicle.

Most of the buildings in Buenos Aires were skyrise, including my hotel. From the second I arrived, the staff were brilliant and nothing was too much trouble.

Keeping your mind occupied with thoughts other than the fight in the week before is very important. Thankfully, we had this media guy called Ariel looking after us and a couple of days into the trip, he organised a visit to see a Vélez Sarsfield football match.

For the press tour a few months earlier, I'd been given an Independiente top, which was red and white. I thought to myself, 'Saints are also red and white. I'll support them.' Then when we went to see Velez play, I saw they had a big V in their logo, just like Saints, so I became a Velez fan from that point on.

I'm not a big football fan, but you couldn't help but love this. We were put in a private box and introduced to the chairman, who was a lovely fella. We even had a good chat with his mum. Then, after the game, they took me out on the pitch to see what it was like and did a few photos. I thought to myself, 'You'll be fighting here in a few days' time.'

Two days later, Ariel said, 'If you do a few more TV interviews today, we'll take you to the Boca Juniors game.' In all honesty, doing media has always been part of the deal with me, so I had no problems doing the interviews. Going to the games just happened to be a massive bonus.

We jumped in this little bus to go to the Boca game and just as we're arriving at the ground, we came to a standstill in gridlock traffic. One of our bodyguards, Cristián, got out and started talking to all these guys from Boca Juniors who he knew. In the meantime, loads of people started coming up close to the windows of the van and started looking in. My mate Lee, who was wearing a Boca Juniors top that he'd been given before the game, got out of the van and started dancing around with loads of Boca fans. I was laughing and shouting out to him, 'Get back in,' but he didn't give a shit. He was out and having a great time.

In the end, we all had to get out of the bus and were escorted through the streets to the stadium entrance. Everybody knew who I was, so wherever I walked I was getting media attention. It turned out Martínez was an Independiente fan, so the Boca fans started cheering, 'MOO-RYE, MOO-RYE, MOO-RYE. (Argentinian for 'Murray, Murray, Murray.)' The buzz was mad.

When we got to the stadium, the atmosphere at the match was amazing. They put us in a private box and Ariel made sure we were treated incredibly well, but also realised that it was best that we didn't stay for the full match. Just after half-time, we left. By the time we got back to the hotel, it turned out there was a big riot after the game and it was all over the news. Good shout. What an experience, though.

\* \* \* \* \*

On the Tuesday before the fight, under the sanctioning regulations, we needed to get hold of somebody to check my weight, but couldn't find anyone. We waited around for ages and in the end I turned to my manager and said, 'I'm starving. I'm going to get something to eat.' He started panicking and stressing, but I still went ahead and had some food. About 30 minutes later, I did this interview with HBO. Straight after, as I came downstairs into the hotel foyer, my manager went over to some Argentine boxing official and started saying in a bit of a panic that he needed someone to verify my weight. This guy said, 'Caaaalm down.' He had someone with him, who I think might have been a lawyer and who could vouch for him. This official turned to me and told me to stand on a spot on the floor a couple of feet away from me. I'm not sure why he wanted me to do that, but I stood on this spot that he was pointing to. He then said, '11st 8lbs.' He turned to the guy he was with, who said, 'I saw it. 11st 8lbs.' And that was that.

Back home, the support in St Helens was amazing. Although Martínez was odds-on favourite to win, the way my fans backed me made me feel like a world champion and fuelled me even more to want to win. The front page of the *St Helens Star* on 25 April 2013 said, 'One of the biggest days in St Helens' proud sporting history takes centre stage this weekend when boxer Martin Murray steps into the cauldron for his world title fight in Argentina.'

Gemma and my dad flew out on the Thursday from Paris's Charles De Gaulle airport, but it was touch and go them arriving on time. Our Danny, Garvey, Ginge and Andy Driscoll should have been on the plane with them, but had been on the duty free all day.

Our Danny was holding a bottle of Jack Daniel's while queuing up to get on the plane and when he refused to give it up to one of the officials, a French policeman arrested him. Driscoll went over to try and sort it out, but they ended up nicking him as well. They were also trying to arrest Gemma, simply because she was with them, but thankfully my dad stepped in and sorted it out.

They chucked our Danny, Driscoll and Ginge in the back of a police van and a short ride later they were in these dungeon-type cells. They were laughing about it but a few hours later, when they realised they'd missed their flights, it wasn't that funny any more. They ended up paying an extra £900 each to get to Buenos Aires. Ginge didn't have the extra cash on him and ended up going back to the UK.

When our Danny did arrive, he was absolutely mobbed. People were flying over to him asking, 'Can we have a picture, please?' 'I'm not Martin. I'm Danny,' he kept replying. But they didn't seem to understand. He even showed them his passport. In the end, he just went along with it.

The day after was the weigh-in and I was on my limit of patience. I had three hot baths that morning as I was struggling to get the last bit off to make weight. When I got to the room in my hotel where the weigh-in was being hosted, the Barmy Army hadn't turned up yet, so the officials waited until they arrived. They knew they were on their way and had timed it to coincide with their flight, just so I could have my support there. Very nice of them. When they did turn up, they couldn't believe the warm reception. The icing on the cake was when HBO and Showtime started interviewing them. You can imagine how made up my dad was to be interviewed live on American television.

The weigh-in was purely a media stunt. We'd already been on the scales behind the stage and then we repeated it for the benefit of the cameras. They basically read out our weight from before.

Michael Buffer introduced me. 'He's the Commonwealth middleweight champion, former ABA middleweight champion (welterweight actually Michael, but we'll let that one slip), reigning WBA world interim champion. The fighting pride of St Helens, Merseyside, Great Britain, please welcome Martin Pooooooooooooweeerr Murraaaaaaaaaaaay.' The Barmy Army were going mad. Even when Martínez walked in with his massive entourage, you could still hear the lads singing, 'There's only oooonnnnnee Martin Murray!' The rest of the room was screaming, 'Ar-gen-tina, Ar-gen-tina.' What a buzz.

\* \* \* \* \*

Throughout the week, we were treated brilliantly. However, at the stadium, come fight night, it was a different story. It went from people loving us to them absolutely hating us with a passion.

The day of the fight, we got picked up by this bus and had a police convoy. Cars, motorbikes, lights flashing, the lot. We drove straight through traffic lights and road signals and never stopped once on the way to the Vélez football stadium.

The atmosphere was something else. Along with a massive thunderstorm, there were about 45,000 people inside the arena and tens of thousands outside. Even though my loyal Barmy Army only numbered around 50, you could still hear them all among the hostile Argentinian crowd. As the Barmy Army made their way to their seats, getting pushed, shoved and spat on, one guy with a massive scar right down the side of his face walked past my dad and did the cut throat sign.

My dad, Gemma, Danny and a few others had ringside seats, but the rest of them were shown to a protective cage, which they use for the away football fans. Craig Lyon, 'The General', could sense how rough it was and turned to one of the guards and said, 'You've all got empty gun holsters. Where's your guns?' 'We don't have any here because the fans take the guns off you and shoot you,' the guard replied. The General at a later date said, 'I've served with the RAF in the Gulf, but was more scared in that cage than anything I ever saw out there. I genuinely feared for my life.'

By the time I'd got to the changing room, I was really calm. I thought to myself, this must be the feeling you get when everything is going to go right. I turned to Ricky Hatton and said, 'How did you feel in the changing room before you fought Kostya Tszyu?' 'I was shitting meself,' he replied. That's not what I needed to hear.

With about 30 minutes to go, I started to warm up with Oliver on the pads, throwing a combination which finished with a body shot. I did it about five times, then accidentally missed the pad with the last shot and dropped Oliver. I barely even remember it happening because I was that much in the zone.

When the time came to do the ring walk, I was as relaxed and focused as could be. As I'm waiting for my music to start, everyone started booing me. Next moment, Bob Marley's 'Don't Worry About A Thing' started playing. I turned to Oliver with a smile and said, 'For you, Ol.' With a big smile on his face, he replied, 'I'll never, ever forget that.'

I don't know if the event organisers did it on purpose, but it felt like we'd walked about two miles before we got in the ring. Every time my face came up on the big screen, the reaction from the packed stadium was pure hatred. In the meantime, this massive thunderstorm was letting loose. Thunder, lightning, the works.

The television camera crew were really close in front of me and I kept having to nudge them back. At one point, I had to hold out my glove to the camera to keep them at arms length, because they kept trying to move into my space. In the meantime, the people behind were trying to push us forward. My mate Lee had a big five-gallon drum of water in his hand and was swinging it at anyone who got in our way, like a man possessed. I carried on walking at normal pace and took my time.

None of it fazed me, though, as I was enjoying the experience. As we're walking, I looked up at the big screen, then did a double-take as I noticed something on the peak of my cap. Someone had spat a massive greeny at me. In all honesty, I thought my reception was going to be a lot worse, so I just wiped it and carried on walking. When I stepped into the ring, almost the whole stadium was booing me. I loved the fact that I was the underdog. That gave me extra motivation.

My dad, Danny and Garvey were sitting outer ringside amongst all these Argentinians, with their Saints flags and Martin Murray t-shirts on. Some fella came up to them and said, 'Are you here for Martin Murray?' My dad replied, 'Yeah, yeah.' This guy said, 'You've got balls of steel sitting there.' Our Danny said, 'Why?' Next thing, they got spat on and started getting loads of things thrown their way. My dad stood up to see what was going on, then took off his jacket and saw the back was totally covered in spit. He threw it on the floor and just left it there.

Our Danny turned around fuming and said, 'Come on, you fucking bastards.' They could see it was all about to get nasty, so my dad went over to the security guards and said, pointing at the cage, 'We need to be up there, please. Now.'

The guard said, 'No problem. I'll sort it out.' Next moment, this bunch of guards came over and walked them over to this cage, fully shielded. On the way up, my dad said to one of the guards, 'I need to go to the toilet.' Not only did they get taken to the toilets, but when they got there they kicked out all the Argentinian fans, just to make sure they were safe.

When Martínez came in with this huge entourage, it was a massive thing. Music, fireworks, lights flashing and his ring walk was definitely much shorter than mine. Next thing I remember was the bell ringing. From the get-go, I could see he was fast and sharp. He also had good angles to his shots, which had a sting to them.

Every time he came in with shots, I'd take a little step back and then get back on him. I knew I'd be able to stay on Martínez non-stop and within no time started to get my own shots off. We knew we could make him feel old the longer the fight went on.

I could tell he was tiring in the fourth, as I hit him with a good body shot and he made a right fuss of it. The referee ruled it a low blow and he got some time off for it. There was nothing wrong with that shot, though.

Next round, I caught him with a right hook, which cut him. The crowd momentarily went quiet.

He predicted he'd knock me out in round eight, but I ended up dropping him with a counter right. It was a shot we'd been practising. Not much power, just good timing. He was more off balance than anything else, but because the punch caught him flush, it put him over.

A 10-8 round to me. I walked back to the corner and noticed it went really silent in the arena again. Up to that point, there was music being played in the stadium and the crowd was non-stop. It's as if the fans could sense an upset might be on the cards.

While putting the pressure on him in round ten, I unloaded with a combination, which finished off with a left hook to the top of the head, and put him down again. This was a proper knockdown. You could see I'd hurt him, but the ref ruled it a slip. Take a look at the fight and you'll clearly see it wasn't.

That was the first fight for which the WBC had brought in 'instant replay', and even when they played it back, it was still ruled a slip. He managed to get a good 16 seconds' rest, whereas what he should have got was an eight count and I could have been all over him then. If you've ever boxed, you'll know how valuable each second after eight is.

Back in the cage, the security guys were trying to get the Barmy Army out straight away for their own safety, as they could also sense an upset. They all replied, 'Not a prayer. We're staying.'

Towards the end of round 11, he caught me with a left hook to the head and I was buzzed. No one knew it, though. When training, Oliver always taught us to have a poker face. If you get hurt, don't show it. As the rounds went on, I knew I'd beaten him but I also knew, if it went to 12 rounds, I wasn't going to get the decision. I was being realistic. Me and Oliver knew that going over.

When the final bell went, Martínez ran over to his corner, stood up on the ropes and started to celebrate. The crowd started screaming straight away. If I'd been in his shoes, I wouldn't have been celebrating. I would have been worried thinking, 'Have I got this?'

On one of the Argentine sport channels, the pundit gave his scores the second the bell went. His card was aired on television and he had me winning 114-113. A couple of minutes later, all three judges gave it 115-112 to Martínez, which was a bit strange in itself. Their TV pundit in the meantime was saying that the best Martínez should have got was a draw. As I said, I knew I was never going to win out there on points, but if you don't try, you never know. It is what it is and I'm happy with the performance I put in.

As soon as the announcement was made, the crowd started launching chairs, bottles and anything they could get their hands on at the Barmy Army – and that's after Martínez won. I hate to think what would have happened if he'd lost. This was another level to anything we'd seen before.

The Barmy Army were pulled out of the cage by security and told to run really fast to this café, while being surrounded by riot shields from the army. My dad ended up twisting his ankle in the rush.

In the meantime, we were escorted back to our changing room straight away, which turned out to be a good thing, as my mate Brownie (Paul Brown) and his missus Kellie were getting pushed and shoved all over the place as they were trying to get to safety. They also ended up getting pickpocketed.

Martínez was still in the ring and getting mobbed. There were that many people in there that the ring collapsed and was rendered unfit for purpose. Gary Buckland was supposed to be up after me, fighting against Fernando David Saucedo for the WBC silver super featherweight title. He'd flogged himself to make the weight and flew 7,000 miles all for nothing.

Back in the changing room, Oliver was upset. Not crying but angry upset. He said, 'How many fucking times do we have to have this?' and Oliver never swears. That was my first loss, but we all looked at the positives. We'd just fought a top pound-for-pound fighter and irrespective of what the judges' cards said, we knew I'd won the fight.

What I did find strange was that I went from being the number one challenger in the WBC rankings to disappearing out of the top ten straight after that fight. It was déjà vu, like after Sturm.

When the security guys were happy that the coast was clear, we were escorted by the police back to our hotel, down this empty motorway. The reason it was empty was because the police had cars blocking every exit. I've never seen security like it anywhere.

When we arrived back at the hotel, everyone was clapping and cheering, which was a great moment to cherish. I'd lost a fight, but gained a lot of respect.

\* \* \* \* \*

Everyone had a story to tell from that trip. Tom Stalker said it was one of the best experiences on the big stage he'd ever seen and that comes from someone who'd fought at the Olympics. Matvienko had his phone nicked, which he was really gutted about. Not because of the phone, but because he'd had pictures taken with Martínez, José 'Pipino' Cuevas, Juan Roldán and loads of others out there.

However, my old mate Sandsy probably won the prize for the best tale. The night after the fight, he and his mate John headed back to their boutique hotel room to freshen up and put most of their valuables in the safe before heading out. As they came bouncing down the stairs looking forward to a good night, three guys were standing there. Sandsy says, 'Alright lads,' and one of them instantly pulled out an old silver revolver and put it in his face. His first thought was his wedding ring. He sunk to the floor and curled up in a ball, so he could hide it. The guy with the gun now bent down next to Sandsy, put the revolver under his chin and made him stand up. Once he was on his feet, the guy put the gun in Sandsy's mouth. The other two were now in a tussle with his mate, trying to steal his watch. Sandsy turns to his mate John and says, 'Give them the fucking watch.' Seconds later, the robbers legged it out of there. Sandsy and his mates lost a bit of money and some valuables, but it could have been a lot worse, considering.

The day after the fight, I met up with the Barmy Army and went all round Buenos Aires and had a great time. People kept coming over and shaking my hand. Two days after the fight, Martínez came over to our hotel as he was getting ready to leave Argentina. We had a quick chat, had a photo taken, shook hands and then we shot off to the airport.

What an absolute gentleman. One of the most respectful and courteous men I've ever met in boxing. Whatever part he played in making my stay pleasant, I'll always be grateful.

\* \* \* \* \*

Our bodyguards took us to the airport, while my dad and Danny had some fun in their own taxi.

They were about halfway to the airport when all of a sudden this cop car appeared behind them, flashing its lights. As it pulled them over, another cop car came in front of them stopping all the traffic. Our Danny was shitting himself as this copper walked over to his door and pulled him out by the arm. He then said, 'Picture please, Martin Murray.' He was just about to say, 'No. I'm Danny,' when my dad said, 'Yeah, yeah. That's right.' They took loads of photographs and our Danny ended up signing loads of stuff. As this was going on, some woman came out of a flat holding a baby and wanted to have a picture of him holding it.

After all the autographs and pictures were done, the cops gave them an escort to the airport.

In the meantime, I'd arrived and the reception was mad. It was like I was a superstar. I was absolutely mobbed. To this day, I've never experienced anything like it.

Before boarding the plane, we said our goodbyes to Cristián, Sebastián and Martín. They were top blokes who we'd spent a lot of time with over the two weeks and really went out of their way to make sure we were looked after. I've never seen them again, but hope they're doing well, whatever they're up to.

As I boarded the plane, I did start to think what the future would hold for me now. I remained positive.

## CHAPTER 34

# SPECIAL AGENT

*'Every time I thought I was being REJECTED from
something good, I was actually being RE-DIRECTED
to something better'*

Dr Steve Maraboli

MIKE Critchley from the *Warrington Guardian* wrote, 'Martin Murray may have lost his first professional bout, but his performance in Argentina at the weekend announced his arrival on to the world stage.' It didn't feel like that coming home, though.

When I landed at Manchester airport, the reception was the complete opposite from what I had left in Argentina. The Barmy Army were on a different flight, Gemma left early to pick up the kids and no friends, family, nothing. It was like coming home to an empty house. If I have to be honest, it was a bit disheartening. I said bye to the team and then headed home.

A couple of weeks after getting back, I had an operation on my elbow. I gave it a few weeks to heal, then was back in Oliver's gym second week of June. My mindset was, everything happens for a reason. I wanted to train hard, because I believed that if I trained positively then positive things would happen. I went to Oliver's with the intention of smashing training and taking everything to the next level.

Problem was, there was no momentum to keep going. After the Sturm fight, I went from fighting at world level to fighting a top 100 fighter. Same thing happened again after Martínez, but even worse. It was one false start after the next.

For the second time, I was offered the Julio Cesar Chavez Jr fight, but this time in Mexico City, which wouldn't have come with any visa problems. Unfortunately, it wasn't that clear-cut. The issue was, I had the elbow operation booked in for the beginning of June 2013 and they wanted me to fight straight away. My thought was, I'd just done 12 rounds against Martínez, so didn't need to be in a rush. Also, there wasn't enough time for me to get in a decent training camp. Finally, Chavez wasn't holding a world title at that point, otherwise, bad elbow or not, I'd have taken it.

The same time I was offered Chavez, we were in talks for a fight with Golovkin. Like with Chavez, I needed the operation but was willing to fight Golovkin if the money was right. Unfortunately, an offer never came to fruition, so I had nothing to agree to.

Not long after, it was looking likely that I'd be fighting Peter Quillin on 14 September 2013 for his WBO world middleweight title on the undercard of Mayweather vs Alvarez. I always thought Quillin was overhyped. Danny Jacobs exposed him badly and I knew it was going to happen sooner or later, but I wanted it to be me. I was still with the Hattons at the time and we jumped at it. It wasn't even a case of how much they were paying. All I thought was, it's in Vegas, chief support to Mayweather vs Alvarez, get me that fight. I was buzzing with excitement.

For the next few months, me and Andy Mikhail went down to London to see an American visa lawyer, so we could go through the process of applying. The problem was, in order to have a visa, we needed to have a fight to show them as they needed to know where my accommodation was. Every fighter knows that you tend to get a maximum of three to four months' notice for a fight. With the embassy taking six months to grant a visa, this basically meant I was never getting over there.

My promoter got in touch with the Golden Boy Promotions lawyer, sent him my criminal record and explained the situation.

He replied, 'The fight's off. You won't get a visa for this fight, if ever.'

*Different kind of boxing*

*Snacking from an early age. But check out the footwork and left hook!*

*From an early age I was trying to get on television*

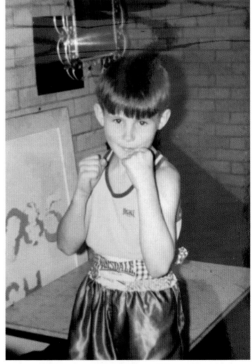

*My very first amateur fight: 5 November 1993*

*Racking up the silverware. Wish I'd kept it…*

*Chizzy wishing the lad the best after my first win*

*With my mother and father*

*Loved a good scrap, me and our Danny*

*The famous mushroom haircut in its prime*

*Me, Danny and Katie posing for the standard school photo*

*Me aged 14, with Chizzy, Birchy and Gary Davies*

*Aged 16. Not a care in the world*

*Posing for a photo in front of an Ali mural in Thorn Cross prison. Aged 20*

*Chizzy and my father*

*My medal from competing in Cyprus 2004. The only bit of amateur silverware I have left*

*Wearing my England vest as an amateur. October 2004, before my fight with Danny Jacobs*

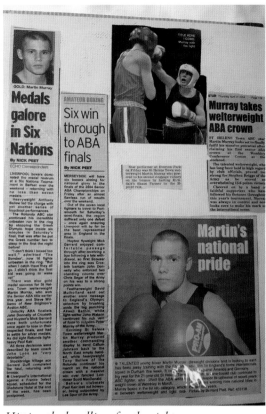

*Hitting the headlines for the right reasons*

*Me and Davo living it up in Malia*

*My 'famous' boxing match in Malia*

*The Barmy Army's in good spirits before heading to Sheffield for the Lee Noble fight*

*Celebrating with the family after winning the Commonwealth title. Gemma is pregnant with Amelia*

*Gotta love the Barmy Army*

*Sparring with Jamie Moore in one of our many wars. As tough as it got [Mike Cleary]*

*Rocking Felix Sturm with a left hook in our world title fight*

*Driving home the right hand against Navarro [Mark Robinson]*

*Me and Oliver buzzing after winning the Interim WBA middleweight world title [Mark Robinson]*

*With Alex Matvienko and Roberto Duran after the Navarro fight*

*The biggest and most hostile crowd I've ever walked out to. Buenos Aires*

*Landing flush on Sergio Martinez*

*Giving Martinez a hard night's work*

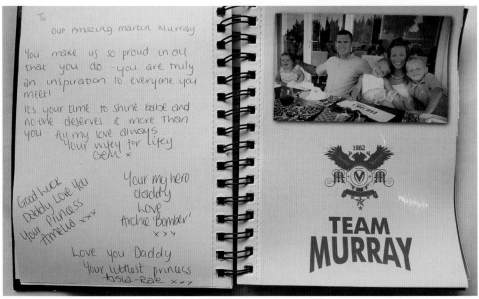

*Messages of support from my beautiful wife and amazing kids before going into battle with GGG*

*Training camp, South Africa. With Harold, Ed, Nav, Rocky and Oliver*

*Landing a right uppercut on GGG*

*GGG repaying the favour*

*Meeting up with GGG the day after our fight*

*Driving the jab home on Abraham's chin*

*Precision hand wrapping from Oliver [Paul Zanon]*

*Local support before the Groves fight*

*Head to head with Groves [Paul Zanon]*

*Catching Groves with the jab [Lawrence Lustig]*

*Tenth round. I almost turned the fight on its head [Lawrence Lustig]*

*An easy night's work against Rosado  [Lawrence Lustig]*

*Landing a clean right hand on Rosado  [Lawrence Lustig]*

*Winning team. Alex Matvienko, Andy, Matt Macklin, Archie, Frank Hopkins, Oliver and Jamie [Lawrence Lustig]*

*At Chizzy's grave [Paul Zanon]*

*Outside the police cells of Paralimni, Cyprus, 16 years later*

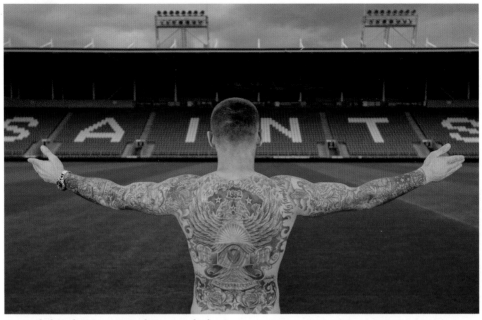

*At my beloved Saints ground [Bernard Platt]*

*My beautiful family. My world*

*With mum and dad*

I decided to go to the American Embassy in London with my full criminal record and come clean about everything so I could get a visa. It was roasting hot on the day and I was wearing a suit, trying to make a good impression. When I got inside the embassy it was that packed, I couldn't find a seat for ages. I pulled my ticket out and spent hours and hours watching this screen, waiting for my number to come up. Finally, I got the call and by this stage I was the last one in there.

I went over to the counter and there was some jobsworth who made a complete example of me. He referred to the time I went to America in 2007 and said, 'You're a liar and dishonest and we don't like dishonest people in our country.' That was that. No visa.

I couldn't have done any more than I'd done in the previous seven years to turn my life around. As I walked out, I looked at him and said, 'People do change, you know.' He said with a smug look on his face, 'I know they do. But for now, you're not allowed in the country.' Prick!

David Lemieux was another one on the radar. We were happy to fight in Canada because we didn't need a visa, but the offer was never made.

In the meantime, I was having some promotional and management issues. Over the next few months, it was probably the closest I'd been to jacking it all in. There was a lot of going back and forth with lawyers to try and get me a decent fight, but I was trying to keep positive by smashing training. Next thing, I got the call to say I'd be fighting Khomitsky again, which was crazy. How did we go from talking about the likes of Chavez Jr, Golovkin and Quillin to Khomitsky? Not to mention my previous fight being against Martínez. It made no sense.

When I walked through the doors of my house, I had a long chat with Gemma and she was heartbroken to see how my career was panning out and seeing me this upset. She said, 'I want you to be happy. If you're not happy, don't feel that you're under any pressure to box. I'm not bothered about the money. We'll always make ends meet. As long as you're happy, then I'm happy. But if you're sad, that will make me sad also.'

I did get down to be honest, but every time things go against me it makes me even more determined to succeed. I was nowhere near ready to retire. Where I'm from, there was always a lot of could-a-beens, should-a-beens, would-a-beens, and I've never wanted to finish like that. I've always said that when I retire, I want to make sure I'm happy with myself, no matter what level I get to.

I never thought I'd get to where I had. Being in massive fights, having a beautiful wife and three incredible kids is more than I could have ever dreamed of. Also, if you'd asked me back when I was a teenager if I'd have been happy to accept being British champion, with so and so amount of money in the bank – of course I'd have taken it. But now I'd reached that and gone beyond it. I felt I still hadn't peaked yet. If I'd have retired then, I would have regretted not giving it my all.

* * * * *

I put my head down and cracked on with the Khomitsky fight. However, I also started to think about getting a new team around me, one that could bring me to that next level and put me in those fights I wanted.

Now's a good time to properly introduce Andy Mikhail. Like myself, Andy's from St Helens but the other end of town in Eccleston. He used to knock around Fingerpost growing up, as his rugby club (Blackbrook) was just down the road from my mum's house, but being eight years older than me, I didn't really know or see him a great deal.

We'd crossed paths at a couple of Saints games and a few boxing matches, then over time, Andy became one of my sponsors. So here I am now, at a bit of a low point, trying to work out how to move my career forward positively, when I thought, 'Go and see Andy.' He's always had this knack of making anything he's done successful, so I instinctively knew he was the person I needed to help me out of this rut.

'Andy. Would you manage me?'

'Martin, I love boxing and I'd love to manage you, but I've never been in that game. I don't know enough to help you. You need someone who's involved in boxing,' he said.

'You don't. You just need to know about contracts and business,' I replied.

Still not confident enough to say yes, Andy says, 'You do in a way as you need to know what money is out there for fighters, in terms of who's getting money for what.'

Once he'd spoken with some people in the business and got to grips with what a good purse was and what a bad one was, he called me and said, 'It's not that difficult. I'm just doing what I do every day. I buy something, and then try to get as much money as I can for it and sell it. The way I'm looking at this is: here's a boxer, try and get him as much money as I can and the right fights.'

That's when I asked him, 'Why don't you come on board as an advisor? Agent type thing.' He said, 'Yes,' and with that, he was officially my agent. In all honesty, if I could turn back the clock, I would have loved to have had Andy on board from my very first fight.

Before I could say hello again to Khomitsky, I firstly needed to say goodbye to someone. One of the good guys.

# CHAPTER 35

# PRECKY'S LEGACY

*'They had a similar philosophy and instantly
clicked. Steve loved Martin's mentality and the
courage he'd shown in the ring. Martin was amazed
by Steve's determination, which I'm sure Martin
will admit gave him some extra motivation to get
through some of his fights, having witnessed what
Steve had been through'*

Martin Blondel, 2016, Secretary of
The Steve Prescott Foundation

WHEN I first starting watching Saints and was getting into rugby, Steve Prescott (Precky) was *The Man*. Someone I genuinely looked up to.

Apart from St Helens, he'd also played for Hull, Wakefield and even got some caps for England and Ireland. He was known for having an incredible fighting spirit on the pitch, but it was the battle he'd started in 2006 that proved to be his greatest.

Having been diagnosed with a rare type of cancer called pseudomyxoma peritonei, Precky was given three months to live. He was prepared to do anything to beat the prognosis and soon after set up The Steve Prescott Foundation in 2007.

He underwent an operation where they removed a gigantic 26lb tumour from his stomach and this gave him the chance of a further six months. Precky, being Precky, got himself as fit as he could and started taking part in all kinds of crazy challenges, raising thousands of pounds. Dragon boat racing, marathons, climbing mountains, you name it. He was convinced he could take a different path than the one that was laid out for him.

In 2007, I bumped into Steve at a retail park in St Helens. He'd not long been diagnosed and I found it a bit awkward to strike up a conversation, knowing his circumstances, whereas he was carrying on as if nothing was wrong, having a proper conversation and being really relaxed. Then in 2010, not long after the Mitrevski fight, I was introduced to a man called Martin Blondel, who was and still is the secretary for the foundation. When he told me Precky was a fan of mine, I almost fell over. I said, 'If there's anything I can do to help, let me know.' Not long after, I was asked to be an ambassador for the foundation, which was a massive honour.

Precky's strength and determination to beat this cancer led him and everyone to believe he could outlive the disease. He was the first one to have this operation, a full organ replacement. The doctors warned him of the risks and that he could die. Unfortunately, on 9 November 2013, as a result of the donor's antibodies rejecting Precky's, he passed away.

When Precky lost his fight, the foundation had to keep living his dream without him. By coming on board with the other ambassadors, we are able to carry on the great work Steve did and continue with his legacy.

RIP Precky. You're an inspiration to your family and what you've done for St Helens is unbelievable. You're a real example of how a sporting hero should behave. I'll certainly never forget you, mate.

## CHAPTER 36

# ROAD BLOCK

*'Fast is fine, but accuracy is everything'*

Wyatt Earp

I'D beaten Khomitsky convincingly the first time, so fighting him again was a hiding to nothing. We were supposed to be on the undercard of the first Froch vs Groves bill on 23 November 2013.

A week before the fight was supposed to happen, I attended a charity boxing event in the afternoon at Langtree Park for The Steve Prescott Foundation, but was on my arse with a nasty virus. As soon as the boxing had finished, I went and met a man called Dr Chris Brooks (Brooksi), under the recommendation of my physio and mate Pinky (Andy Pinkerton). Brooksi was Wigan's rugby league doctor. Legend of a bloke. I'd heard stories about him, but this was the first time I'd met him.

Brooksi recommended some things which made me feel better but it was obvious I was in no condition to fight. The week after, I went and saw him and he said I looked good, but not 100 per cent. As much as I improved for a few days, we had to postpone the fight until 14 December as I felt like shit. In all honesty, though, it was a fight I didn't need and shouldn't have risked my health in, but the problem was I was contractually bound and needed the money.

Although I beat Khomitsky comfortably on points, I was drained. However, the real dramas for the evening started after the final bell. I got back to the changing room and my hand was proper throbbing, so me and Andy went off to the hospital as it was obvious I'd done some damage. Turns out I'd broken a bone. Three hours later, we were driving back to the hotel, when my dad called Andy in a right panic.

'Andy. It's fucking kicking off in here. Our Danny is fighting. It's like a riot.'

All I could hear was Andy saying dead calm, 'Yeah. Yeah. Will do. OK mate.'

Andy hung up, then turned to me cool as ice and said, 'Listen. You're going to get to the hotel and there's most likely going to be a bit of trouble. I want you to ignore it, go to the lift and straight to your room and forget about it. OK?' 'Alright mate. Will do,' I replied.

Reverse the clock back ten minutes earlier and this is what was happening in the hotel. Our Danny, Garvey, Gemma and Andy's wife Vicky were having a drink, minding their own business. This massive Cockney fella came over to our Danny and just stood there. Our Danny says, 'What's up, mate?' 'Don't be giving us the fackin big-un sunshine. I've got a fackin knife,' he replied. Ten minutes later, we were just pulling up.

When I walked in, it was like the doors had swung open to an old saloon bar in a Western movie. There were bodies flying everywhere, fists being thrown and chairs being smashed up. Even worse, our Danny was in the thick of it with his shirt ripped off. He was standing in front of this massive guy in the crane kick position, laughing like some psycho, thinking he was the Karate Kid. I shouted out to him, 'What the fuck are yo doing?'

He's my brother and can handle himself, but I didn't want to see any harm come to him. I flew in and shoulder-barged our Danny out of there and straight to the lift.

It was good timing because seconds after getting into the lift, the police pulled up and started throwing people in the back of vans without even asking questions.

Never a dull day in the Murray household.

\* \* \* \* \*

After all the letdowns before Khomitsky, it looked like I was going to get another title shot and one which I could win without any problems.

The opponent was Jarrod Fletcher and we'd be fighting on a show promoted by Rodney Berman. It looked like it was a done deal. We'd booked in provisional dates for 2014 and even had the press conference at Langtree Park, at the Saints ground, and had one lined up for Monte Carlo. I was the WBA interim world champion at the time and this was supposed to be for the WBA (regular) middleweight world title. Finally, some light at the end of the tunnel.

Then we were told that the fight hadn't been sanctioned. Why? You tell me. To this day, I've never had an answer.

I decided to speak with top hand specialist Mike Hayton and he said that going ahead with the fight could be irreparably career-damaging. Without a world title on the line, it was now a nothing fight, so we decided to pull out.

I went from being the number one contender with the WBA to completely dropping out of the top ten. I also ended up forking out over two grand in legal expenses on a fight that never happened and lost money on a cruise that I cancelled, because it looked like the fight was going ahead.

It was one disappointment after another.

CHAPTER 37

# DONE DEAL

*'Change is not merely necessary to life – it is life'*

Alvin Toffler

O NE of Andy's personal tasks he'd set himself when coming on board was to get me a big payday. When he heard how much I'd been paid for the Martínez and Sturm fights, he was disgusted.

Soon after the Fletcher fight fell through, Andy said, 'I think we should go to that Monte Carlo show.' Golovkin was fighting Osumanu Adama and Fletcher was fighting Max Bursak for the WBA international middleweight title.

After pulling out of the Fletcher fight, I was a bit hesitant. I wasn't sure of the reception we'd get and whether it was a waste of time. Andy, on the other hand, had a plan. He was thinking about the promotional options on the table, which included Matchroom and Frank Warren, but it was the shows in Monte Carlo that interested him the most.

Andy e-mailed Rodney Berman from Golden Gloves. 'Hiya Rodney. It's Andy Mikhail, Martin Murray's agent. Sorry we couldn't make the fight (referring to the Fletcher bout), but we still want to come over and watch the show. Can you let me know about tickets?'

Rodney replied, 'Andrew. You and Martin are not welcome to come to the show. You let me down and that's not what Golden Gloves are about.' He went on to say, 'You almost put the whole show in jeopardy by pulling out.' The response was cold but you could understand Rodney's reasons because from his side it looked like we had pulled out because we didn't want to fight. He wasn't given the full picture at that time.

Either way, we went to see the fights in Monte Carlo. We never saw Rodney, but we did see Golovkin stop Adama in seven rounds to retain his titles. I'd never seen him from ringside before but you could tell he was a quality fighter and operator. I knew that if a fight was to happen, I'd have to take it to him. There was no other way.

A couple of weeks later, I was out of contract with Hatton. Andy messaged Rodney. 'Great show the other week, Rodney. Well done. Me and Martin really enjoyed it. I wish you every success in the future.' Rodney replied very appreciatively, then Andy added, 'Martin's out of contract now. Would you still be interested in getting Martin over to Monaco?' He replied straight away. 'Absolutely.'

Rodney had been promoting fights since 1977. He'd had some of the biggest names under his wing over the years, but it was his strong relationship with the Golovkin camp, especially Tom Loeffler, that interested us.

Negotiations with Andy and Rodney went on for a few days, but to be fair to Rodney the offer was good from very early on. Andy called me to say the contract had been finalised, then drove round to the gym to present me with some figures for a three-fight deal. I was absolutely shocked as it was life-changing cash.

When we left the gym, we were in the car chatting with Rodney, talking through the details again, getting ready to accept the deal. This was the first time I'd really spoken with him. He was going on about a plan of when I'd fight. A proper plan. One that sketched out four fights, with dates and an amount of money for each fight in advance, as opposed to me getting a call and someone saying, 'You're fighting in a few weeks for this amount. Take it or leave it.' Before this deal, I was training non-stop because I didn't know when the next call was going to come, which meant I was often getting burnt out by over-training. I'd never had structure like this before.

Firstly, I'd have a tune-up fight in South Africa against Ishmael Tetteh, then a three-fight deal in Monte Carlo, with the intention of topping the bill with a fight against Golovkin in early 2015. The only thing was if I lost any of the fights along the way, I wouldn't get Golovkin or the purses. Also, I would have lost my mandatory [position] and that would have sent me right down the slide again in terms of rankings and reputation. But that's always been the kind of pressure I've thrived off.

Apart from the package Rodney had put together, the other thing I liked about him was that he understood family values. Over the next few weeks, whenever we'd talk, the first thing he'd say was, 'How's the wife and children?' He knew I boxed for my family and a better quality of life. Also, most of the fighters Rodney has promoted over the last four decades he's still close with now. That says a lot.

\* \* \* \* \*

Once my hand had fully recovered from hitting Khomitsky's head, I stopped Tetteh in six rounds in South Africa.

The most memorable part of the trip was having my family with me and being able to enjoy a nice holiday with them. But the craziest memory involved my mates Stu McCulloch and Lee Atherton. They decided to go drinking in the most dangerous township in Johannesburg. I'd already gone to bed, as Gemma was over with the kids and I was fighting.

In the morning, I saw Dean at breakfast and he said, 'You should have seen the state of them two last night.' 'Why? What went on?' I replied. Next thing, they walk in still pissed. It turned out they started having a few drinks and decided to make a night of it. They went back to their room, put all their valuables away in the safe, bar a few quid to go out with, and got a taxi outside the complex where we were staying. They said to the driver, 'Take us to the roughest pub in Johannesburg.' He took them to some shed in Soweto, right in the middle of the township. They left there absolutely bladdered, with their 'Team Murray' t-shirts on, giving it the big-un. The locals must have thought they were nutters.

When they pulled up for breakfast, a close friend of Andy's, Mike Wittstock, was also eating with us. Mike's from Joburg and also happens to be the Princess of Monaco's dad. He's a good friend now and I'd never seen him lose his shit before.

As Stu and Lee start talking about what they'd done, he threw his knife and fork down on the table and said, 'Do you realise how stupid you've been? People get killed over here for just walking down the wrong road and you think it's funny going to hang out in a township?' Lee and Stu put their heads down, with smiles on their faces, like they'd just been told off at school.

Back to the boxing. With a three-fight schedule planned over the next ten months, I decided now was a good time to get some expert help for my overall fitness. Firstly, I went to see the St Helens rugby club physio Nathan Mills, who gave me a full body screening, and then I started working with Bittaz (Mark Bitcon), who is the director of performance for Wigan Warriors rugby team.

First session, he worked out the areas I was lacking in strength and conditioning, and he built up a programme for me. Instead of getting me to just do it, he explained it. 'This is why we are doing this exercise, these are the benefits and this is how it will help you as a boxer.' It made sense.

Bittaz deals with teams and individual athletes of all shapes and sizes, but understands that each sport has different needs. In rugby or football, the season is set for the year and the routines in training tend to be similar, whereas in boxing, technically, we're year-round athletes. I might have to take a fight with five or 12 weeks' notice and Bittaz designs a plan accordingly.

With three fights on the horizon and the right support behind me, I was now ready for my Monte Carlo adventure.

# CHAPTER 38

# MONTE CARLO OR BUST

*'Gambling is entertainment. People go to the
casinos to be entertained'*

Eric Schneiderman

A COUPLE of weeks after getting back from South Africa, I
went over to Monte Carlo with Andy. We met up with a close
mate of Andy's called Mike Wittstock, who also happens to
be the Princess of Monaco's dad. I'd first met Mike at the Tetteh fight
in Johannesburg, which is where he's from. He kindly took some time
to show us around and then when we came to Monte Carlo, he did it
all again, showing us places we hadn't seen on my previous visit and
introducing us to some of his mates. Basically, he made us feel at home.

Monte Carlo is a totally different world to where I'd been brought
up. Some of the scenery and the money was something to take in.
Luxury cars, designer gear and fancy watches all around you. I like
seeing people do well and it inspired me to want to get to that next level.

The Bursak fight was in the main casino in Monte Carlo, which
like everything else was breathtaking. The décor inside was like the
set of *The Antiques Roadshow*. However, as a boxing venue, it was tiny
with little atmosphere.

Going on that trip to Monte Carlo made Andy realise I've got a
touch of the obsessive compulsive disorder (OCD). In the week leading
up to a fight, my OCD goes up a few notches. Fast forward to the week
of the Bursak fight and I'm in the same hotel with Andy. He walks into
my room and says, 'Have you not unpacked yet?' 'Yeah, yeah. I've put

everything away.' He starts looking around and sees my trainers and shoes are immaculately clean, then sees everything around the room is perfectly placed. Even the painting on the wall was straightened as I wasn't happy with it.

Shaking his head, he walks into the bathroom and says, 'It's like being at home here. Everything is tidy. You should see my room.' Before coming out, he spotted my toothpaste, toothbrush and all my toiletries were placed in a certain way, all facing the same direction. Andy being Andy, he couldn't resist mixing everything up.

As he walked out, he said, 'Going for a piss in your toilet is like going for a job interview. Everything has to be spotless. I had to check I didn't leave any piss around the rim.' We both laughed but I was thinking, 'I wonder if he left any piss around the rim?'

As far as the Bursak fight was concerned, it was a comfortable win over 12 rounds. It also sent a message out that I could outclass a good European-level fighter without too much bother.

* * * * *

There was another reason I had a good following ringside for this fight. My mate Dean had decided to double up the trip as a stag do. He had asked me to be his best man about a year before and had given me dates for the wedding. Normally this wouldn't have been a problem but after signing with Rodney Berman, my diary was busy. Thankfully, in the end, the stag do coincided with the Bursak fight (21 June 2014) and the wedding would take place on 22 July in Cyprus. This was a bit strange because even though I was the best man I didn't take part in the stag do.

Dean travelled over with 25 mates and had no idea of the prices in Monte Carlo. They'd booked a hotel in Nice because it was a lot cheaper. Or so they thought. It cost them £90 for a taxi each way, so maybe not that cheap in the long run. First night they hit Monte Carlo, Dean pulled up to the first bar they passed and said, 'Twenty six pints of beer please, mate.' The guy at the bar slid over a menu. Dean looked at him and repeated, 'No, no. We don't want food. Lagers, 26 of them please.' The barman was just trying to be polite. When Dean looked down at the menu, the cheapest beer was 20 euros a pint. Dean's response was, 'One lager, mate.' In the end, they found an Irish bar.

Dean explained to the owner the size of their group and that they'd be there a few days drinking, and asked if he could cut them a deal. And he did. Eight euros a pint. Thankfully, Andy Mikhail also found another bar for everyone called Slammers and the man who ran it, Terry, was a cracking bloke who also gave them a good deal.

The Barmy Army were on their best behaviour but a few of the lads got arrested for being drunk and disorderly. Silly stuff like walking across the road pissed. However, they did say they were the nicest cells they'd ever seen. Better than the hotel they were staying at in Nice and no need for a £90 taxi to get there. A few of the lads did consider getting nicked every night as the cheaper and more comfortable option.

* * * * *

A month after the Bursak fight, I was on best man duties in Cyprus for Dean. However, it's funny how you can bump into people and end up becoming friends straight away.

Three days before the wedding, I went down to the ironing room in the hotel and next minute this lad walks in, who introduced himself as Johnny Fear from Merthyr, Wales. I'd not met him before. We got chatting and he suddenly recognised me. 'Are you Martin Murray?' 'Yeah,' I replied. We had a little chat about boxing, then I mentioned me and the lads were going out if he fancied coming along. 'Yeah. Sound. Great mate.' We met up the day after, went to Ayia Napa and had a top night out.

We kept in contact after the holiday and that was the start of the Welsh division of the Barmy Army. Top bunch of lads who've followed me everywhere. Thanks for the support.

The wedding itself kind of turned it all into a mini-adventure from start to finish. As sensible lads do, we stayed up to about three in the morning the night before the wedding. One of the lads was found asleep in a bush and later that morning spewed up all over his wife and kids.

There were a few sore heads on the day of the wedding but the ceremony was fantastic. I wrote a poem that went on for a good few minutes. Dean is convinced I stole it from somewhere but I swear,

I wrote it myself. It was so hot that by the time I'd finished, I was sweating that much you could see my entire tattoo on my back straight through my white shirt.

Last day of the wedding trip, we all decided to go for a day out to a different town. After a while, we were getting ready to head back when I spotted this bus which was signed to go to Paralimni. I wasn't ready to go back yet, so I turned to everyone and said, 'Paralimni! I was in jail there. Anyone fancy seeing if we can find my old prison cell?'

Me, Dean, Barry and Shaun jumped on this bus, while the girls and kids went back to the hotel. We got off straight in the middle of the town. Bear in mind it was midday and the heat was stifling. We stepped off the bus and it looked like an old ghost town from a cowboy movie. In the meantime, the bus drove off and we looked around to see everything was shut.

We started walking and after a while spotted a taxi rank. We went over and all the drivers were playing cards as the rank was shut. I asked where the local police station was but it took a while for them to understand what I was saying. Thankfully, in the end, we managed to get some directions from them.

We started walking down this road, which seemed to go on forever, in about 40 degrees of heat, following the directions this guy had given us. We got to near where the taxi driver said it was but couldn't see it anywhere. As we were deciding whether to head back to the bus station, one of the lads suddenly said, pointing to a building, 'Is that it?' I looked over and said all excited, 'That's it! We're here!' We were at the back, so we ran around to the front and buzzed on the door, and they let us straight through.

When we entered the building, there were two policemen sat behind a desk. I've said, 'Hello mate. I was banged up here 13 years ago. Just wanted to know if we could look around?' You could see them looking at these four lads, thinking, 'Who are these guys?' They couldn't understand us and had to call some woman to translate.

'I know it's a long shot but is there any chance I can show my mates where I stayed?' 'No. There's nothing to see. The cells are full up with stationery, old police files,' he replied. A few seconds later, he asked, 'What were you in for?' 'Drugs,' I replied. You could have cut the atmosphere with a knife. After about five seconds of dead silence, I said, 'Annnnnyway. We're going to go now.'

We asked them to call us a taxi but the second the front door of the prison locked behind us, I started thinking at a hundred miles an hour. 'Drugs. Why did I tell them that? They might think we've got drugs on us now. I wonder if they've called us a taxi or if they've called a van to nick us?' Thankfully, it never happened.

We stood outside and took some pictures. I was so happy to go back there. Not to visit the prison but because I was proud of how far I'd come since then.

# CHAPTER 39

# GGGRUELLING
# PREPARATIONS

*'If we want something we've never had, we
need to do something we've never done'*

Martin Murray discusses the Golovkin
training camp with Oliver Harrison, 2014

THREE months after Dean's wedding, I fought Domenico Spada on 25 October 2014. I wasn't nervous about the fight at all. For me, it was one step closer to Golovkin and I was confident I could beat him easily. Andy, on the other hand, was petrified.

The night before the fight, he came to my room and said, 'I don't want to put any more pressure on you but you need to box clever here. Whatever you need to do to win tomorrow, do it. This is your ticket to the big one. This fight and the next will secure your future.' No pressure then, Andy.

It turned out to be a messy fight. Spada was constantly putting the head in, holding and doing his best to make it a scrappy fight. Spada's eye was cut from a clash of heads, so I won on a technical decision in the seventh. Not the way I like to win fights but a win's a win.

The only reason we'd agreed to fight Spada was because he was the only one who wanted to fight me.

We'd offered Marco Antonio Rubio the bout for good money as he was holding the interim WBC world middleweight title. That would have been a step in the right direction but he didn't take it. Instead, he went and fought Golovkin for less money and got smashed in two rounds.

\* \* \* \* \*

Golovkin was ringside for the Spada fight, knowing he'd be up against the winner on 21 February 2015. After the fight, there was a small press conference to officially announce the contest between us. Everybody was excited as they knew that I'd be fighting for the world title against the best middleweight in the world. I turned to Gemma and said, 'We've done it. Whatever happens now, we're going to be OK.' I was referring to our financial security.

The first big press conference for Golovkin took place in London that December. I introduced him to our Arch, Danny and my dad. He started playfighting with Archie, holding his hands up, telling him to throw a combination. That was a nice touch.

Back to business. With three months to go before the fight, I was aware that the training camp needed to be perfect in every way. The 15 weeks I'd done for Sturm and Martínez had me up, then down, up, then down. You should only peak once in camp. Physically and mentally, it can make a massive difference over a 12-round fight. By now, I knew that nine weeks was the perfect length of time for me.

The tactics and strategy for this fight were very different to anything we'd prepared for before. We knew we were going to be in for a hard fight. We'd even anticipated that due to the way he hit, there was a possibility I was going to go down at some point, so we needed to prepare for that. The only time I'd hit the canvas before was against Khomitsky, which was more of a slip. The kind of knockdowns we were preparing for were the type that give you triple vision, a bit like when Rocky fought Ivan Drago in *Rocky IV* and Paulie says to Rocky, 'Hit the one in the middle!'

We did some mad drills, like forward-rolling three times from corner to corner of the ring, and then turning around and doing the same again non-stop. I'd do 12 rolls, get up and I swear, I couldn't move. My senses went. Oliver then started attacking me with big shots, getting me to defend, until my senses came back. I'd then throw shots for about five seconds and by that time, my head was clear. He would also spin me around until I was ready to fall over, then get me to hit the pads while dizzy, just to get me used to having my wits about me.

We knew Golovkin had a great jab, so we worked on getting around that and getting our own shots off, including targeting his body. We also did a lot of stuff off the ropes, because again, we knew we'd be there at some point. Avoiding his left hook was something we focused on, as that was one of his big shots. Every time he'd throw the left, we'd take the sting out of it by taking a little step away to the side. One week into the new year, we headed off to South Africa for the main part of the camp.

For the Spada fight, I'd only seen my kids eight days in the last four weeks of the camp and that tore me in half. I'm a family man and try to do as much as I can with my kids. Even on Christmas Day 2014, I woke up really early and went for a run just because I wanted to be able to get back to see them open their Christmas presents. They're in my every thought. The fact that I wouldn't be able to be with them for the next couple of months scared me if I'm honest.

Around a week later, Gemma and the kids dropped me off at Warrington Bank Quay train station, before me and Andy headed down to London. We had ten minutes together sitting in the car talking and I won't lie, it was horrible. The kids were asking why I was going and we were all getting upset. We gave each other hugs and kisses and as I got my case out of the car, our Archie started screaming, 'Dad, dad, dad.' I went back to the car and said, 'What's up, Arch?' He said, 'I just want to give you one more hug.' It broke my heart leaving them like that.

I knew I didn't want to go but I had to. There were loads of advantages to me going to South Africa. When I fought there in April 2014 against Tetteh, I only went ten days before the fight, so I didn't have time to acclimatise to the lack of oxygen. Every time I was going back to the corner, I was breathing heavy. I knew that going back to South Africa, training at altitude would push me to my limits. Secondly, there was a constant source of vitamin D with the sun. January is one of the hottest summer months in South Africa, so the weather was perfect, the complete opposite to winter in the UK.

I'd have needed to wear about five layers back home to start sweating. Over there, you could get into your shorts and t-shirt, and in no time you'd broken a sweat and you were ready to go. Finally, I had a round-the-clock chef, which meant everything was done for me. As it turned out, the cooking was so good, I'd never eaten so well trying to make middleweight. All of this would give me time to focus. Who knows what the outcome of the fight would have been if I had not gone away? I can always live with the result but if it had been a devastating loss, I'd have always thought, 'I should have gone to South Africa.' I hate looking back regretting 'what ifs'.

I was over there for five weeks. There was me, Andy, Oliver, Rocky, Nav Mansouri and Ed Tooley, the nutritionist. Harold and Michelle Volbrecht were incredible. They allowed us to train at their gym and always made us feel nothing was too much bother. They'd pick us up every day, take us down the gym and really looked after us.

Routines were pretty simple. We'd wake up in the morning and do a little fat burner running around the Emperors Palace complex, but were given strict instructions not to stray from there as Johannesburg can be a dangerous place. Then around 3pm, Michelle would pick us up and take us to the Hammer gym to do our evening session.

Oliver maintains it was the worst camp I'd ever had but I don't think that's true. For the first week, I was on my own and during that time, I overdid it. There's no way you can go in there at high altitude when you first arrive and start smashing it without something giving. By the time he came over, I was on my arse. He's since told me he was very close to pulling me out after seeing how some of the sparring sessions went. After a couple of weeks, he had me doing nothing but footwork, shadow boxing and going over the fight in my head. When I did start sparring again, it was the way it was supposed to be.

＊ ＊ ＊ ＊ ＊

A few days before getting ready to fly to Monte Carlo, I wanted to get my hair cut. It was kind of part of the finishing touches of the training camp. The only thing is, I'm very sceptical about letting anyone else near my head other than my barber Ilham back home in Warrington.

I went to this hairdressers and straight away she put me on a chair, with no mirror in front of me. I wasn't happy with that, so I moved my chair in front of a mirror so I could see what was going on. She then sprays me up with loads of water and I was absolutely dripping. Then she got out the scissors and chop, chop, chop. I was thinking, 'What the fuck is going on here?'

Rocky and Nav were staying at a different hotel but had come over to meet me straight after for breakfast as they wanted to have their hair done also. Rocky was sat next to me and asks, 'You get your hair cut then?' 'Yeah,' I replied. Rocky looks over to check it out, then does a double-take and bursts out laughing. 'What? What's so funny?' I said. 'Looks like she's cut half and left the other half. Seriously mate. Where it's long, she's left it and just cut around the back of your head. Is she coming back tomorrow to finish it off or something?' 'Don't mate. Don't start,' I've replied, laughing nervously.

Then Nav's started adding his bit and he's even more particular than me when it comes to his hair. He's now pointing every little thing out, which was winding me up even more.

We had the afternoon off from training, so decided to get this haircut sorted. We got the driver from the hotel to take us to the local shopping centre as we thought there might be someone there who could do it properly. In the end, we drove around for hours, went to four different shopping centres all over Johannesburg and not one had a barber's. Then the driver said, 'I know where there's one.' I was thinking, 'Now you tell us.'

He drove us to this dingy old market and finally a barber's shop. I jumped in the chair and said with some relief, 'You see there, where it's shaved along. That needs sorting out.' The fella put the cloak on me, got me all ready, then said, 'What's wrong with it?' It was fucking obvious what was wrong with it, but I said, 'You see where there's a big massive step there at the back of my head? I need it blended in.' 'What do you mean blended in?' he asks.

Nav and Rocky are sitting there pissing themselves, thinking this was great entertainment as I was starting to lose it. I started saying in a bit of a panic to the barber, 'You know. With scissors and shavers and stuff, so it's blended.' He replied, 'I don't know what you mean.' I ripped the cloak off and said, 'Fuck this. Come on lads, we're going,' and stormed back to the car, with Nav and Rocky walking behind me creasing up laughing.

Five hours and nothing. When we got in the car, I turned and looked at Nav and Rocky dead angry, then burst out laughing myself. Rocky was taking loads of photos throughout the day, like my haircut was going to be the feature of a documentary. Unfortunately, Rocky ended up dropping his phone and smashing it, so he couldn't upload any photos. Real shame, that, although it always seemed to be them who were having the last laugh.

We went back to the hotel and I went back to my room to relax. Michelle was picking us up a couple of hours later. In the meantime, Nav and Rocky had found out there was a barber's by the airport and got their hair done.

When I came downstairs to meet them, there they were slick as fuck, looking proper smooth, all gelled over and dead fresh. I said, 'Hold on. What's gone on here, lads? Where have yous been, you crafty bastards?' Rocky replied with a big grin, 'We thought we might lose an ear but actually they did a good job.' Typical that those two landed on their feet.

As for me, I never got it sorted and ended up fighting Golovkin with a shocking haircut. It took Ilham months to get it back to how it was before the training camp.

I REMEMBER it was a great atmosphere in Monaco. Martin had a lot of fans and I had a lot of fans and the energy from both sides was great. Nobody wanted to fight Martin because of his performances against Felix Sturm and Sergio Martínez. I wanted to test myself against the best competition and was happy when we could make the fight together.

Martin was very tough, he showed the heart of a champion and desire to win the titles. He kept fighting even after I knocked him down and wouldn't quit during the fight unless his trainer stopped the fight.

I have a lot of respect for Martin as a fighter and as a person. We met the next day at a restaurant. I've never done that with any other opponent but it shows the amount of respect we have for each other.

I know Martin is a great family man and I wish him all the best for the future.

**Gennady Gennadyevich Golovkin (GGG), 2018**

# CHAPTER 40

# GOLOVKIN

*'The fight was the worst experience of my life. Every part of me wanted to stand up and walk out, but I couldn't. I'd never forgive myself. I just wanted the fight to end. I knew that Martin would never give up, but I could see he was physically hurt and I'd never seen that before'*

Gemma Murray, 2016

AFTER a couple of connecting flights from Johannesburg, we arrived in Monte Carlo on the Monday. In the five days leading up to the fight, I did the press conferences and all the media stuff but I didn't go out much. I just wanted to ride my time out behind closed doors, especially as Gemma didn't fly over until the Friday because she didn't want to leave the kids for too long. We'd been given a hotel to stay at in the heart of all the action, but we also booked a separate hotel that was out of the way, so I didn't have to interact with people too much as I need to keep my head focused.

Come the day of the weigh-in, I was a bit grumpy trying to make the middleweight limit, so I went to the sauna to see what I could sweat off and Andy decided to join me. The second he got in, he was sweating his tits off and spent most of the time getting out to cool down. After 15 minutes, I went out to weigh myself. Andy walked out with me and as we sat down for the next session, he turns to me and says, 'We've done the weight easy this time, haven't we?' I turned, looked at him, while thinking about the months of training and dieting, then said, 'We? What the fuck have you done? You've been in here 15 minutes and keep popping out every 30 seconds!' We both burst out laughing.

The atmosphere at the weigh-in itself was unreal. Loads of people had come over from England to support me, which I really appreciated. Good memories.

\* \* \* \* \*

Fight night. Unlike for the Sturm and Martínez fights, the casino was a really small venue, which meant a short ring walk. By the time I was out of the changing room, I was in the ring facing Golovkin. We listened to the instructions, touched gloves and I walked back to the corner. Oliver popped in the gumshield and the bell went.

The tactics in the first couple of rounds were to try and keep him at bay by out-boxing him. He wasn't finding his big shots but I could feel he was getting closer and closer as the rounds went on.

By round three, he had started to get on top. He showed that he could take a shot brilliantly and was a master of cutting the ring off. It might sound silly but I thought he was going to be more powerful. Don't get me wrong, his punches were harder than anyone else's I'd been hit by before, but mentally I'd prepared myself for him to be hitting like a heavyweight. When he did start to hit me, from the beginning, I thought to myself, 'I can deal with this for 12 rounds, no problem.' However, the issue wasn't the power, it was his variety and constant pressure. Nobody had ever opened me up the way he did and given me no time to breathe.

He tried to throw the left hook to the body a few times but it wasn't fully connecting. The tactic we'd practised in training, of riding the punch, was working. Then, in round four, I started talking to him when it wasn't landing flush and said, 'What's that?', making out the punch was having no effect. The next time he threw it, I slipped to my left with my hands up and all of a sudden he threw this massive right hook to the body. Wallop. All I remember was this searing pain ripping through me. I'd never experienced anything like it. The pain in my stomach was excruciating. If I have to be honest, I actually thought I'd shit my shorts.

It took me ages to get over that shot. The rib he caught was prominently sticking out after and it took Pinky about six weeks to get it back in place. It was purely my grit, determination and will to win that got me back on my feet, but that shot changed the dynamics of the fight. The second the ref finished the count and walked away, Golovkin was on me. The tactics of practising on the ropes came into play. I tried to grab a hold of him, but he was just too physically strong. He put me down again. Same shot. Right hook to the body. It was only a little shot, but I was still feeling the effects of his last one 20 seconds earlier.

It took me from rounds five to eight to get back into it but I took a lot of shots during that time. Going back to what I said about his variety, he doesn't have just one big shot. Every shot is hard. Round six, he hit me with a short left uppercut, then another straight after. Bang, bang. It pushed my nose almost up my face. I instantly thought, 'He's going downstairs now.' I bent my elbow down to cover up the body and he instantly hit me with exactly the same shot. Bang. Straight on the nose. I thought, 'Surely, he's gonna go for the body now,' and bang, he hit me on the nose once again. I thought, 'You twat! He's got you again.' My nose was a mess from that point on.

During the fight, I caught him with a right uppercut, a left uppercut, a right hook and a left hook. A nice, solid four-punch combination that we'd been working on in training. Every one of them caught him. They'd have done damage to quite a lot of people, but he just shook them off and kept coming forward.

Rounds nine and ten, although tough, I felt like I was starting to mix it with him. He was still on me non-stop but I was starting to land some good body shots on the inside, which managed to slow him down a bit. That was up until he caught me with a shot on the top of my head in the last five seconds of round 10 and had me on the canvas again. As the shot landed, it rattled my brain.

Going back to the corner, even though I'd been down three times at this point, I still thought I was going to pull off the fightback from somewhere. He landed with a combination in the 11th, which finished with a big right hand to the head. It looked like I'd sagged a little bit but I didn't. It was just a little drop we'd practised on the ropes to help take the sting out of anything being thrown. Even so, the referee decided I'd had enough and jumped in. The fight was all over.

My team wanted me to sit down in the corner and I said, 'I'm alright.' They just had my best interests at heart. They kept asking again and again, and I eventually snapped and said, 'I'm fucking alright. I'm not sitting down in that chair, so just get it in your head, it's not happening.'

After the official announcement, I went back to the changing rooms, then went to the toilet with Gemma and burst out crying. That was the first time after a fight I'd ever done that. I was absolutely gutted. I thought I was going to win, did everything I possibly could, took myself away from my family and it still didn't work. All the emotion just built up.

It wasn't just me, though. Andy was pale white in the changing room. He walked over, put his arm around me and proper broke down. Gemma was in a terrible state. She'd been shaking throughout the fight and I can't imagine what she had to go through seeing me taking the shots I did.

The night wasn't over yet. I still needed to give my piss sample. Me and Gemma walked into this room and Golovkin was also there waiting to have his done. My face was battered and bruised, and he put his hand on his chest, looked at Gemma and said very sincerely, 'I'm sorry.' He's a nice bloke and he's purely about business. I really do wish him well. That said, I was still thinking, 'Let's fucking go again!'

Andy had now walked in and was furious. He'd been waiting for the doctor to get me checked out but found out he'd already left. When we came out of the room, I knew Andy was still going to ask me to see the doctor. Here's the thing, Andy rarely loses his temper with me but he's done it twice and only ever for my benefit. This was the first time.

I can be pretty stubborn and once I've made my mind up, that's it. So when he asked me to see the doctor to get checked over, I've said, 'I don't need the doctor.' That was all it took. Andy shouts back, 'I don't give a fuck what you say. It's my responsibility to make sure you're alright. If you don't get checked, I'm never speaking to you again.' I tried talking my way out of it, but in the end Andy said, 'I don't give a fuck. You're seeing the doctor. That's the end of it. Stop arguing with me.'

There was an ambulance waiting outside but I said, 'There's no fucking chance I am getting in an ambulance.' You could see Andy was about to lose it again but he took a breath and said, 'Calm down. We'll get a taxi. But be under no illusion, we're going to see a doctor.'

We ended up jumping into a minibus that had been laid on for the boxers and drove round to the other side of the hotel. We found out which room the doctor was staying at and Andy got him on the phone. 'I'm in bed,' he says. 'I don't give a fuck. Get out of your bed, bring your stuff down and come and see Martin now.'

He came downstairs pretty quickly and after checking me out, said to Andy, 'He's concussed. I think you should take him to hospital.' Andy said, 'Are you telling me to take him to hospital because you can see something is wrong or are you telling me as a precaution?' 'Precaution,' he said.

When I heard the word 'precaution', I refused to go to hospital. I just wanted to get back to my room. By now, it was about three hours after the fight. It wasn't just the concussion, I was badly dehydrated. On top of that, the adrenaline was wearing off, which meant all the pain from my body was now starting to surface.

When I got back to the hotel, I knew I wouldn't be able to rest, so I took a couple of sleepers. They never work properly, though. I usually only get a couple of hours' sleep tops after a fight. When I woke up in the morning, that's when the sleepers kicked in and I felt spaced out all day.

Unlike the previous times when I'd fought and we'd partied the day after, this time was different. I just wasn't in the mood because my pride was dented. However, the Barmy Army were still buzzing, so we went to Stars and Bars first, then Slammers about lunchtime. I owed that to them at the minimum for their incredible support. I spent a couple of hours with everyone and I even ended up behind the bar pulling pints as everyone started to sing pissed, 'There's only oooonnnnnee Martin Murray'. I was proud of my performance, but obviously I was a little bit down, which was understandable. I wasn't in a slump. Yet.

Next thing, Tom Loeffler, Golovkin's agent, called Andy asking if I would like to meet with him and Golovkin. I'd said my goodbyes and was ready to go home at this point, but I knew it was the right thing to go over and see them. Me, Gemma, Andy, Vicky and Mike Wittstock went over. They were sitting around a table being dead quiet, having some food and a few drinks. Certainly different to the scene I'd just left at Slammers.

As I walked in, Golovkin came over, we shook hands, had a little chat and discussed stuff like who he might fight next. By now I was struggling to stay awake, so we only stayed for about half an hour. I wished him all the best and then went back to the hotel and crashed out.

The day after, me and Gemma flew back. The kids were waiting at the airport with my mum and came running over. We had a big group hug and all broke down in tears. I'd not seen them for six weeks and they're my absolute world. From the time I'd left to go to South Africa, all I was bothered about was seeing them. After everything that happened with Golovkin, I still had them to come back to and that was priceless.

Up to this point in my career, I looked at Golovkin as my only genuine loss. It was new territory for me and I didn't really know what to do or how to react. Unfortunately, the way I ended up dealing with that defeat wasn't great.

# CHAPTER 41

# DOWN-TIME

*'It's always a wake-up call to get beaten'*

Usain Bolt

ABOUT four weeks after getting back from Monte Carlo, it was Gemma's 30th birthday and I'd organised a surprise party at the Saints ground, Langtree Park. I'd planted the seed months before and told her that we'd been invited by the board of directors and that it would be a quiet evening dinner there.

That camp away in South Africa helped massively in arranging it because I was able to talk and plan it with our family and all her friends, without her knowing I was talking to them. How I pulled it off I'll never know, because Gemma is the most inquisitive person you could meet.

After dropping the kids off at my mum's earlier in the day, I'd given strict instructions to everyone to park their cars around the corner from the main entrance, so Gemma wouldn't suspect anything. I'd booked the hotel just near Langtree Park, so we went in and picked the key up and then headed to the stadium.

As we pulled up, I saw our Danny's car right in front of us and I thought, 'Shit!' and put my arm around Gemma and walked her quickly to the entrance without trying to make it too obvious. Once the car was out of sight, I started texting everyone to let them know we were coming up.

She was dead nervous going in for this quiet dinner but she didn't realise I had a DJ, singer and loads of people waiting for her. She was a bit hesitant walking in because everything was dead silent, then as she walked in everyone came out and shouted, 'Surprise!' Her face was a picture.

To carry the party on, we headed to The Imperial nightclub in St Helens, had a few more, then in the early hours we headed back to the hotel. We got to the room and Gemma says in a panic, 'Martin. There's people in the bed. What's going on here?' She wasn't wrong. There was this lad in bed with this bird and they were bang at it.

You'd think this lad would have been surprised but he turned around all happy, turned to his bird and says, 'It's Martin Murray!' He grabs a sheet, covers himself up and says, 'Can I have a picture?' 'Yeah, yeah mate,' I says. I asked Gemma to take it and that was that.

Turns out the hotel had double-booked the room.

The laughs didn't finish there. My father-in-law Pete had also stayed at the hotel with us but had left his car parked at the Saints ground. The day after was the St Helens 10k, with benefits going to The Steve Prescott Foundation. Martin Blondel had told us where to park our cars, just to make sure we didn't obstruct the course. Well, when I woke up in the morning, I noticed loads of missed calls from Martin. Pete had only gone and parked his car on the starting line of the 10k race. Because they couldn't get hold of any of us, they ended up having to move the starting line.

Unfortunately, all the laughs from Gemma's party weren't enough to keep my spirits up after the Golovkin fight. A couple of weeks after the birthday celebrations, we went to see Gemma's brother Anthony and his wife Sabine, who lived in Abu Dhabi. Anthony had come over for Gemma's birthday, so it was nice to be able to go and see him and his wife over his side. We spent four days there and then another four in Dubai. From the get-go, me and Gemma started arguing a lot and it was all down to me.

In the past, I'd be drinking after a fight to have a bit of a laugh and enjoy passing the time with good friends. This time round, I was drinking to get absolutely hammered. The last time I'd drunk like that was when I had my flat in Peasley Cross. What I didn't realise, or perhaps didn't want to admit to myself, was that I was depressed.

I'd been occasionally depressed when I was working in Malia but for different reasons. Back then, I felt low sometimes because I knew the future held nothing for me. Some nights I'd finish work and I'd be walking around drinking to the point of unconsciousness. This time, depression had kind of been forced on me because of the result of the fight, but I had that empty feeling again. I kept saying, 'It is what it is,' instead of trying to look for a way to get through it.

From Gemma's perspective, it must have looked like she had married two different people. There was one version who sat at home, not speaking, out of shape, totally unmotivated and another who was down, but wanted to party all the time. Gemma did her best to motivate me and be understanding, but it didn't work. I was throwing her support back and getting her upset.

People always say about depression, 'It's OK to talk,' but in my case, I didn't know I was depressed at the time. Whenever Gemma did try to get me to speak, I was really snappy or I'd walk away. She said on a number of occasions, 'There's something wrong,' but I'd dismiss it each time.

The turning point came after a three-day bender. I decided to go to Merthyr for the weekend for a session with the lads. Me, Dean, Brownie, my dad and a group of other mates from St Helens all went. We got down there on the Saturday and had a good night. We woke up Sunday morning at the hotel and by 10am we were on the Jagerbombs.

On Sunday evening, we were getting ready to head back home. We got a taxi to Abergavenny train station and had a few drinks at the local there. It's a pretty quiet pub usually but we had a docking station and started blaring music out of it.

We were supposed to be getting the 4pm train but I said to everyone, 'Let's have a few more.' We then missed the 5pm train and only just caught the last train, which was indirect to Warrington. Out came the docking station again and the ale. I'm sure we pissed off quite a few people in our carriage. Then, as we were getting close to Warrington, Brownie says, 'Let's stay on to Manchester.'

We all got off the train then, without anyone noticing, me and Brownie jumped back on. Dean was there on the platform looking around for us when we've suddenly banged on the window, laughing and waving bye to everyone as the train pulled off. They looked at us bemused shaking their heads. Next stop, Manchester.

When we arrived, we booked into a hotel in Deansgate and went out to the local bars. We were in a bit of a mess by this stage. Loads of people kept coming up to me asking about the fight. Even though I wasn't at my best, I tried to remain polite. After a while I'd had enough, so we went back to the hotel.

When I woke up on Monday morning, first thing I thought was, 'What have I done? You're in shit street with Gemma.' I knew I'd really taken the piss out of her and I felt like I'd let myself down. I'd managed to get used to living a new way in life, then resorted to my old ways. Massive step back.

I called Dean up. He answers, 'Alright mate. Where are you?'

'I'm still here in Manchester. I'm feeling rough.'

'Fucking hell, Mart. Get yourself home.'

'I'll have some brekkie, then I'll head back.'

'Good lad.'

The problem now was that I was in my own little world. I knew I was doing wrong but couldn't get to grips with myself. Instead, there I was with Brownie having a pint of Magners for breakfast contemplating what to do. One pint led to two, then two became an all-day session.

We left the hotel and went up and down all the bars of Deansgate again. Later that evening, I called Gemma saying I'd be back soon. When I got home, I was expecting to get a right bollocking from Gemma, but the house was empty. She'd gone to her mum's with the kids and decided to sleep there. I gave her a quick call and said we'd catch up properly in the morning.

The night went from bad to worse. I ended up having a few more drinks on my own at the house, getting more depressed, trying to block everything out with alcohol. That Tuesday morning, I woke up and the realisation of what I'd done hit me like a steam train. I knew I needed to drive over to Gemma immediately to apologise, but more than anything just to show my face.

I got to Liz and Pete's, and saw Gemma, who wasn't best pleased to see me. She told me to take the kids to the park, whereas selfishly, all I wanted to do was lie down and sleep off my hangover. After taking them to the park, I returned to an empty house, while Gemma stayed at her mum's again. Bad times.

The day after, Andy came over to see me and brought me some dinner. He also gave me a massive bollocking. 'Where have you been? What are you up to, lad? You're a family man. You can't behave like this.' I didn't want to listen to what Andy had to tell me, so I went on the defensive and said, 'Don't start burning my head out. I don't need this shit. When's my next fight? How much will I get? I need to be in big fights.' Andy lost it. This was the second time I'd ever seen him do so.

'Who are you? Seriously. Because I don't recognise the person in front of me. You're going on like you're Floyd Mayweather Jr and Muhammad Ali rolled into one. Sort your head out.' I bowed my head down. Andy carried on, 'You're Martin Murray and you've just got beat by the best fighter in the world. Now you need to get a grip of yourself and stop acting like a dickhead. I understand why you're down but you've got a family to consider here. You've got responsibilities as a father and a husband. I'll stand by you through anything but when what you are doing is wrong, I won't.'

Andy's a top mate but he's also someone I look up to and listen to. When he bollocks you with a verbal slap like that, you listen. Boxers need agents, managers and promoters to get them the deals but when they need them most is when they hit the bottom. I'll never forget Andy for coming round and speaking to me the way he did that day, and for being the friend he is.

Gemma was still staying round at her mum's with the kids and I was at the house on my own. I started to fill out NHS surveys online about depression. At the end of the survey, it suggested I went to visit my doctor because I was officially depressed. The thoughts going through my head that night were horrible. Suicide thoughts and everything. I'm not saying there was any substance in what I was thinking, because I'd never do that to Gemma and the kids. I love them too much and love the life I have with them.

My main focus in life had always been about being a good husband and father, and I'd let myself and my family down on both counts. For the last couple of months, between going away to South Africa and then coming back and going on a bender, I hadn't been there for them.

I used this experience as a wake-up call, to be that better husband and dad and to get back into my training. It took me a couple of months to move on from the depression but I'll be honest when I say a bit of the depression from the Golovkin fight stayed in my system long term. It turned out to be a positive, though. I've learned never to let myself ever get in that state again.

Thankfully, I had something to take my mind off things. A new fight in the diary. The training camp helped me to sort out my priorities. Boxing's always had a way of doing that throughout my life, giving me that essential focus. I was now ready to jump back in the ring and show that I was still able to mix it with the best.

# CHAPTER 42

# KING ARTHUR

*'Competing in sports has taught me that if I'm not
willing to give 120 per cent, somebody else will'*

Ron Blomberg

AFTER the Golovkin fight, the idea was to re-sign with Rodney.
The problem was I wanted to be fighting more at home now
and Rodney couldn't provide that from Johannesburg.

I sent him an e-mail thanking him for looking after me and
delivering everything he said he would. He sent me a really nice reply
saying that he completely understood and not to hesitate if he could
be of any help in the future. Class. The way I parted company with
Rodney was different to any promoter I'd ever worked with. I'm not
having a go at the others but with him it was faultless.

After weighing up the options, we ended up going with Matchroom.
The first fight with them was on 26 June 2015, against Giorgi
Beroshvili. Although it wasn't top of the bill, the big attraction of the
fight for me was the location.

From the first show I saw at the Echo Arena in Liverpool, I knew I
wanted to fight there. I'd been to see the likes of Tony Dodson, Tony
Quigley, Bellew, Pricey, Smigga and always loved the reception the
Liverpool fight fans give their home fighters. So I was over the moon
to be joining that list of names. This would also be my first fight at
super-middleweight.

The Beroshvili fight turned out to be a quick night's work as I
stopped him in the second round. I was fully aware this wasn't world-

class opposition but it was good to get back to winning ways and to start looking again at the bigger picture.

Knowing I'd hardly broken a sweat and wanting to keep me active, Matchroom sorted me with another fight three weeks later. I was up against Mirzet Bajrektarevic, who was a big lump. He'd fought at light-heavyweight his whole career and was the Croatian champion. I went to work on him from the first bell. Despite taking the shots well, by round four he was wilting. In round five, the ref stepped in, which at the time I thought was a bit too early. I was looking to get a definitive end to the fight but when I looked at it the day after, I realised the ref had made the right decision, as Bajrektarevic didn't need to take any further unnecessary punishment.

Jose Miguel Torres was my next opponent six weeks later, on 5 September 2015. He'd fought David Lemieux at middle a couple of years earlier and was stopped in seven rounds, so he'd been in with good company. I knew Torres could punch a bit, but he'd come up from light-middleweight, so I knew I was going to be too big for him.

It turned out to be the weirdest fight I've ever been involved in. I don't know if it was the right hand I put him down with that knocked his senses, but he was like a yo-yo. He dropped to the canvas so many times it became a joke. I even turned to the ref at one point and said, 'I've not even touched him.' It was eventually stopped in the fifth.

The biggest positive about the fight was that it moved me up the WBA rankings as it was for their intercontinental belt. Before the Torres fight, we kind of knew that a fight against Arthur Abraham for his WBO world super-middleweight title was a possibility. However, we were also realistic and didn't think I'd get another world title shot so quickly.

Soon after the Torres fight, negotiations started with Abraham's team. It was on, then off, then on. An agreement was finally reached and a date was set. We were hoping it would be in 2016 to give me a bit more time for the training camp, but we took the gamble and agreed to take it on with seven weeks' notice. I knew the risks I'd be taking fighting in Germany, but I wasn't arsed about travelling to the champion's backyard, as I'd been there, done that. A couple of weeks after signing contracts, we flew over for the press conference in Germany and thought it was going to be like the Felix Sturm show with the whole promotional video thing, but he was totally different. Abraham was just a regular guy with a small team around him and no fuss. We were in and out in a day.

Five days before fight night, we flew back out there. I was calmer than I'd been for any title fight before but still aware that Abraham was no mug. We knew he would be very strong but that he would give rounds away and then come on with his best work for the last 20 seconds to impress the judges. When you're up against the home fighter, especially in Germany, you don't get judged on how well you do and how much you do, it's always about the home fighter getting judged on what he does, no matter how little that is.

The fight went as predicted. He was like a massive tough sponge, who easily looked like a cruiserweight on the night. He'd soak, soak, soak it all up, then bang, he'd release big, thudding, wild swings. One thing he was deceptively good at was with his little lean and stepbacks, which he doesn't get much credit for. It was hard to catch him cleanly. I did rock him in round eight but couldn't nail him as he kept tying me up.

The fight went the distance and when it came to the scorecards I thought I'd done the better and busier work. Unfortunately, it didn't go my way. It's easy for me to say because I have a biased opinion but I thought the judge who scored it 115-112 to me had it spot on. If I look back, there's things I would have done differently. I held on more than I needed to, which definitely went against me, but I thought I was the classier fighter and produced the more eye-catching work.

With Christmas coming up, I took a well-earned break and looked forward to what 2016 had in store.

CHAPTER 43

# A VALUABLE LESSON

*'He's natural. So grounded. He doesn't focus on what
they can't do, he looks at what they can do and helps
them out. Our kids have got a lot to offer but many
people don't see that. Martin does. He's such a role
model and he's one of us, from St Helens'*

Peter Eden,
Head of PE, Mill Green School, June 2016

IF it wasn't for the people of St Helens, I would never have got as far as I have in boxing. Chizzy, my friends and family, the Barmy Army, they've all played their part.

Since turning professional, I've been very lucky to be in a position where I can help improve the profile of St Helens, through sharing some of my past mistakes and helping to spread the word about the benefits of boxing. However, in 2014, I was asked to go to a place that I instinctively knew I'd have a bond with for life.

Marie Cunliffe, who was at our school, in Danny's year, was married to one of my old school mates Dave. Years later, it turns out Marie was a teacher at Mill Green, which is a school for pupils with a wide spectrum of special needs. Mill Green provides them with incredible support and opportunities, which positively impact their lives. We need more schools like this.

When Marie asked if I'd do the official opening of the school on 11 December 2014, I was honoured and agreed straight away. Me and

Andy went down not knowing what to expect but were absolutely blown away. When we walked into assembly, I thought it might be a case of take your chair, sit down, say a few hellos and sign some stuff. Far from it. The reception we received was unbelievably humbling.

When I was in Monte Carlo, a couple of days before the Golovkin fight, one of my mates brought me over this big parcel of stuff which I'll never forget. The kids from the school had hand-made me a stack of cards, wishing me luck. When I opened the parcel, I was absolutely made up. I was just imagining them making them and the effort they put in.

I went back to do a boxing session with them a few months later. Bit of pad work, that sort of thing. What we didn't realise is that during the week, the teachers had been telling the kids about my boxing in the classroom and it turned out a lot of them were big into their sport. They'd jumped on to Google and started looking at pictures and videos of me, and were asking the teachers all kinds of questions. When I walked in, they were really excited and couldn't wait to get cracking.

The enjoyment you could see in each and every one of their faces was brilliant. Some kids were able to punch on their own and others needed the teachers to hold their arms and do the punching with them. Some of the students who were in wheelchairs were very limited both physically and mentally, but we managed to involve them all. One of the kids was in her wheelchair and we brought one of my championship belts over for her to feel, for the sensory benefits. The smile on her face as the teacher helped her run her hand over the crest of the belt was something else.

I don't know how long the experience lasts in each student's memory but it's there for that moment in time. Whether anyone remembers me or not, that's not important. What's valuable is providing quality time for them when I am there. Creating a new smile and some positive new memories is what it's all about.

\* \* \* \* \*

Fast forward to 2016. After the Abraham fight, I had a couple of months off, then fought and stopped Cedric Spera in two rounds on 7 May. Around that time, I had confirmation that I'd be fighting George

Groves for the WBA international super-middleweight title on 25 June 2016 at the O2 Arena. The fight was a world title eliminator.

Eight days before the Groves fight, I went down to Mill Green. I probably should have been in the gym or resting but the truth is, no amount of padwork, sparring or running could provide me with the inspiration or motivation I came away with that day.

At the time, Sky and Matchroom wanted to do a bit of promo for the Groves fight and I told them I was at Mill Green and suggested they come up and do the filming at the school. The kids loved seeing the big cameras around and the crew from Matchroom and Sky made a right fuss of them.

I was only supposed to be there for a short while and do a bit of padwork with a few of the students, but I ended up staying for hours. I made sure every student from every class had a go. I was absolutely dripping in sweat by the time I was finished and can't describe the buzz I had from interacting with all the students. I then did a presentation at the end as it was sports week and handed out prizes.

The cherry on the cake is that the school recently became a registered charity and in January 2017, they asked me to became an ambassador. I obviously accepted straight away. What an honour.

CHAPTER 44

# RUNNING ON EMPTY

*'You've been spitting greenies in the bucket in sparring
for a couple of weeks now. You don't need me telling
you that isn't right. Call the fight off'*

Oliver Harrison talking to Martin
a couple of weeks before the Groves fight

THE day at Mill Green was unbelievable, but unfortunately things behind the scenes on the boxing front were far from that. The training camp for Groves kind of went in two parts. Healthy up to 1 June 2016 and not so good from there on. After the Abraham fight, I went to Cancún with Gemma and the kids in early January, then I trained up until Spera in May and then straight through to the Groves fight. I should have taken a few weeks off.

Up to 1 June, the training camp was flying. The problem was I'd peaked and still had three and a half weeks of sparring and training ahead of me. I was absolutely drained. Ten days later, after taking a set of antibiotics and a stack of different vitamins, I was still feeling like shit. Every day I was having a hot toddy before going to sleep. Lemsip, a little bit of Jack Daniel's, hot water and some chopped-up fruits.

I kept telling Oliver it would be OK but the Wednesday before the fight I started another set of antibiotics as it was the worst I'd been during the whole camp. The problem with those antibiotics is that they retain water, which is not great when trying to make weight. Nothing was coming together the way it should have been but I kept telling myself, 'Don't worry, you'll be alright on the night.'

The morning of the weigh-in, I was in and out of the sauna checking my weight and my head was pounding badly. The idea was to get bang on the weight on my scales and then walk to the weigh-in, which would take about half an hour. That in theory would then put me a bit under the weight.

The problem was that it took forever to get rid of the weight and in the end the guys at Matchroom had to take me round in a van, otherwise I wouldn't have made it in time. When I arrived at Covent Garden, I was a bit over when I jumped on the scales. I ended up going round the corner and getting a bit of a sweat on going through a few moves with Oliver, then came back and weighed bang on the 12 stone limit.

After some food, I went back to the hotel, took a Lemsip and had a banging headache right through to the morning. It was purely down to dehydration. When I woke up, I had another Lemsip and some breakfast. Usually I'm champing at the bit in the morning but I was flat with no energy. I still went in with the mentality of 'It's worktime, let's get the job done,' but there was only so much I could bring to the table. Come fight night, my range, timing and distance weren't there, and I had no snap in my shots. First five or six rounds, I didn't do enough. A lot of people thought Groves, like Abraham, would be too big for me, but it had nothing to do with his size. The difference between him and Abraham was that Groves could box really well and had a good straight right, but I still stuck in there.

I was having a good round nine and was getting back in the fight when, in the dying seconds, he caught me with a big right hand that went through my guard. After the bell went, I fell into the corner and couldn't feel my legs. Oliver and Frank Hopkins tried to pull me out of the fight and I said, 'No way.' 'You've got one round,' Oliver replied.

I stood up, getting ready for the tenth round, and I could feel my legs still tingling. Next second, I heard David Haye shouting from ringside, 'Get straight back on him, George. He's still buzzed.' I'm thinking, 'Shut the fuck up, ye prick!'

I went there and nearly spun the fight on its head in that round. I had Groves up against the ropes and caught him with an overhand right, which buzzed him and had him holding on. The last two rounds were a free for all, but in all honesty, with my energy levels, it's amazing that I heard the final bell. I lost 118-110 on all cards.

After the fight, it was the same old routine. Piss test, then take a sleeper. As always, I couldn't sleep. I woke up in the morning and went for a few drinks with Gemma and my mates around Covent Garden, then got the train home and had a few more back at the house.

I went to bed at around two in the morning, then not long after and with absolutely no warning, I woke up and started vomiting profusely in bed. I'm talking projectile. The worst part was, as I was running to the toilet still vomiting, it went over Gemma's face. It was that bad I had to put a new carpet in.

Five days after the fight, I hadn't been able to shake what was basically a permanent headache. I'd been taking paracetamol every day thinking, 'It'll get better tomorrow,' but it didn't. In the end, thanks to Brooksi, I got a brain scan done almost instantly. The doc at the hospital said there was no damage to the brain but I was concussed, which I'd have never known.

I always like to take a positive out of a negative and the positive from this is that everyone thought I was past my best and that I was finished. Admittedly, that performance didn't do me any favours but it can't have been that bad, because I was still ranked in the top ten super-middleweights in the world by *Boxing News* right the way through into 2017.

But where would I go from here?

All I can say is, fair play to Matchroom and to the team at MGM management (now MTK), especially Daniel, Anto and Matt for getting me a big fight after Groves. My old opponent from exactly one year earlier, Arthur Abraham. This was a fight I wanted badly. It was unfinished business. I felt I did enough to win the last time and would now have the chance to prove that. With the fight being in Monte Carlo, I knew that I would get a fairer shake from the judges than fighting in his backyard of Germany, but I also instinctively knew I had the beating of him this time round.

This would be a final eliminator, which put me next in line for Gilberto Ramirez, to challenge for the WBO world super-middleweight title. I was buzzing. The date was set for 12 November and the camp was going well. That was until Abraham pulled out due to injury.

Minutes later, it was all over social media saying who his next opponent was. Call me pessimistic if you like but I don't think he wanted to fight me. Thankfully, Dmitry Chudinov stepped in.

This camp especially had a nice twist to it as my good friend and old sparring partner Jamie Moore was brought in to help. I've always spoken with Jamie for years about my fights and he's always given me great logical feedback.

Forty-eight hours before the fight, we got dealt another blow. Thursday morning, Andy pulled up to the house to take me to Monte Carlo.

'Y'alright mate,' I said.

'You're not gonna be in a minute,' he replied.

'What d'ya mean?'

'Chudinov pulled out last night.'

The second he told me, it was like something popped. Like all the enthusiasm was drained from me. As daft as it sounds, I was more up for Chudinov than Abraham, because I thought it would be a harder fight. When I found out the replacement would be Nuhu Lawal, who came with an unbeaten record but no real form, the buzz had gone. It would be for the vacant WBA continental super-middleweight title, but not a world title final eliminator.

I won the fight by a wide points decision but I felt like I was in a bigger tussle against the referee, who was letting Lawal get away with murder and was on my case throughout the whole fight. It wasn't my best performance and wouldn't have been as good as a win against Chudinov or Abraham, but I was happy that I won. By not losing, it meant that the big fights were still a possibility.

I gave the WBA belt to Andy as a small token of my appreciation for everything he'd done for me in boxing. It was the very least I could do.

After the fight, one of the journalists told me that no other British fighter had ever fought in Monte Carlo as many times as me. At least that's one title I've got that nobody else has!

\* \* \* \* \*

Thankfully, 2016 ended on a high note and it had nothing to do with boxing.

Getting motivated for fights is not easy but when it comes to my kids' achievements, I'm instantly inspired. In 2016, Amelia started going to gymnastics and to be honest she wasn't very good at it, but we kept telling her 'With practice, you'll get better.' She always worked hard in training and slowly started to improve. Later that year, she did this competition for the vault. The whole family were there and obviously we cheered her on like mad. For us and her, it was never about getting a medal but showing how much she had improved in just a few months, simply by putting her mind to it.

After the competition was done, they did the awards ceremony. When they read out who had come in third, then second, you could see she'd kind of given up hope of getting a prize, then next thing they said, 'First place, Amelia Murray.' I'll never forget the look on her face. She was genuinely surprised to have won. She didn't boast or make a fuss, which was a change to the usual. It was as if she'd recognised that determination and persistence does get you results and she's never lost that mindset. God help her if she ever laces up a pair of gloves. In fact, God help any of her opponents.

CHAPTER 45

# RAY OF LIGHT

*'Injury makes the comeback sweeter'*

www.debruns.com

AFTER a nice holiday over Christmas, I was straight back into training. I kind of had a feeling that a big fight might be around the corner and a few weeks later, towards the end of January, I was asked if I'd like to fight Gabriel Rosado on 22 April 2017, headlining at the Echo Arena, Liverpool. We'd be fighting for the WBA intercontinental middleweight title, which I'd previously won in 2010, then won again at super-middle in 2015. I didn't really care about the belt and in all honesty only found out about it the day before the fight. In fact, I'd made quite a big thing in the build-up that me and him, from our reputations, could sell a fight without anything on the line. So the belt was almost irrelevant.

I'd always liked Rosado's style and respected his toughness, but I'd always felt where I've been unlucky in world title fights, he'd always come up short. The training camp went really well and the only adjustment I had to make for this fight was to drop back down to middleweight. The main reason I'd moved up to super-middle in the first place was because of the opportunities available at the time. Almost two years later, the better opportunities for good fights were back again at middleweight.

Come fight night, Rosado was expecting me to stand in front of him and let my hands go, and he'd do the same. In all fairness, in the build-up we'd dressed the fight up to be a big war. I knew I'd never get caught up with something like that but it wouldn't have helped the promotion if I'd have said during the press conferences, 'Well actually, it's not going to be a war,' because you want people to come to the fight. However, Rosado bought into that.

In terms of the fight, you can never knock Rosado for his toughness but I always knew I was a better boxer and better all-round fighter. Rosado wanted a war but he was never good enough to take me into the trenches and get that. I proved that on the night as I felt I was always a step ahead of him. He was quite slow on his feet and predictable. About round six, when he knew he was far behind, plodding forward, he said, 'Come on. Let's have this war, bitch.' I laughed as I picked him off, and said, 'This is too easy. No need for a war.'

He had a good push the last couple of rounds but it was too little too late. The biggest drama came after the fight. Rosado knew he got beat but what he wasn't happy with was the 119-109 score, which obviously wasn't fair. But on the flipside, it was never a draw. The score of 116-112 was about right.

Anyway, he starts shouting at Eddie Hearn over the ropes, 'This is bullshit.' I've said, 'What ya mouthing off at?' I turned to his trainer and said, 'You don't seriously think he won that fight, do you?' The trainer turned and with no conviction in his voice said, 'Yeah.' 'You're fucking on glue, mate,' I said, with a thick St Helens accent. I don't think he understood.

Next thing Rosado was in front of me and it got heated for a second. Nothing happened but it was close I'm glad nothing kicked off because I had our Archie in the ring with me while that was going on. Fighting Rosado, winning titles, nice purses, it's all great, but having him in the ring was priceless. We're like best mates and I know how proud he is of me, but that night the look on his face said it all. The second the decision was announced, I went up to him and we hugged each other straight away.

I'm creating positive memories for him that he'll never, ever forget. In 20 or 40 years' time, he'll be showing his kids and grandkids them photos, looking back on that moment. You can't put a value on that. Another thing you can't put a price on is your health and throughout the Rosado training camp, our Aisla showed she's a champion in her own right by coming through a very tough journey. From a young age, we had a suspicion that something wasn't right with the way she was walking. The health visitor should have picked up on it but never did. Aisla didn't start walking until she was nearly 15 months old, whereas our Arch and Amelia started at ten and 12 months respectively. But when she did start to walk, she had this little waddle.

As she got older and her body started developing, we used to joke and say she had a big booty. But it wasn't that, it was because her thigh bone had fused to the side of her hip bone, instead of being inside the socket. But at this stage, we didn't know that. Aisla had always complained about her legs being tired but we used to think it was her way of blagging to get carried by me or Gemma. One day we took her to the GP and like the health visitor, he basically said that everything was fine. The only person who did pick up on it was her gymnastics teacher, who realised that she couldn't raise her legs too high.

We ended up going back to the GP in January 2017 and he said he'd sort a scan date. After waiting for a few weeks, I thought, 'Fuck this. I'm taking her private.' I phoned my mate, Doug Jones, one of my old physios, and explained the situation to him. He spoke to a paediatrician, who recommended a hip surgeon called Dr Farhan Ali, at The Alexandra Hospital, who's one of the best in his field.

We went up to see him and straight away he got her to walk up and down and he said, 'I think she's got dislocated hips (commonly known as 'Clicky hip') but I need to do a scan. If it is, then we need to operate ASAP.' The reason being is that the cut-off age to have this op done is four and she was only a few off months off that. We just made it.

The first op was on 3 March 2017. We had a chat with her to prepare her but obviously you've got to put a positive spin on the reason why she's going in to hospital, as she was only a three-year-old girl. 'You know why you always get tired legs? Well, this operation will sort all that out. You're going to go to this nice hospital, with a nice bed and the nurses are lovely. You're going to have a needle, then you're going to go to sleep and when you wake up and everything's been done. Your leg will be in a big plaster for a few weeks, then it will get better. Then we'll get your other one done and once your legs are completely better, you'll be able to run faster than Amelia and Archie. They won't be able to catch you, like they can now.'

What an absolute trooper. Obviously, on social media, you only put up all the happy bits of her recovery, but after the first op she was bad for a week in hospital and then bad for a week at home. Me and Gemma were heartbroken. The colour of her, seeing her in pain, it was horrible. After that second week passed, she was brilliant. She had her right leg in plaster and her good left leg out and she was starting to crawl, then balancing, then walking.

She had the other leg done on 19 April, only three days before the Rosado fight. Unbelievably, when we were driving her home after the op, we got a call from the NHS to say, 'Aisla was due in for a scan today.' 'Are you joking? She's already had her second operation,' I replied. This was the appointment we'd been waiting for since January.

The only thing we didn't anticipate was that whichever leg was in plaster wasn't getting used and became really weak. As a result, she had muscle wastage, looked dead scrawny and her appetite went. Thankfully, by the end of May, when we picked her up, she wasn't making pain faces and she'd get herself down off the couch and crawl again. To have to go through it once was bad enough but back to back, she's shown serious guts. Our little hero.

Incredibly, a year later, she's now taken up taekwondo, which has improved her core, flexibility, balance and strength. If that wasn't enough, she recently took part in The Lantern Walk and raised a couple of grand. As a family, we're buzzing with how she is now and it's hard to look back and see how she was a year before.

We'd just like to say a special thank you to Dr Farhan Ali. What an absolute legend of a man. We can't thank him enough for fixing our little girl.

# CHAPTER 46

# HERE WE GO AGAIN

*I don't know where I'm goin'*
*But I sure know where I've been*
*Hanging on the promises in songs of yesterday*
*An' I've made up my mind,*
*I ain't wasting no more time*

Whitesnake

AFTER the Rosado fight, we were trying to weigh up where I would go from here. I was with Matchroom and knew they'd just signed Daniel Jacobs and thought that's a fight that could happen. We'd fought twice in the amateurs, so I thought maybe that could now be an option for us as professionals. Nothing came of it, though.

I'd booked a holiday away with the family to Cyprus and just before we went away, everybody was going on about Julio Cesar Chavez Jr. He put a post out on Twitter about fighting me, then he messaged me and I replied back. I was thinking the fight could happen in Mexico, where there would be no visa problems and it would be a big draw. But again, it didn't come to fruition.

So there I was a couple of weeks into the holiday in Cyprus thinking about who I might fight next, when I had a chat with MTK, my management company. They asked if I fancied going in as a reserve for the World Boxing Super Series (WBSS) super-middleweight tournament. I agreed to it. Erik Skoglund and Callum

Smith were headlining the tournament, and if either of them pulled out, I'd be in.

When I got back from Cyprus in August, I knew I'd only have a four-week training camp and was straight in the gym. However, the set-up was different for this. Jamie took charge of my training.

Here's what happened. Jamie was officially on board from the Nawal fight in 2016, but Oliver was still in charge. However, not long after the Rosado fight, he fell ill. Twice we went to see him at Tameside Hospital to say our goodbyes to him. It was heartbreaking. But thankfully, he hung in there and pulled through over the coming months.

Jamie now stepped in to train me. I'd been working with him at Oliver's from when I turned pro and always respected his opinion in boxing, so it was a natural progression.

I basically did the last four weeks of a normal eight-week training camp and jumped in feet first. I'd always over-trained in long camps and it turned out that going into this fight a little 'underdone' worked in my favour.

Both Smith and Skoglund made the weight and, in the end, I fought Arman Torosyan on the undercard back at the Echo Arena, Liverpool on 16 September 2017. We looked at his fights and knew that the German could be a potential banana skin, as he'd only lost three fights and stopped 15 of his 18 opponents.

We trained accordingly for someone of his style and although I didn't have an eight-week training camp, I entered the ring in good shape. The bout was scheduled for eight rounds, but in the end I stopped him in four.

Oliver thankfully came out of hospital a few weeks after the fight, but was still very fragile, so Jamie carried on as my full-time trainer. We still did a session once a week at Oliver's practising technique and going through various drills, but Jamie was now in charge.

I didn't know this at the time, but Jamie was actually getting ready to retire from being a trainer. His intention was to pull away after Tommy Coyle decided to stop fighting. Then when Oliver got sick, I went with Jamie and became the second fighter he was training. Rocky and Stevie Ward then asked where I was going to train because they'd also been trained by Oliver. I explained why I was going with Jamie. They came down for a session to see if they liked it and the rest is history.

Within a couple of weeks, Carl Frampton and Conrad Cummings came on board. Then Jack Catterall, a few months later. I was absolutely buzzing for Jamie. He's one of the nicest and most positive guys you could ever meet, speaks sense and I genuinely believe he will go on to be a great trainer for years to come.

I also need to give Nigel Travis a big mention. When I started my boxing career, training at Oliver's in 2007, Nige was fighting professionally and we had a few spars. He's a cracking guy and I've always got on with him. Even when he retired, time allowing, I've always tried to attend his amateur boxing shows at Moss Side Fire Station Boxing Club, where he's the head trainer. He's just a lovely guy who always brings top banter with him. When he walks into the gym, he's like a band leader. You're guaranteed he'll get everyone happy, buzzing and ready to get stuck into training.

Apart from my amateur days, I'd never really experienced the camaraderie and banter in a group as a professional. As a result, at times, I became a lonely, depressed fighter. Now with Jamie and Nigel, everyone had a permanent smile on their face.

The overall set-up was incredible and couldn't have come at a more perfect time for me in my career. It was a new environment for me, but with old faces. Jamie, Nigel and a great bunch of lads to bounce off. We go to each other's fights and motivate one another during training. My enthusiasm for boxing was right back up there. As the old boxing saying goes, a happy fighter is a dangerous fighter.

\* \* \* \* \*

Three months after the Torosyan fight, I got the news that I was waiting to hear: a fight against Billy Joe Saunders for his WBO world middleweight title. We had hoped to fight him before Lemieux, but it never happened. We were told that if Saunders came through against the Canadian, I'd be in line to fight him as a voluntary defence.

I was now promoted by Frank Warren and a few weeks after the Lemieux fight, shortly after Christmas, we'd been told the fight would take place on 14 April 2018. I was absolutely buzzing. Just want to say a big thank you to Eddie Hearn and the awesome team at Matchroom. We parted on good terms and I'm very grateful for everything they did for me as a promotional outfit.

When I went to South Africa to prepare for the Golovkin fight, it was really hard to leave my family behind, because I was away for a number of weeks and it felt like I was on the other side of the world – which I was! This time, I was off to Tenerife for two weeks, but it was different. Even though it's a four-hour flight, you still feel you're in touch with the real world. If something happens, bang, you can get on a flight and be back home before you know it.

The other thing was that I genuinely enjoyed myself out there, whereas South Africa was at times a miserable training camp. I also didn't understand the science of altitude training back then. I just went there all guns blazing. This time, I knew more and was looking forward to going over with a top bunch of lads, staying at this fancy villa. In all honesty, it could have ended up going really wrong, but it ended up being right. I refer to it as a holiday because it was literally that much fun, but it was also the most productive training camp I'd ever been on.

There was me, Dean, Tommy, plus Carl, Stevie, Conrad, who I nicknamed the Irish Kenyans. When we got there, they said, 'Do you fancy going for a wee trot?' To me, that meant going for a plod, a slow run. Fuck me. Their 'wee trot' was like shit off a shovel. We started and, bang, they were gone. All five of us did the run up Mount Teide, but me and Dean just did 'my' plod as I didn't want the altitude to mess me up.

Having run at altitude before, I knew it could affect you a few days later and thought it might do that with the Irish Kenyans. Not to be. They absolutely smashed it. They're big runners. Stevie Ward for a big lad can really run. Frampton is an all-round quality athlete and Conrad can definitely run a bit as well.

The mix of characters worked brilliantly and everybody had the craic. Tommy is always up for a laugh, Stevie is known as the quiet man, but he's a funny fucker. Frampton is hilarious. Really dry sense of humour and quick-witted. Conrad, again, funny as fuck, whereas Jack Catterall was dead chilled out and a top lad.

First day, we set the tone for the holiday. What happened was, we'd all gone to the supermarket to do a little shop and I had no t-shirt on. You couldn't go into the supermarket without a top, so Tommy says, 'Go on, Mart. Get in my t-shirt with me.' Up and under I goes, with my arms hanging out alongside Tommy's, standing in front of him.

Nige is murder for kegging (whipping your underpants down) and next thing, without me knowing, he'd whipped Tommy's pants down. All I could feel and hear was Tommy panicking and then you could hear loads of slapping. That's when I realised they were slapping his arse and he had no pants on. I was laughing like mad, but then thought, 'His dick is on me!' I was throwing him about like a bucking bronco, trying to get him off, while thinking, 'They're going to keg me next. They're going to get my pants down!'

We knew Saunders was a very slick southpaw. We looked at the things he did when he threw shots, which way he was turning, what he did when he was under pressure. We also knew he was coming off a career-best win against Lemieux, but I thought that performance flattered him. Lemieux is not the best boxer, he's a puncher. Rosado took a bit of a beating against him in their fight and was stopped with a badly swollen eye. But up to that point, he was outboxing Lemieux. I'd fought Rosado and didn't think he was the greatest boxer, either. I found him quite slow and predictable in moving his feet. Going in against Saunders, he knew I was no Lemieux. I had more to bring to the table and was a far more dangerous fight.

We started working on tactics, using educated pressure in certain rounds. How to make him turn into shots, then land our own little counters, that sort of thing. The only thing we didn't do out in Tenerife was sparring, because that was planned for when we got back.

Soon after coming home in March, we received some bad news. We got back on the Wednesday and on the Saturday, I went for a run. I came back content, the sun was shining, I was in the best shape of my life and couldn't wait to fight Saunders. Then I got a phone call off Jamie. 'You alright?' I says. 'No. He's only gone and pulled out, hasn't he,' he replies. 'You're fucking joking,' I said. 'No, no.' Then there was a few seconds' silence as we both didn't know what to say. I was gutted, but part of me wasn't surprised that he'd pulled out. There was nothing I could do.

Billy Joe messaged me and apologised and said we'll definitely do it on 23 June. I accepted it and hoped he was a man of his word.

The problem now was that the new date was almost three months away. I'd been flying in training, peaking, then the fight was scratched. Mentally, I found it difficult to unwind as I wanted to fight, but I knew I needed to take some time off. I ticked over with some strength and conditioning, once, maybe twice a week at the boxing gym, then seven weeks out from the fight, started back in the proper training camp again. I also got a bit of southpaw sparring in with Oliver's lads. We tried things in sparring that we'd been practising for the first camp and some stuff didn't work. The cancellation was a blessing in disguise because it was like we'd had two chances to get it right.

Off we goes again to Tenerife, had a great craic again and smashed training. It was a smaller camp this time round, with Jamie, Nigel and the Irish Kenyans, but Rocky was also over, getting ready for his world title shot against Tyrone Zeuge. Rocky's a top lad and was the only one missing from the first training camp, so I was made up that he was part of this one.

One day during the second week of the camp, I'd gone to drop the van off to Jamie as he needed it. As he got inside, I said, 'You alright mate?' 'No,' he replies. I didn't click. Jamie then says, 'He's only gone and pulled out again.' 'You're fucking joking.' We were gutted. It's not just two training camps for me, but two for Jamie also. I'd lost about 15 grand but more importantly, I'd lost six months of precious time away from my family that I'll never get back. I kind of expected the first pull-out, but not the second. I was fuming. I knew the fight wasn't happening and came home early.

With Saunders off the table, I was still waiting to hear about a possible replacement fight, because the rest of the show at the O2 Arena still had to go ahead. I was thinking, 'Even if they just get me a Noddy to fight,' just so the training camp wasn't wasted. Then out of the blue, the WBC silver world middleweight champion, Roberto Garcia, called me out on Twitter and said he'd be willing to come over to the UK and fight. Happy days!

I've got to thank MTK and Frank Warren massively for sorting it all out very quickly from there on. They could have cancelled the show or got me a journeyman, but instead I was fighting for a title against someone who was highly ranked in the world by the WBC.

After the Saunders fight had been cancelled, we kind of knew there was a good chance that the replacement fighter would be orthodox, so Jamie had me sparring Sam Eggington, even though I didn't have a confirmed opponent. That turned out to be perfect preparation for Garcia as Sam's a good, solid, come-forward fighter. I also sparred Johnney Roye's fighter, English light-heavyweight champion Liam Conroy. I could have probably done with a few more spars, but with time not on our side I think we did well. We went from training for a southpaw runner to someone who comes forward all night long.

Jamie sent me the link of Garcia against Chavez Jr and told me to look at certain shots he threw in certain rounds and how he reacted under pressure. Even though he was a solid fighter, I knew pedigree-wise there wasn't a lot to him. He plodded forward with a high workrate, throwing clumsy shots. The game plan was to put in a controlled performance and outbox him.

At the press conference a few days before the fight, Garcia kept saying, 'I want it more than you. I want it more than you,' while staring at me. He was fighting in my backyard giving it the big'un, but I let it go, even though that did get under my skin a bit.

On the day of the weigh-in, I was hungry and narky and it didn't help when I had a massive argument with some woman in the sauna about an hour before. I'm at the InterContinental Hotel at the O2, while Jamie, Nige and Andy were sitting outside on the loungers by the pool as I'm trying to get this last bit of weight off. This woman was laid down in there, flat out, motionless. Every now and then, I'd pop my head out the door and say stuff like, 'Jamie. Can you call Dean and tell him so and so,' then five minutes later something else would come into my head and I'd asked Andy. Then I called Nige and he walks into the sauna, looks at this woman lying down and jokes, 'What have you done to her? Have you knocked her out?' He's not called Captain Chaos for nothing.

This woman then sits up and says, 'You can't talk in here.' Bear in mind, I'm hungry and narky, I've replied, 'Says who? Who said you can't? Every sauna I go into, you can't shut people up.' 'This is for peace and quiet,' she replies. 'You show me a sign anywhere in here that says you can't talk and that it's for peace and quiet.' 'I'm going to get security,' she says, and then walks out.

I'm there in the sauna sweating away and can see that two security men went over to Jamie, Andy and Nige. I burst open the door and proper lost my shit. 'Don't fucking speak to them. I'm the one who's had the argument with her. Come and speak to me. I go in saunas all over the UK and not once can you not talk in there.' The security guys had that, 'Oh God' look on their faces. Andy's walked over laughing as I'm losing my shit and smoothed it out with them.

The woman then came back in and made the security guys stay outside of the sauna because she said she didn't feel safe. I said, 'I'm fucking getting out anyway. It's all yours!'

By the time of the weigh-in, it was going to take very little to put me over the edge. Before we got on the scales, behind the weigh-in area, Garcia's looking over at me, snarling, and his trainer is doing the same. I'm not into all that disrespectful stuff, so I ignored it. I just wanted to do the face-off and weigh-in, shake his hand and go home. Anyway, when we got on stage, we're looking at each other and his coach is shouting, 'Easy work, baby, easy work!' and all that shit. I've done the face-off, then faced the front, but when I turned back to look at him, he's pulling this stupid face, so I pushed him. I got in trouble for that and decided to contact Mauricio Sulaiman from the WBC and the BBBofC afterwards to explain the situation and apologise for my actions. They said that I'd always been well behaved during my career and took no further action.

Come fight night, I had Mad Benny walk out with me. He'd walked me out when I fought Torosyan, but that was in Liverpool. Benny's 75 and the furthest place he'd ever been before coming to London was on his honeymoon, when he went to Towyn, North Wales. That's not even 60 miles from St Helens.

I spoke with Benny and asked if he wanted to come to London and stay over, but he wanted to go back the same night. My mate Webber drove him down and said he'd do Benny a packed lunch. I don't think anyone had ever made Benny a packed lunch before and he was more made up about that than the fight or the trip to London.

When Webber and Benny got to the O2, Simon Legg, the whip, took care of Benny and gave him the VIP treatment and made sure he was there ready to walk in with me.

The fight went as planned. I tried to keep it clean, keep him on the end of the jab and bring him in to shots as he was always coming forward in a clumsy, unorthodox way. Within no time, it became obvious he was a dirty fighter, though. He started with the low blows, using his head, hitting me at the back of my head and kidney blows.

Then, in round three, he threw this big clubbing left hook, which just got round my guard and hit my ear. The second it landed, I felt my ear go 'pop' and could hear whistling. It also sent me off balance straight away. I didn't realise it at the time, but he'd just perforated my ear drum. As it happened, it made me really focus, because I realised I needed to box smart and cute to not get injured any further.

When I got back to the corner I said to Jamie, 'Put your finger in my ear,' because it felt like I'd been in a pool and just needed to clear the water out. I thought it might just be a bit of water. He put his finger inside the ear and then said, 'Everything OK?' 'Yeah, yeah. Sound,' I replied. I had the cameras on me and didn't want them making a mountain out of a molehill. I just got on with the job for the next nine rounds.

The low blows kept coming. I think one of my bollocks is still in lost property at the O2 as he landed so many times. Occasionally, I gave him a few borderline shots back, just to see if the ref got on to me for doing it, which he never did. However, in the 12th round, I gave him a proper low one in the last minute because I knew I'd won the fight. I threw it thinking, 'Let's see how you like it.' He started moaning straight away! I'd been taking them all night and the first one he gets, he started moaning. The ref gave me a warning.

I won the fight by a very wide points decision and moved up to number two in the WBC world middleweight rankings. It was the second time I'd won the WBC silver title, the first time being against Max Bursak in 2014.

The moment the decision was announced, I got Archie and Amelia in the ring. For me, boxing is a job. But to be able to create another new memory that will last a lifetime for my kids along the way, that's what it's all about. Amelia didn't let go of that belt for the next few days. She even took it to school. When they had assembly, I went in with Amelia and Aisla, and stood up with them at the front and talked about the belt and what it stood for. The kids asked some questions and then Amelia finished off by saying, 'My daddy fights for his family.' That pretty much sums up my boxing career.

## CHAPTER 47

# LIFE LESSONS

*'Summing up Martin, I'm really proud of him. He pushes himself so hard for his kids. He's a brilliant dad. I'm so proud of what he's achieved in boxing but I'd be proud of him whatever he did.'*

Gemma Murray, 2016

WHEN me and Gemma first got together, we used to watch *Friday Fight Night* on the telly in my room. If I went to her place, it would be the same thing. It used to drive her mad. I'd say to her, 'That'll be me one day, you watch.' She was always supportive, even though she didn't follow the boxing then.

Nowadays, honestly, I couldn't tell you the last time we've watched a fight together. My weekends at home now with my kids mean the world to me. That doesn't mean to say I'm not appreciative of boxing. Far from it. Throughout my life, my family have supported me through thick and thin and I'm one of the few lucky ones to be able to say that boxing has given me the opportunity to pay them back.

I'd been saying to my mum from about 2012, 'Why don't you buy your house off the council? It would be good security for you for when you retire.' The response was always the same. 'We've tried but your dad's too old to get a mortgage.' Back then, I'd have loved to have bought the house straight out for them but I just didn't have the money. In the meantime, they just cracked on paying the rent to the council every month.

At the end of 2015, I was able to help them. I started the conversations again about the house and suggested different locations locally that they could move to. She said, 'No. I love where I live. I've been here 30-odd years.'

'Go to the council and tell them that you want to buy your house.'

There was a bit of a silence and she said, 'What do you mean?'

'I want to buy the house for you. Tell the council you want to buy the house outright. No mortgage.'

'No Martin, you can't do that. You put that money away for you, Gemma and the kids.'

'It's what I want to do, mum. I'd have done it earlier but I couldn't then. Now I can.'

There was a small silence and I could tell she was a bit emotional.

My concern was that they were getting older and even though both of them were working, neither knew how long they'd be in work for. This gave them security and a chance to put the rent money away and enjoy themselves a little bit. Get a better quality of life.

When the completion of the house went through towards the end of 2016, it was a lovely moment. One less worry for them and for me.

\* \* \* \* \*

Chizzy used to tell me, 'You can't buy experience,' and it's true. In my life to date, I've made some mistakes, fallen in love, lost some very good people, reached some sporting highs and learned some very valuable lessons along the way.

If someone had said to me when I was in a prison in Cyprus at the age of 18 that I'd have a book written about my life when I reached 35, I would have been shocked, because I genuinely didn't think I'd live to see my 30th birthday. If it wasn't for boxing, Gemma, our kids and the love of good family and friends, then this book may never have been written. And in terms of my boxing career? Be assured, I'm not done by a long way. I'm still fit, able to campaign in two weight divisions and still intend to win a world title. With Jamie Moore and Oliver Harrison in the trenches with me, I know the best is yet to come.

Well – that's my life so far. It's had some mad twists and turns and if it's meant that I've had to go through all the shit that came with it to get to where I am now, then I can accept that. As someone once said, 'I may not have everything I want in life but I have everything I need. For this, I am grateful.'